PROFILES
IN
PEACE

D0730382

Voices of Peacebuilders
in the Midst of the Israeli-Palestinian Conflict

Ron Kronish

©2022 Ron Kronish

All rights reserved. No part of this book may be reproduced, scanned, or distributed in any printed or electronic form without permission. Please do not participate in or encourage piracy of copyrighted materials in violation of the author's rights. Purchase only authorized editions.

Version 1.0

15 August 2022

ISBN: 978-1-7344700-9-3

Library of Congress Control Number: 2022914221

L.E.A.R.H.N. Peacebuilding Publications

Jerusalem/New York/San Francisco

waynegoodmanbooks

waynegoodmanbooks@gmail.com
Twitter: @WGoodmanbooks

Print versions at independent booksellers
Electronic versions on Kindle and Nook
Audiobooks from Audible and iTunes

Praise for

PROFILES IN PEACE

Rabbi Dr. Ron Kronish has devoted more than 30 years of his professional life to being a peace-builder in Israel. As a master educator, Kronish helps us understand the context for the current conflict, lifts up the stories of some of the most inspiring and audacious peace-builders on both side of the Israeli-Palestinian conflict, and shares their wisdom for a path forward. *Profiles in Peace* is essential reading for everyone who feels invested in peace between the Israeli and Palestinian communities, and who needs inspiration to continue on that path.

Rabbi Angela W. Buchdahl
Senior Rabbi,
Central Synagogue, NYC

This book is a must read for anyone interested in the efforts of Jews and Palestinians, six of whom are highlighted in it and whose own words we can read, to bring about a peaceful co-existence in Israel and its neighboring communities. It provides lessons in interreligious and intercultural dialogue that readers around the world can adapt for use in their own communities, to work together across religious and ethnic divides for the betterment of all, especially those in need. Highly recommended!

Dr. Eugene J. Fisher
Distinguished Professor of Theology,
Saint Leo University

Peace is not forged by documents or treaties, it is made possible thanks to the efforts of people, individuals of courage borne by compassion and seasoned by the pain they see and feel around them. Courage needs strategic wisdom and the ability to see beyond the moment. Some of these agents of peace are identified here by Ron Kronish, who is, truthfully, also one of

i

these agents of peace. This book is a small testament to the larger-than-life people our world needs.

Prof. Azza Karam (PhD)
Secretary General,
Religions for Peace

In this beautiful book, Rabbi Ron Kronish, master peacebuilder and peace educator, brings us an incredible window into his sacred work of interreligious peacebuilding between Israelis and Palestinians. After an insightful dual-narrative history of the conflict, Kronish profiles six brilliant peacebuilders–Israeli and Palestinian; Jewish, Christian and Arab; and male and female. Each of these leaders has contributed mightily to the relational infrastructure of peace between Israelis and Palestinians. Every reader will be moved to pray for their continued success.

Rabbi Amy Eilberg
Peacebuilder and Social Justice Advocate,
Palo Alto, CA

The conflict between Israel and Palestine appears to be so intractable, that many fear that a peaceful resolution to the conflict will never emerge. In *Profiles in Peace*, Rabbi Ron Kronish provides compelling portraits of six Israeli and Palestinian peacebuilders who refuse to surrender to such despair. Through their voices as well as his own, Rabbi Kronish offers much-needed hope for the future of these troubled nations.

Rabbi David Ellenson
Chancellor Emeritus, Hebrew Union College-Jewish Institute of Religion and past Director of the Schusterman Center for Israel Studies, Brandeis University

Over 15 centuries of Arab-Jewish interaction, the default engagement was peaceful, despite the history of the past 75 years. Rabbi Ron Kronish is among those who contend that a better, more prosperous and more faithful realization of our respective religious imperatives between Arabs and Jews lies in re-establishing peace between these communities. In this book, he shares with the reader the stories of other peace builders from both sides who share his contention and are committedly working to achieve peace.

Imam Feisal Abdul Rauf
Founder and President,
Cordoba House, NYC

Rabbi Ron Kronish has been an advocate for peace for as long as I have known him, and longer. His commitment has never wavered in spite of the many challenges he has faced and he, in my mind, is foremost among the courageous peacemakers and is worthy of celebrating as the six other re-markable peacemakers profiled in his new book. I have also been more than blessed to know Rabbi Kronish as a source of inspiration, and I believe that this book will inspire many people around the world. Rabbi Kronish's book is a must read for those of us who wish and pray for peace and wellbeing for all the people who call the Holy Land their home.

S.A. Ibrahim
Retired businessman and interfaith leader, USA

Rabbi Dr. Ron Kronish has provided us with the core principles of interre-ligious work by highlighting the work on the ground and activism of some of the most amazing peacebuilders. It is a challenging time for interreligious dialogue and peacebuilding especially between Israelis and Palestinians but Dr. Kronish has stood up for the realization for peace and continues to offer us hope in Jewish-Muslim Relations.

Dr. Mehnaz M. Afridi
Professor of Religious Studies, Director of the Holocaust, Genocide, and Interfaith Education Center,
Manhattan College, NYC

Rabbi Ron Kronish has written an important book. Most people, when they think of making peace, think of high-level diplomats negotiating on behalf of nation states. This book instead tackles the equally important work of grassroots peacebuilding and offers the reader the intimate stories of people doing work on the ground to offer different perspectives on the difficult yet critical work of peacebuilding. A must read for anyone interested in understanding Middle East peace.

Dr. Jonathan Golden
Director, Center on Religion, Culture and Conflict,
Drew University, NJ

Table of Contents

Preface

When I was a teenager growing up North America, I was impressed by the presidency of John F. Kennedy, whose assassination in Dallas, Texas, in November 1963 shocked the nation and the world. Not only was he a man of vision, but he was also a man of decisive action. Moreover, he was a person of courage, not only bravery during war (he was famous for saving other American soldiers in a PT boat during World War II), but he was also revered because of the courage of his convictions. He was also a pursuer of peace, and his establishment of the Peace Corps was a legacy which continues until this very day.

In addition, Kennedy was a man of great intellectual abilities, and he wrote some important books. Perhaps his most admired and most widely read book was the one he wrote in 1956 entitled *Profiles in Courage* in which he talks about what he means by courage:

> To be courageous requires no exceptional qualifications, no magic formula, no special combination of time, place or circumstance. It is an opportunity that sooner or later is presented to us all...The stories of past courage can teach, they can offer hope, they can provide inspiration. But they cannot supply courage itself. For this, each man [or woman] must look into his [or her] soul.

I have taken the idea of *Profiles in Courage* to write this book about *Profiles in Peace*. I have long been interested in the work of Israeli Jews and Palestinian Arabs in Israel and Palestine who have sought to build peaceful relations among the two peoples as well as between individual people who simply seek to live in peace and harmony with one another. As the reader of this book will discover, these people have acted courageously and consistently in their work for peace, which has become the hallmark of their lives.

In this book, I will profile the lives, thoughts, feelings, and actions of six important peacebuilders–men and women, secular and religious: three Jewish Israelis: **Rabbi Michael Melchior**, **Professor Galia Golan** and **Hadassah Froman**; and three Palestinian Arabs: **Professor Mohammed Dajani**, **Huda Abuarquob**, and **Bishop Munib Younan**. The reader will learn about their visions for peace and their actions to bring their ideals to fruition, as much as possible, in the real world of the Israeli-Palestinian conflict.

Researching and writing this book has been a labor of love. I have followed the work of the peacebuilders who are the heroes and heroines of this book for many years, and in some cases, I have been involved with them in the sacred work of building peace from the ground up in Israel and Palestine. I have labored in the fields of interreligious dialogue for the sake of peace for more than 30 years, during which I partnered with many people and organizations who were committed to peaceful coexistence among Israeli Jews and Palestinian Arabs (both Christians and Muslims) in the land which we all call holy.

I came to this work somewhat by accident. From 1988-1992, I worked for an American Jewish organization in Jerusalem whose former director had been very involved in interfaith relations. He took me to many meetings and introduced me to many of the players in the field at that time. There was another interfaith organization that was falling apart at the time, and people who were abandoning it came to me and asked me to help start a new organization which could become the voice for people engaged in interfaith dialogue in Israel, and which could serve as a central address for these activities. Accordingly, in 1991, together with a small group of people, I founded an interreligious peacebuilding organization which was known as the Interreligious Coordinating Council in Israel (ICCI), which operated in Jerusalem from 1991 to 2015. This broad coalition of institutions grew up in the 1990s, parallel to the political/diplomatic peace process which changed the trajectory of Israeli and Palestinian societies dramatically. As such, it became not just another interfaith relations group, but a council of organizations which used the method of interreligious dialogue as a tool in peacebuilding throughout the 1990s, until 2015.

Through this organization, I brought together a diverse group of people (from more than 70 institutions all over Israel), who cooperated together in many dialogue programs and cooperative projects of significance and substance. In so doing, I came to know both Israeli Jews and Palestinian Arabs from all over Israel, including and especially in Jerusalem, and also from the West Bank. I saw the powerful impact that many of these peace activists had on their communities and in their societies and beyond. Moreover, I formed lasting professional relationships and personal friendships with many of these people, including the six peacebuilders in this book.

In addition, I became a practitioner of dialogue in the service of peace, and a spokesperson for this method of peacebuilding in Israel and abroad. Not only did I write a great deal about the obstacles and challenges, as well as the successes and achievements of this work in many journals, newspapers, blogs, and books that I edited or authored, but I became a facilitator of these dialogues, as well as a lecturer and panelist–about their significance in helping to transform the Israeli-Palestinian Conflict into a situation of peaceful coexistence in Israel and in the region–at many international conferences, seminars, workshops and programs all over the world.

Why have I written this book?

One reason that I have chosen to write this book is that the media and most books about peace in the Middle East, especially about the Israeli-Palestinian Conflict, focus almost exclusively on the political peace process–and all too often the war and violence–which dominate the headlines. This is the "A" story in most newspapers and magazines and on most television news reports. According to writers and editors, this is all they have room for in their daily newspapers or broadcasts. Or perhaps this is just their excuse; they don't have space or time to get into non-essential stories. In fact, most media outlets have ignored the peacebuilders for many years since they have undervalued their importance, and as a result, they rarely publish human interest stories about people who actually pursue peaceful relations among people in conflict. One of my main goals in this book is to highlight this mistake, especially because the peacebuilders have been the only game in town for many years, while the political/diplomatic peace process has been frozen for most of the past two decades.

Another reason that I have written this book is that I believe that peacebuilders–those who have been active in interreligious, intercultural and intergroup dialogue and activism for peace for a long time—have important stories to tell, based on their extensive experience in enriching and energizing encounters with "the other" in the conflict and based on their significant activism for peace for many decades. Despite overwhelming obstacles and complex challenges, the peacebuilders who share their insights throughout this book have demonstrated over and over again that peaceful relations among former enemies is possible, that relationship-building takes dedication and time but is vital for peaceful living, that difficult dialogue is not only possible but fruitful, and that persistence and personal commitment to a vision of peace and to the methods of achieving it are vital for the common future of Israeli Jews and Palestinian Christians and Muslims who live in the same region.

For whom have I written this book?

Firstly, this book is for the general reader who is interested in contemporary Israel, in the Israeli-Palestinian Conflict, in the prospects for peace, in the future for both Palestinian Arabs and Israeli Jews in the land which they both regard as holy or as special to them in their religions and cultures. I believe that anyone who cares about the intertwined destinies of Israel and of Palestine will find this book of interest and of importance.

Secondly, I have written this book for the younger generation, for those young people who are studying in universities and are still interested in peace and in a better future for both peoples. They are not as tired or worn out as many of their elders. Yet, they are swamped with misinformation and disinformation from many sources, including and especially social media, which provide mostly negative news about what is going on in Israel and Palestine. In addition, they have been inundated with propaganda from various governments, which tend only to share their biased narrative of the conflict. This book is an attempt to change the narrative, to focus on people who have a positive story to tell and who have not given up on a vision for peaceful coexistence for the benefit of both peoples.

Thirdly, this book is for scholars, lecturers and writers, who study, teach and write about peacemaking and peacebuilding and who focus particularly on the Israeli-Palestinian conflict. It is my hope that this book will add perspective and context to their research, teaching and writing. Many lecturers and professors who are teaching about the Israeli-Palestinian Conflict in colleges and universities around the world in courses on Israel Studies, Peace Studies, Conflict Resolution and Transformation, History and other disciplines are looking for new books and articles to enrich their curricula. I am hopeful that the stories and the peacebuilders in this book will serve as a rich resource of information and inspiration in their teaching at the university level for undergraduates and graduate students.

Clarification of terms that I use frequently in this book

It is important for me to clarify at the outset some of the key terms that I use throughout this book:

Peacemaking: refers to the work of politicians, diplomats, international relations experts, lawyers and governmental officials who try to reach peace accords, which are agreements between governments. They are often engaged in the official peace process, which involves negotiations between various governmental representatives.

Peacebuilding: refers to the work of non-governmental organizations and people in civil society (not in government) who engage in dialogue and co-operative programs and projects to enhance peaceful living between people in a region where the formal conflict is either still raging or where it is beginning to be resolved by the politicians.

Palestine: refers to the name which the Palestinians give to their political entity in the West Bank and Gaza. It is officially called the Palestinian Authority or the Palestinian National Authority by others. There are ambassadors from Palestine around the world and at the UN. When you meet someone from the government in Ramallah, his business card will say that he works for Palestine. I use the term Palestine in this book since it is the name that Palestinians use, even though there is no agreed geographical entity recognized by the international community that constitutes Palestine.

The Occupation: refers to the continued military and administrative control of the West Bank by the Israel Defense Forces since 1967. Some say that because of the continued military blockade of Gaza -and the fact that Israel controls the border crossings, the electricity and the water—that the Gaza Strip is also under some form of occupation. But for the purposes of this book, the word is usually used to refer to the situation in the West Bank in which the Israeli military controls the lives of the Palestinians on a daily basis. Some prefer to use the term "disputed territories." Others—mostly those who wish to annex the West Bank to Israel or are already doing so de facto by what is known as creeping annexation–prefer to refer to the West Bank with its Biblical names of Judea and Samaria. Occupation is the term preferred by international relations experts, and it is the term that most reflects the situation of control and oppression on the ground. I use the term throughout this book to describe the situation in the West Bank.

The Israeli-Palestinian-Conflict: While the conflict used to be known as the Israeli-Arab Conflict (in the days when Israel was at war with the Arab countries surrounding it), it is not called this anymore, especially since Israel has already made peace with Egypt and with Jordan, and because the fighting in Lebanon from time to time is not with the state of Lebanon but with the Iranian-backed Hezbollah militia. In recent decades, the conflict has become known throughout the world as the Israeli-Palestinian Conflict. However, in my view, this label is a bit unsatisfactory since the conflict is essentially about two nationalisms—Zionism, the national movement of the

Jewish people which has resulted in the Jewish state of Israel, (which includes a Palestinian Arab minority of about 20% of its population) and Palestinian nationalism, which seeks to have a state side by side to the state of Israel in part of historic Palestine or Israel. Therefore, if one wants to be fully correct, I prefer to say that the conflict is between Israeli Jews and Palestinian Arabs, which I believe is the most accurate description of the two groups in this conflict.

The double narrative: There are two meta narratives to this conflict—the Israeli Jewish narrative and the Palestinian Arab narrative. They use the same dates but tell radically divergent stories. These narratives do not agree on the history of the conflict. Both narratives interpret the facts differently. Moreover, when one talks to many diverse Palestinian Arabs and Israeli Jews about the conflict, one quickly discovers that there are multiple narratives about the conflict on each side. Each person's narrative is based on his or her family, education, community, place of residence and his or her interpretation of history and the contemporary situation. Throughout this book, I portray both the meta-Israeli and meta-Palestinian narratives concerning many events and turning points in the conflict. I also include multiple narratives, since each peacebuilder has a different story to tell which is intertwined with his or her unique biography.

The Structure of the Book

The first section of this book will offer a brief history of the efforts of the peacemakers—the politicians, diplomats and civil servants who are entrusted by their governments to create peace accords, treaties or agreements between governments, which attempt to resolve the Israeli-Palestinian Conflict on the formal diplomatic level. In this way, the reader will learn about the ups and downs of the peace process—and the all-too-often war process—between Israelis and Palestinians, largely with the help of American mediation, over time. This will constitute the background and the context for the rest of the book.

Part two of the book will focus on the personal profiles of the six peacebuilders mentioned above, all of whom live and act in the midst of the ongoing, seemingly intractable Israeli-Palestinian conflict outlined in part one. The reader will learn what has motivated these peacebuilders to be active for peace for so long, what has kept them going, and what have been their successes and achievements, as well as how they dealt with setbacks and obstacles along the way. In this book, the reader will hear from these peacebuilders in their own voices, based on extensive interviews that I have conducted with them, as well as upon articles or selections from books that they have written. Each profile will end with a major "lesson learned" which the readers of the book can take away with them.

In the third section of the book, the six peacebuilders will reflect on their work in past decades and think constructively and creatively about what still needs to be done in the future. Representing a wide diversity of views and strategies, they will share their different perspectives—those which are religious and those which are secular, those that use dialogue and those that use advocacy—towards the goal of envisioning and activating a better future for Israeli Jews and Palestinian Arabs who share the same land. In addition, I will bring in voices of four young peacebuilders—two Jewish Israelis and two Palestinian Arabs.

In an afterward, I will offer my own conclusions and thoughts for the future, especially vis-a-vis the need to interweave peacemaking and peacebuilding in the years ahead. Ultimately, both will be needed to create a sustainable peaceful way of life in Israel and Palestine. Furthermore, I will share my insights and lessons learned from engaging with these six peacebuilders and others, as well as from my own peacebuilding work.

Acknowledgements

I wish to thank all those people who gave me inspiration as well as information over the years in order to write this book.

First of all, I express my heartfelt gratitude to the peacebuilders who agreed to be interviewed at length for this book: Huda Abuarquob, Professor Mohammed Dajani, Hadassah Froman, Professor Galia Golan, Rabbi Michael Melchior, Bishop Munib Younan. As you will see, their life stories and their work for peace are an inspiration and a sign of hope.

In addition, I am grateful for the willingness of young peacebuilders-graduates and staff of recent and ongoing peacebuilding programs-who continue this vital work now and for the future, for their willingness to be interviewed for the concluding chapter: Hoda Barakat, Rabbi Tamar Elad-Applebaum, Rabbi Elhanan Miller, and Tareq Saman.

I want to acknowledge the inspiration that I have received from many people in the field of interreligious and intercultural dialogue, peacemaking, and peacebuilding in Israel, as well as people who supported this work, who are no longer alive, but are still with us in spirit: Edward Idris Cardinal Cassidy, Professor David Cobin, Br. Jack Driscoll, William Frost, Judge Mayer Gabay, Nathan Hacker, Ambassador Shmuel Hadas, Mayor Teddy Kollek, Abdelsalaam Najjar, Dr. Mithkal Natour, Dr. Ron Pundak, Dr. Bernard Resnikoff, Archbishop Pietro Sambi, Rabbi Professor Michael Signer, Alan B. Slifka, Fr. Thomas Stransky, Sr. Rose Thering, Rabbi Professor Eugene Weiner, Dr. Geoffrey Wigoder. All of these people paved the way for me in dialogue and peace work over many years.

I have been privileged to be a library fellow at the Van Leer Jerusalem Institute, since 2015, where I have researched and written much of this book. I would like to thank the librarian Bayla Pasikov for her assistance and to express my appreciation to the professional leadership of this institute for affording me the opportunity to think and reflect on all aspects of the topics of this book in a beautiful setting in the heart of Jerusalem.

My book agent, Susan Cohen of Pearl Literary Agency, has helped me in many ways in creating the kind of book that would be of interest to both scholars as well as the general public and has urged me to write it and publish it. In addition, she read several of the chapters at various stages of the writing and offered helpful suggestions. I also express my gratitude to additional people who read various chapters of the book and offered valuable comments: Professor Joel Migdal, Rabbi Marc Rosenstein, Rabbi Amy Eilberg, Sari Kronish, Dahlia Kronish, Ariella Poni Kronish.

Special thanks go to Judy Kupchan, who copy edited the entire book on a voluntary basis, and to Andy Ross, who guided me in writing the original book proposal. I wish to express my gratitude to Wayne Goodman for his professionalism in formatting and preparing the book for publication as a paperback and an e-book.

I would not have been able to write this book-or anything else that I have written or done in my life—without the abounding love and companionship of my wife of 53 years, Amy Kronish, with whom I have shared my thoughts and dreams for all of my adult life.

Part One
Introduction

Profiles in Peace

In the Midst of the Conflict: Historical Background and Context

From the 1948 War of Independence/*Nakbah* until the Abraham Accords in 2020

While the focus of this book will be on the profiles of six prominent peacebuilders who promote peaceful relations between people in the midst of the Israeli-Palestinian Conflict, it is important to provide the context and the background in which these peace activists live and function. They attempt to pursue peace in a very difficult neighborhood, which has known many wars and too much violence. Parallel to the wars, there has been a political peace process that has provided the backdrop for the work of people and NGOs in Israel and Palestine, especially since the 1990s.

This chapter will provide a brief history of the peace processes–and the war processes–between Israel and the Palestinians, which is essential to know before the reader encounters the courageous work of our indefatigable peacebuilders over several decades.

Peacemaking

When most people in the world hear about the search for peace in Israel and Palestine, they tend to think about the political-diplomatic process which has become known as "the peace process." This is what makes the front pages of newspapers, or the lead stories in newsfeeds. If, on the other hand, there is a war or some terrorist or counter-terrorist incidents, violence will always trump the search for peace.

The peace process–or what I will call in this book "peacemaking"–is the work of the politicians and diplomats and their staffs, people who are often trained as lawyers or professionals in the field of international relations. In addition, this process often includes outside mediators, usually from a foreign government, like the United States or Norway, in the case of the Israeli-Palestinian peace process, who invite the parties in conflict to the negotiating table and mediate the process. The common goal of all these peacemakers is to help governments craft peace treaties. In our case a peace accord would be between the State of Israel and the Palestinian Authority (which governs the Palestinians of the West Bank) and has relations with *Hamas* (which governs the Palestinians in the Gaza strip); or between Israel

3

and an Arab country, such as Egypt or Jordan-agreements that have already been concluded.

The peacemakers have an important role in the search for peace between Israel and her neighbors. They function on the governmental level, representing the state in negotiations with their counterparts from other states and political entities. It is frustrating, complicated work, but when they work well together, they create the framework for peaceful living between peoples who were previously seen only as enemies.

Not surprisingly, peacemakers often get into gear after a war has disrupted the status quo. Indeed, there have been many wars which have then set the stage for peace negotiations between Israel and her neighboring Arab states. It seems that war processes and peace processes are very much related.

Diverging Narratives: The Establishment of the State of Israel and the *Nakbah*

The State of Israel was established in May of 1948 and can be seen as the historic result of many decades of preparation that began in Europe during the last decades of the 19th century with the creation and development of the Jewish nationalist movement known as Zionism. Beginning with immigration to the land of Israel in waves during the first decades of the 20th century, the Jewish population grew gradually, enabling the settlement of Jews from many countries in Europe and Russia, who faced anti-Semitism, pogroms, and marginalization in their communities. During the period of the British Mandate (1923-1948), the development of Jewish national institutions included well-organized fighting forces—the *Haganah* ("Defense") and the *Palmach* (an elite strike force)—both of which morphed into the Israel Defense Forces (the Israeli army, who initials are IDF) after the founding of the state. Without a doubt, the establishment of the State of Israel is considered one of the most important developments in Jewish and world history of the 20th century.

At the same time, parallel to the development of Zionism, another national movement was developing in the land of Israel, or the land of Palestine, known as the Palestinian national movement. This movement sought to prevent a Jewish state from being established in what they perceived was their land. Accordingly, it was not a forgone conclusion that the state of Israel would actually arise, due to major opposition from local Palestinian Arabs and the armed forces of neighboring Arab countries, as well as many of the countries in the world at that time.

Israel's War of Independence, which actually began before the announcement of the state, lasted for ten months until the signing of the armistice accords with Egypt, Syria, Lebanon and Jordan in early 1949. For a long time, the Jewish Zionist achievements in this war were perceived in Israel in nearly miraculous terms of a victory of *the few against the many* (as in the historic days of the Maccabees). Some considered it to be a divine miracle; others saw it mainly as an achievement of tremendous human proportions.

Later, in the 1980s, a group of young scholars who were called "new historians," making use of newly revealed archival documents, revealed that the Israel Defense Forces was actually better trained and better organized than the Arab armies or the local Palestinian militias, and that even though they had small numbers in manpower, their superior organization is what helped them win this war. In addition, historians and philosophers have argued that the existential reality of Israel in the immediate aftermath of the Holocaust led to great courage, daring and determination among the soldiers of the IDF at the time—and among the Jewish population. Losing this war for survival was simply not an option.

This same war, which the people of Israel call the "War of Independence" or the "War of Liberation" is understood in a diametrically opposite way by the Palestinian Arab side to the conflict. Palestinian historians refer to this war as the *Nakbah*, Arabic for "the great catastrophe." As a result of this war, about 700,000 Palestinian Arabs fled, and/or were expelled from Israel to the neighboring countries of Jordan, Lebanon Syria and Egypt, creating what has become known as "the Palestinian refugee problem." Hundreds of thousands of Palestinians live in neighborhoods that are still called refugee camps in Syria, Lebanon, Jordan, the Gaza Strip and the West Bank, and even parts of East Jerusalem (which is today part of the state of Israel.) Even now, many Palestinians abroad retain keys to their former homes in Israel, with the professed dream of returning someday, when there will be a peace agreement, or when, according to some, they will liberate Palestine and retake the entire country. neither of which appear to be very likely to happen in the near future.

When we look back at the period of the emergence of the State of Israel and the rise of the Palestinian refugee problem, we see that there have always been two conflicting narratives of the conflict: the Israeli one of independence and liberation, which celebrates the return of the Jewish people to their ancient homeland after 2000 years in exile, but which generally ignores the suffering they have inflicted on the other side; and the

Palestinian narrative, which sees the Palestinians as a people who have suffered a great national tragedy—the loss of their land and the emergence of the Palestinians as refugees, living in exile in the neighboring Arab countries as well as in lands all over the world to which they have immigrated, but which ignores the suffering they inflicted on the Jews of Israel. These two parallel and conflicting historical and contemporary narratives will accompany us throughout this book. Coming to grips with each narrative is one of the central tasks of both Israeli and Palestinian peacebuilders.

The Sinai Campaign of 1956, The Six Day War of 1967 and a Missed Opportunity for Peace

In the years following the establishment of the State of Israel, the main tasks were to stabilize the country, develop it economically and socially, and to welcome and absorb hundreds of thousands of new Jewish immigrants who were dispersed from Arab countries in North Africa and the Middle East, as well as to take in the "saving remnant"–Jews who had survived the Holocaust in Europe. Within a few short years, the Jewish population of Israel doubled, from 600,000 in 1948 to 1,200,000 by 1951.

In addition, the Israel Defense Forces needed to constantly be strengthened and developed to protect the country against attacks by *fedayeen* (Arab irregular forces, who would today probably be called terrorists) and to be prepared to defend the country against possible aggression by the hostile neighboring countries of Syria, Jordan and Egypt. As part of these policies, a controversial war was launched by Israel against Egypt in 1956 known as the Sinai Campaign, or the Suez Crisis.

In this lightning war (October 29-November 5, 1956) led by Israel's famous general Moshe Dayan, the IDF achieved a quick and decisive victory. Under Egypt's President Gamal Abdul Nasser, the situation on the Egyptian border had been going from bad to worse. When Nasser closed the Straits of Tiran, thus preventing Israeli shipping from using the Red Sea, the Israeli government saw this as an act of war. In addition, Nasser's decision to nationalize the Suez Canal inspired Great Britain and France to identify with Israel's plight and to form an alliance with her. Israel captured the Sinai Peninsula and the Gaza Strip, but withdrew from both by March 1957, due to strong international pressure.

For the next ten years, there were no wars between Israel and any of the neighboring Arab countries, but there was constant tension on the borders, with periodic terror attacks and counter-terrorism operations by the IDF.

Israel was always on guard, and continued to develop its armed forces to defend the country.

At the same time, there were developments on the other side. Palestinian nationalism, which had existed since the early decades of the 20th century, had been largely dormant during the initial years of the State of Israel. After the *Nakba* and loss of much of their lands and properties in 1948 and the years following, Palestinian nationalism began to re-surface, this time in a new form. The Palestinian Liberation Organization (PLO) was founded in 1964 at a conference in Cairo. The organization's original goals were to unite various Arab groups for the purpose of liberating Palestine, which was understood by the Israeli side as a serious threat to destroy the Jewish state. In the course of time, the PLO would claim to represent the Palestinian people as a whole, but at this time, it was still a relatively small organization. It became famous or infamous, depending on one's point of view, through extremist rhetoric and horrific terrorist actions against Jewish and Israeli targets inside Israel and in many places in the world. The Palestinians, through the PLO, saw themselves as liberators of their land, just as the Israelis did by referring to their War of Independence in 1948 as a War of Liberation.

In 1967, the largest Arab country, Egypt, issued threats of war which culminated in President Nasser's decision to again close the straits of Tiran to Israeli shipping. This led to the famous three-week waiting period in May of 1967 when the people of Israel were digging mass graves in anticipation of an Egyptian attack, with many people in Israel fearing another Holocaust. Similarly, there were threats of Syrian aggression against the north of Israel. These developments catalyzed the government of Israel to launch pre-emptive strikes against the air forces and armies of both Egypt and Syria, which led to Israel's decisive victory over these Arab states and Jordan, in what became known as the Six Day War of June 1967.

The Israelis-and Jews around the world-saw this war as a miraculous military victory, the hand of God in history once again. On the other hand, their Arab neighbors-Syria, Egypt and Jordan—viewed it as a war of aggression, during which many parts of their lands were captured and then occupied by Israel. Israel captured the entire Sinai Peninsula, and held on to it until the peace agreement with Egypt in 1979. The Israel Defense Forces also captured the Golan Heights from Syria; this area was later officially annexed by Israel. Israel captured the West Bank from Jordan, which remains "administered" or "disputed territory" or territory under "occupation," depending on your point of view. In addition, former Jordanian Jerusalem, known today as East Jerusalem (which included areas to the north, east and south of pre-1967 Jerusalem), was officially annexed to Israel. This created one Jerusalem municipality, in which Palestinians could vote in the city's elections but not in Israel's national elections, leaving Palestinians who live in Jerusalem essentially stateless.

The war of June 1967, which the Arab countries saw as aggression and the state of Israel viewed as self-defense for survival, created a totally new situation in the region. After this lightning war, Israel ruled over the Golan Heights, the West Bank and the Gaza Strip and all of the Sinai Peninsula. By humiliating the Arab armies and conquering large swaths of territory, it had become a mini-empire in the Middle East. This led to feelings of over-confidence and hubris in Israeli society, which turned out to be very dangerous in the years ahead.

Moreover, the Israeli victory in the Six Day War of June 1967 turned out to be a double-edged sword. This remarkable military victory could have become an effective opportunity to trade land for peace, an idea proposed by some of Israel's leaders at the time, which was ultimately rejected. Instead, the captured land became the foundation for a new era of expansion via settlements and ongoing military occupation by Israel in the West Bank and Gaza over the coming decades. Depending on your viewpoint, Israel was able to return to its Biblical roots in Judea and Samaria, securing and safeguarding the "Promised Land," or Israel's expansion was inflaming the conflict over land that had been in Arab hands, laying the groundwork for more wars, terrorist violence, counter-terrorism and the prolongation of the conflict. It was a missed opportunity for peace—due to errors and miscalculations on both sides—which was to haunt the region for many years.

From the Six Day War of June 1967 to the October War of 1973

In the years following the Six Day War, Israel's image changed from that of the Biblical David to the contemporary Goliath. Back in 1948, the emerging state of Israel was seen as David with his slingshot taking on all of the Arab armies in the region. But after the '67 war, Israel was considered the major military power in the region, backed extensively by the United States. The Six Day War also exacerbated the Palestinian refugee problem, with hundreds of thousands more Palestinian Arabs fleeing–and/or being expelled–from their towns and villages in the West Bank to neighboring Jordan, Lebanon and Syria, and to the far-flung diasporas all over the world. Israel's overwhelming military victory also led to the humiliation of the Egyptian and Syrian leaderships. This led them to plan to take revenge on Israel via a war that they managed to keep a secret from the world until the last moment.

On the Saturday morning of October 6, 1973, which was the Jewish holy day of *Yom Kippur* (Day of Atonement), the armies and air forces of Egypt and Syria launched massive surprise attacks on the Sinai Peninsula in the South and the Golan Heights in the North. Israel was caught off guard and unprepared. Thousands of Israeli soldiers were captured, killed or wounded. Yet again the Israeli army and air force rebounded and repulsed the Egyptian and Syrian forces and after several weeks eventually won the war, but at a very high cost in both numbers of the dead and the implications for the future of such a devastating loss for the nation.

Yet, the double narrative persisted, even if it was reversed for a brief time. The Egyptians called it the October War. Even though they eventually lost militarily, they regained their pride as a nation through the success of their surprise attacks at the beginning of the war. On the other hand, the Israelis called it the Yom Kippur War since it began on the holiest Jewish day of the year, when the country was closed down and most of the Jewish population were in synagogues. This time they were humiliated, and this was one of the reasons that it became a time of national soul-searching. This led to a change in the leadership of the country a few years later, which would have ramifications for Israel and the region for decades to come.

During the six years between the Six Day War and the Yom Kippur War, Israeli society began to change dramatically. During this period, the new Jewish messianic movement known as *Gush Emunim* (the Bloc of the Faithful) began to establish settlements in the occupied West Bank and Gaza Strip with great fervor and religious determination. They saw all the land captured in the Six Day War as belonging solely to the Jewish people, as divinely ordained in the Bible, and not to be shared. They turned the settlement of the land of Israel in the West Bank and Gaza into a kind of holy war, which they waged with the backing of most Israeli governments since 1967. Both the government and *Gush Emunim* rejected the notion that there was such a thing as the Palestinian people. They engaged in constant denial of Palestinian nationalism, just as Palestinians rejected Zionism, which to them meant conquest and occupation. It was a zero-sum game for both sides.

During this period, the PLO-the national liberation movement of the Palestinian people-greatly increased its terrorist attacks against Israel, both in Israel and abroad. In 1970, Palestinians launched terrorist attacks against five Israeli airplanes. In 1972, Palestinians massacred Israeli athletes at the Munich Olympics. In the Israeli mindset, the word "Palestinian" became equivalent with "terrorist" at the same time that Israel continued to formally reject Palestinian nationalism.

On the other hand, Palestinians saw themselves as freedom fighters, like Jewish nationalists (Zionists) in the pre-state underground movements of *Etzel* and *Lechi*. It seems that one person's freedom fighter is another person's terrorist. Similarly, Jewish settlers, during these years, did not see the suffering on the Palestinian side. Most of the Jews of Israel saw only Palestinian terror and they viewed all measures by the Israeli army, as protective and defensive.

Both sides of the conflict–Israeli Jews as well as Palestinian Arabs–were largely invisible to the other. The double narrative of denial and mutually exclusive histories and identities continued to grow and strengthen in the years following the Six Day War. Neither side formally recognized the existence of the other as a people with any rights to any part of the land of Israel/Palestine. This mutual non-recognition phenomenon was not to change for a long time. The PLO would finally change its position vis a vis its recognition of the state of Israel in the late 1980s and both sides would eventually embark on the Oslo Peace Process in the early 1990s.

The Peace Process with Egypt, 1977-79

Nevertheless, there were some positive developments for peace in the 1970s, especially on the southern front. After the October War of 1973, President Anwar Sadat felt that Egypt's honor had been restored and it was time to make a dramatic overture to Israel for peace. In November 1977, he made a historic pilgrimage to Israel to speak to the people of Israel in their parliament, the *Knesset*.

Since the debacle of the Yom Kippur War four years earlier, the people of Israel had become increasingly frustrated with the entrenched leadership of the Labor Party, which had led the country since 1948. This ushered in the growth of the *Likud* party, led by Menachem Begin, a veteran right-wing leader who had been a freedom fighter in a Zionist underground movement in the pre-state years. After the state was established, he led the *Herut* (Freedom) party for many years, a party which was always in the opposition until 1977. In forming the *Likud* (Unity) party, he merged *Herut* with the Liberal party (which no longer exists.) During all those years, from 1949-1977,

Begin had been an extremely vocal hawk and had been labeled by the Labor establishment and the mainstream media as an extremist. Yet, he surprised everyone by being extremely receptive to Sadat's overtures and to the idea of making peace with Egypt, the largest Arab country in the region and the one with the biggest army.

The visit of Sadat to Israel in 1977 and the warm reception that he received led to the signing of the Camp David Accords, which had been negotiated between President Jimmy Carter, President Anwar Sadat, Prime Minister Menachem Begin and their teams in September 1978, and to the signing of a full peace agreement between Israel and Egypt in March 1979.

This took place just four months before I immigrated to Israel, in June 1979. I remember feeling at the time that I was moving to a country which had succeeded in making peace with its major Arab enemy, which gave me optimism for the future of Israel. I was not the only one who had very positive feelings about the peace with Egypt.

If you had asked anyone in Israel or in Egypt or probably anywhere else in the Middle East at that time whether or not there was a chance that the states of Egypt and Israel could make peace with each other, you would have been told "No!" After four wars and constant military tension since 1948, it was assumed by most people that the state of belligerency would continue for a long time, if not forever. Yet, at that time there were courageous leaders who caught everyone by surprise by successfully reaching an historic peace agreement, which has now been in place, without hitches for more than 40 years. This was a lesson for the future: daring leaders with vision and determination could indeed make peace between countries which had been in bitter conflict for a long time, even if it seemed impossible at the time

This first peace agreement between Israel and a major Arab country in the region created a new reality. Peace was now seen as a possibility even though it was not a panacea. It did not solve all the problems of the region, but it greatly lessened the probability of another war between Israel and the Arab countries. Still, Sadat's extraordinary vision and courage cost him his life. He was assassinated in Egypt by factions who opposed the new peace with Israel. Likewise, the new peace plan left the Palestinian problem unsolved, or at least it pushed the resolution of this issue further down the road.

Growing Palestinian Nationalism, The First *Intifada* and the War in Lebanon

In the 1980s, the major focus of the conflict shifted from the south to the north. Lebanon emerged as the main battlefield between Israel and her enemies, especially after the Palestinians had established a mini-state known as *Fatahland* in southern Lebanon (*Fatah* is the name of the main faction of the PLO). Since the leaders of the PLO were expelled from Jordan in the mini-war waged against them known as *Black September* in 1971, they moved to southern Lebanon, with many of their followers. For years, the Palestinians, led by the PLO, attacked Israeli towns and villages in the Galilee with mortar fire and via terrible terrorist attacks. Eventually this led to the outbreak of war in 1982, with the military goal being a limited incursion to restore peace and security for the citizens living on Israel's northern border. However, this was not to be the case. The war turned into a nightmare for the people of Israel, as well as for the civilian populations living in the south of Lebanon, made up mostly of Christians who allied with Israel. It was especially devastating for Israeli Prime Minister Begin, who resigned in 1983, due to his despair after the death of his wife and after learning about the deaths of so many young soldiers in this unnecessary war. He believed that he had been misled by Defense Minister Ariel Sharon who had sought a much broader war in Lebanon.

One of the worst events in the history of this extended war in Lebanon was the infamous massacre of more than 3,000 Palestinians in the refugee camps of *Sabra* and *Shatilla* in Beirut between September 16-18, 1982. Even though the massacre was carried out by Lebanese Christian allies of Israel known as *Phalangists*, it was perpetrated with the support and knowledge of the Israeli army. It was a staggering and shocking event, which led to a massive demonstration organized by Peace Now against the government's handling of this war. More than 400,000 Israeli citizens turned out in Tel Aviv to protest Israeli involvement in this massacre (even if it was indirect) and to demand the investigation of the role played by Defense Minister Ariel Sharon in this horrific incident.

Together with many other people we knew, my wife and I were part of this outpouring of protest against the policies of the Israeli government at the time. We were exercising our civic responsibility by participating in the largest anti-war demonstration in Israeli history. It reminded me of some of the major anti-Vietnam war protests that I had participated in when I was a student in the USA in the late 1960s. I was proud that I was there with hundreds of thousands of Israeli citizens who cared about our country. However, this massive demonstration unfortunately did not end the war in Lebanon very quickly. In fact, it did not prevent the war from continuing for a very long time. And, although it led to an investigation into the role of Ariel Sharon, it did not stop him from becoming prime minister in later years.

As the 1980s progressed, the PLO–which had been mostly engaged in the armed struggle with Israel via terror and violence over many years–was going through some changes in its thinking about the conflict. The launching of the First *Intifada* (uprising or shaking off of the occupation) by the Palestinians in the West Bank and Gaza was a gamechanger. Beginning in December 1987 and lasting almost four years, this sustained Palestinian resistance for such a long period of time made the PLO stronger and provided the backdrop and the catalyst for peace negotiations in the 1990s.

It all seemingly began with a car accident, when an Israeli truck crashed into a station wagon, allegedly by mistake, which killed four Palestinians and wounded ten. The Palestinians did not, however, see it as an accident. Rather, they saw the incident as an act of retaliation against the killing of a Jewish Israeli in Gaza. Palestinians took to the streets in protest in the Gaza strip where they threw rocks and Molotov cocktails at Israeli police and soldiers. The violence quickly spread to the West Bank.

The reaction of the State of Israel was one of great shock and surprise, as if the leaders were not aware of the seething Palestinian despair and nationalist sentiments which were growing in the West Bank and Gaza during the 20 years of Israeli military occupation. Yitzhak Rabin, who was Israel's Minister of Defense at the time, reacted famously—or infamously—with a public announcement that called for breaking the bones of those Palestinians who were resisting the occupation through mass demonstrations. This led to more widespread Palestinian demonstrations and to a massive Israeli military response to try to crush the uprising, which took a long time to accomplish.

In the meantime, the PLO became more popular and dominant in the West Bank and Gaza as a result of this uprising. What began as a grassroots movement became highly organized. Palestinian leaders formed the United National Command of the Uprising, a coalition which had strong ties with the PLO. In addition to violent protests, with rock-throwing and Molotov cocktails hurled at Israeli soldiers, more and more Palestinian groups from civil society joined the uprising with strikes and boycotts and other forms of protest

In stark contrast, the Israeli narrative saw this uprising in a very negative light. The leaders at the time did not want to recognize the existence of Palestinian nationalism, and tried to portray the Palestinians as nothing more than a group of rabble and terrorists, which was the way that Israeli leaders had viewed the PLO for a long time. However, since so much of Palestinian civil society had joined the protests, this narrative could not be sustained forever. Also, the PLO was going through serious internal debates as to how to make progress towards their dream of statehood as a result of this *intifada*, which they viewed as a success, despite large numbers of Palestinians wounded and killed.

After much internal debate, the PLO changed its diplomatic course and in a famous speech at a UN meeting in Geneva in December 1988, Yasser Arafat, the iconic chairman of the PLO for decades, actually recognized the State of Israel and argued for the two-state solution. At the same time, the Palestinians issued their own Declaration of Independence, which is largely unknown in Israel or the western world.

Throughout the 1980s, Israeli politics was ruled by the right-wing *Likud* party which was highly militaristic. This party supported the ongoing War in Lebanon for too many years. It was virulently anti-Palestinian and pro-occupation (and remains so to this day, along with several other political parties on the center-right in Israel). At that time, Israeli governments refused to recognize the existence of the Palestinian people, and their rights for self-determination which would lead to a Palestinian state. Moreover, throughout the 1980s, the governments of Israel continued to see the conflict as the Arab-Israeli Conflict, rather than understanding that the core of the conflict was now between Israel and the Palestinian people, despite the fact that they spent a great deal of time fighting against the PLO in Lebanon during these years.

At the same time, the PLO continued to not only fight a mini-war with the Israeli army in southern Lebanon, but also to engage in terrorism against Israeli targets within Israel and beyond. Moreover, their spokespeople were virulently anti-Israel in their public rhetoric. The speeches of PLO leaders mostly had a violent tone and spoke consistently about the need for armed resistance and liberation of their former lands by force, not by negotiations. The persistence of terrorist attacks on innocent Israelis and the negative language of non-recognition of Israel, referring to it only as the Zionist entity, continued to engender hostile feelings for Palestinians by Israelis at the time.

Fortunately, all of this was to dramatically change just a few years later, in the early 1990s, when back-channel talks led to a very surprising and unexpected development: mutual recognition between the Jewish-Israeli people and the Palestinian Arab people.

The Beginning of the Decade of Peace: The Madrid Peace Conference

On March 6, 1991, the president of the USA, George H.W. Bush told the US Congress that the time had come to put an end to the Arab-Israeli Conflict. This then led to eight months of shuttle diplomacy by Secretary of State James Baker between Israeli, Arab and Palestinian leaders as well as international stakeholders, which culminated in the Madrid Peace Conference (October 31-November 4, 1991). The conference was co-chaired by President Bush and the President of the Soviet Union, Mikhail Gorbachev, who had recently opened up his country to the world. It was attended by delegations from Israel, Egypt, Syria, and Lebanon, as well as from the Hashemite Kingdom of Jordan. The Jordanian delegation included Palestinians. This was an event of unprecedented historical importance since it was the first time that all the parties to the Arab-Israeli Conflict had gathered together.

One of the groundbreaking parts of this conference was that this was the first time that Palestinians were included in negotiations for peace. As such, this represented a giant shift in the definition of the conflict: a new recognition that resolving the issue of the future of the Palestinians (especially those who still lived in the land of Israel/Palestine) was at the core of the conflict.

The Madrid Conference did not reach any important conclusions but it was the catalyst for everything else that happened in the 1990s between Israel and the Palestinians and between Israel and Jordan. It set the precedent for direct negotiations between the parties to the conflict. Following the conference in Madrid, representatives of Israel, Syria, Jordan and the Palestinians met for bilateral talks in Washington DC and for multilateral talks in Moscow in 1992.

However, these diplomatic channels became riddled with radical disagreements. It became clear to the leaders of Israel and to those of the Palestinian Liberation Organization (PLO) that these talks were not producing results, and that new ideas and modalities would be required in order to move forward. This led to some amazing back-channel dialogues, which changed the course of history in the Middle East.

The Oslo Peace Process, 1992-95

Since the formal diplomatic channels were not working well, the leadership of Israel at the time–Prime Minister Yitzhak Rabin and Foreign Minister Shimon Peres–as well as the leadership of the PLO–Yasser Arafat, Mahmoud Abbas (Abu Mazen) and Ahmed Qurei, (Abu Alaa) and others–began exploring alternative paths to peace through secret talks which became known as the Oslo Peace Process, since they were sponsored by the government of Norway and actually took place in Norway, in and around Oslo. Secret meetings between representatives of Israel and the PLO took place for nine months during 1992 and 1993, under the guise of academic conferences. These off-the-record dialogues–which took place in informal retreat settings–developed great mutual trust among the partners to these talks, so much so that they were able to agree to a Declaration of Principles by the summer of 1993.

Thus, in July 1993, Prime Minister Rabin of Israel contacted PLO Chairman Yasser Arafat and received a response on August 4th. This led the leaders of Israel — especially Prime Minister Rabin and Foreign Minister Peres, who were keeping this a deep secret–to consider the idea of mutual recognition, i.e., the Palestinians would recognize the State of Israel, and the State of Israel would recognize the Palestinian people and their right to self-determination.

By September both sides had agreed on the major principles for moving forward. This led to the famous signing of the Declaration of Principles– known as the First Oslo Accord–on the White House Lawn on September 13, 1993, presided over by President Bill Clinton, with Prime Minister Yitzhak Rabin and Foreign Minister Shimon Peres of Israel on one side and PLO Chairman Yasser Arafat on the other side. The iconic photo of this major milestone in modern diplomatic history became a hopeful symbol of the new era of peaceful possibilities between Israelis and Palestinian. This was a major event in both Palestinian and Israeli history, which brought great hope to the peoples of Israel and Palestine, and to people all over the world.

The historic First Oslo Accord of September, 1993 was only the beginning of the process. It stimulated much new dialogue between people at all levels—from the grassroots to the top leadership—in the years ahead. It also led to more peace accords between the state of Israel and the PLO during the decade of the 1990s, a decade of positive momentum for peace.

The Oslo Accords actually comprised a series of agreements. The second agreement, signed in May 1994, known as the Cairo Agreement, dealt with the arrangements for the Gaza Strip and the region of Jericho in the Jordan Valley. This accord enacted the provisions which had been set forth in the original declaration of principles of September 1993, which had endorsed the idea of a five-year interim self-rule for a Palestinian Authority, which would be a provisional government for the Palestinian people. After this, talks on final status were to begin after three years, with a proposed two-year deadline for an agreement to be reached. Issues such as borders, the return of refugees, the status of Jerusalem, and the status of Jewish settlements in the occupied territories, were all delayed until then.

Unfortunately, the plans laid out in the Oslo Accords in 1993-1995 were too ambitious, and many obstacles and challenges remained to be resolved. Violent resistance to the plans by rejectionist portions of both the Palestinian and Israeli publics undermined the future of the Oslo Accords and only some portions of the initial plans were actually implemented. Many interim arrangements became permanent, and final status talks were bogged down and ultimately abandoned in the years ahead.

The Agreement between Israel and Jordan, October 1994

On October 26, 1994, a little over a year after the signing of the First Oslo Accord, a peace agreement was signed between Israel and the Hashemite Kingdom of Jordan in the Arava desert, in southern Israel, symbolically on the border between Israel and Jordan. President Clinton was the master of ceremonies again. The agreement was signed by Prime Minister Rabin and Prime Minister Abdul-Salam Majali and King Hussein of Jordan.

In contrast to the negotiations with the Palestinians, the talks to achieve a peace treaty with Jordan progressed easily. Even though Jordan was an official enemy of Israel, it was widely known that King Hussein had held many secret talks with Israeli leaders and that he genuinely desired peace. The agreements with the Palestinians now made it possible for Jordan and Israel to achieve their common goals for peace. Most importantly, the agreement normalized relations between Israel and Jordan. In this sense, the peace treaty was meant to be much more than just a cessation of war. It implied that normalization would take place between the peoples of the two countries. There was hope expressed by the negotiators that economic co-operation would lead to productive and peaceful relations between the two peoples.

Imagine that you were living in Israel, as I was, in the fall of 1994, after the signing of the peace agreement with Jordan. The State of Israel had signed two agreements with the Palestinians within a year! The peace treaty with Egypt had been in place since 1979, which meant no more war on our southern border. And now Israel had just signed a peace agreement with Jordan, the country with a very long border to our east, ending the state of war and normalizing relations with their people. At the same time, there were even negotiations going on with Syria!

It was an amazing time. The mood in Israel was euphoric. There was tre-mendous momentum in the peace process, with one agreement after another being signed and sealed. Many of us in Israel, including myself, felt that it was almost as if the messianic era of peace was upon us. In fact, dur-ing the years 1993-1995, I organized a series of seminars (in cooperation with a Palestinian organization in East Jerusalem headed by Ziad Abu Ziad), which we called *Educating About Each Other in the Era of Peace*. We actually believed that we were in a new period of history, and we wanted to think about next steps right away.

In addition, in the spring of 1996 I was invited to Amman by the Royal Institute of Interfaith Studies for three days, to meet with senior officials and to present a lecture to diplomats and other invited guests at the insti-tute. It was an amazing experience for me, a direct result of the peace agreement between Israel and Jordan signed the previous year. However, as I was to discover on my visit to Amman, this was to be a cold peace, since the rejectionist anti-normalization forces were still very strong there. Never-theless, I viewed this as an opening for dialogue, a positive step towards peaceful relations.

The Assassination of Prime Minister Rabin

Even though many people and groups in Israel and Palestine tried to tor-pedo the peace process in the months after the signing of the accord between Israel and Jordan, the most serious blow to the process came on the night of November 4, 1995, with the assassination of Prime Minister Yitzhak Rabin, an event which shook the people of Israel and Palestine, and the people of the world, to their core. Rabin was killed by a Jewish extremist, Yigal Amir, who had learned from his extremist rabbis that Rabin was a traitor since he was prepared to give up parts of the holy land of Israel, and that therefore it would be for the good of the Jewish people to remove him from the political equation.

Some people say that the assassination of Yitzhak Rabin actually killed the peace process. He and Arafat – two highly respected leaders of their peoples – had developed a real chemistry for peacemaking. They had made the move from war to peace in their hearts and souls. Arafat even attended Rabin's funeral, along with leaders from around the world. I believe that the peace process was severely wounded after this assassination, but it was not killed. On the contrary, it continued to move forward under the leadership of Shimon Peres, who became acting Prime Minister following the assassination. Peres committed himself to proceeding towards peace, despite all the obstacles of the rejectionists on both sides. However, on May 29, 1996, Peres lost a very close election to Benjamin Netanyahu of the Likud party, which dealt another blow to the peace process. Even Netanyahu, however, continued the process, at least for a brief period, as we shall see.

Another Peace Accord between Israel and the Palestinians

The Wye River Memorandum was the last of the peace accords signed by Israeli and Palestinian leaders. The negotiations were held at a place known as the Aspen Institute Wye River Conference Centers, not far from Washington DC, during October 15-23, 1998. This agreement, under the patronage of President Bill Clinton, was the result of the efforts of both sides to continue the negotiations to bring an end to the Israeli-Palestinian conflict and to continue implementing the decisions of the Oslo Accords. President Clinton was very involved in the negotiations and he invited King Hussein of Jordan to attend, to help mediate between the Israeli and Palestinian leaders.

Surprisingly, this agreement was signed by Israeli Prime Minister Benjamin Netanyahu, who had been a fierce opponent of the Oslo Accords only a few years prior. This was Netanyahu's first term as Prime Minister, when he was relatively young. Somehow, President Clinton and the American mediators coaxed him into signing the agreement, although as we learn from later history, his heart was never really in it and he later rejected all attempts to reach peace with the Palestinians during his 12 years as Prime Minister (2009-2021).

Upon returning to Israel, Netanyahu faced massive opposition to his sign-ing of the Wye River agreement, mostly by right-wingers and settlers (Jews who had settled in the West Bank and Gaza since 1967) and therefore not much of it was ever implemented. In addition, the opposition eventually brought about a no-confidence vote against his government, which caused the government to fall, leading to new elections. In the elections of May 1999, Netanyahu and his Likud party were defeated by Ehud Barak and the Labor Party, in a landslide victory. This signaled that the people of Israel were still interested in pursuing peace. Barak and his colleagues pledged to continue the peace process.

The Negotiations for a Comprehensive Settlement at the Camp David II Summit

After his election as prime minister, Ehud Barak did renew the peace pro-cess. During his first year in office, he made serious efforts to re-engage the Palestinians, and in early July of 2000, he urged President Clinton to invite him and Chairman Arafat to Washington DC for another serious round of talks. This led to what has become known as the Camp David II Summit, which took place at the presidential retreat in the Maryland mountains, outside of Washington DC for two full weeks from July 11-25, 2000.

Twenty-two years after the successful Camp David I negotiations which brought about the peace agreement with Egypt, President Clinton–an American president who cared deeply about helping Israel and the Palestinians reach peace–was clearly hoping to pull off another diplomatic miracle when he convened this summit meeting at the same historic loca-tion. Arafat and Barak ostensibly agreed to attend the meetings since they both somehow thought that an agreement was achievable. In fact, I remem-ber vividly a headline in a newspaper in Israel which said *End of Conflict in Sight!* There was actually some hope in Israel that a final comprehensive accord was in the works.

It was the last year of President Clinton's eight years in office, during which time he had devoted a great deal of time and resources to trying to serve as an honest broker to mediate between the Palestinians and the Israelis to resolve what so many pundits had characterized as an intractable conflict. Moreover, ever since both Clinton and Arafat had attended the huge state funeral for Prime Minister Rabin, in 1995, it seemed that enough trust had developed between them that Arafat agreed to come to Camp David II with a genuine desire to reach an agreement. Prime Minister Barak, like Rabin, had come from the Israeli military (he was a decorated officer and had served as Chief of Staff), now supposedly sought peace with the Palestinians in a sincere fashion.

This summit at Camp David was meant to achieve a comprehensive agreement between the Israelis and the Palestinians, which the organizers of the conference thought was actually possible at the time. Unfortunately, however, an agreement was not reached and both sides went home profoundly disappointed.

This was the beginning of what I call *the blame game*. Each side, like in a bad divorce, blamed the other for the failure of the talks. The Israeli leadership said that they had offered the farthest-reaching compromises that were possible and that Arafat had simply "chickened out" at the last minute. On the other hand, the Palestinian leadership, which was afraid of the reactions of their people, accused the Israelis of not going far enough, specifically by not offering the Palestinians enough contiguous land in their new state-to-be, but just a series of cantons amidst many Israeli settlements in the area.

This blame game went on for years, with each side developing a mantra which said "we don't have a partner for peace." The bottom line was that each side lost trust in the other's sincerity to finalize an agreement. Since mutual trust had been the basis of the Oslo Accords in the early '90s, the absence of trust was a serious blow to the possibility of continuing the political-diplomatic peace process in any meaningful way.

The War Process Replaces the Peace Process: The Second *Intifada* 2000-2005

Following the failure of the Camp David II summit, a somber mood overtook the people of both Israel and Palestine. The peace negotiations had failed, and there was a feeling of pessimism and stalemate in both societies.

Then in September 2000, about two months after the collapse of the Camp David II talks, Ariel Sharon, a veteran representative of the right-wing Likud party in the *Knesset* (who would later become the Prime Minister) made a provocative visit to the Temple Mount, or *Harem el-Sharif* as the Palestinians call it, in Jerusalem. It was as though Sharon decided to demonstrate to the world, and especially to the Palestinians, who was the boss in Jerusalem. Lest there be any doubt, he was surrounded by a security detail of over a thousand soldiers and police officers.

This event led directly to the outbreak of the Second *Intifada* (uprising or shaking off of the occupation). Despite the fact that the Israeli leadership tried to say that the *intifada* had been planned before Sharon's walk on the Temple Mount, it was clear that his stroll was the match that lit the fire at that time. The rioting soon spread to other towns, villages and cities in the West Bank and the Gaza strip, with harsh but unsuccessful attempts by the Israeli security authorities to quell the rioting and bring calm to the situation. Thus, began a five-year period of violence and counter-violence which would leave deep scars and much trauma in both Israeli and Palestinian societies.

The previous *intifada* of 1987-1993 was very different. In that uprising, the Palestinians used rocks and sling shots and knives and were portrayed as David and the Israeli army was described as Goliath. In contrast, this uprising featured suicide bombings in the name of the religion of Islam, or more correctly a radicalized and politicized version of Islam. The more the Palestinians used suicide bombs as a weapon against the Israeli occupation— and the more that they killed innocent civilians in deadly terrorist attacks— the more that the Israeli security forces responded with great force. Accordingly, the cycle of violence and counter-violence escalated from day to day, week to week, month to month, with no end in sight. It was a very dark period in Israeli and Palestinian intertwined history.

This uprising began during the rule of Prime Minister Ehud Barak, of the Labor Party. Barak, who came from a distinguished military career, did succeed in withdrawing the Israeli army from the quagmire of Lebanon in summer 2000, but he was apparently caught by surprise by this *intifada*. As a military man, who had risen in the ranks of the IDF to become Chief of Staff and then later joined the Labor Party, he responded primarily by military means to the very complex new situation on the ground.

The Second *Intifada* became known as the *Al Aksa Intifada*, since it began with Ariel Sharon's walk on the Temple Mount/*Harem El-Sharif*, where the Al Aksa Mosque and the Dome of the Rock are both situated. Many Palestinians, including and especially Muslim radicals, saw this as an attack on one of Islam's holiest sites, and as a result they invented conspiracy theories which circulated widely via word of mouth and their own media to the effect that the State of Israel was planning to destroy the Al Aksa Mosque. It didn't matter that these ideas were completely unfounded—what would be called today "fake news." Many Palestinians, especially young people, were incensed by these rumors, which they fervently believed to be correct, since they heard statements repeatedly about this from their religious and political leaders. This clearly enraged them to engage in more violent, futile and irrational acts of resistance, which is one of the reasons that the *intifada* lasted for nearly five disastrous years, with thousands of Palestinians and Israelis killed or wounded physically and emotionally.

In the midst of the second year of the *intifada*, Prime Minister Ehud Barak stepped down, and in a snap election in February 2001, he was resoundingly defeated by the right-wing Likud leader Ariel Sharon, who formed a national unity government. Sharon had been a war hero and was known for his tough policies against Palestinians. After about a year in office, in March 2002, Sharon's government undertook two major initiatives which fundamentally changed the situation on the ground in the months and years ahead. First, at the end of March 2002, they launched a major military campaign against the Palestinians, which they called Operation Defensive Shield, to quell the Palestinian uprising in the territories; then, they began construction of what they called the *security fence* and what the Palestinians called the *separation wall*, to stem the tide of terror attacks by Palestinians inside Israel.

According to sources at the IDF, the main objective of Operation Defensive Shield was to strike Palestinian terrorist infrastructures and to put an end to the wave of terrorist attacks against Israel. One of the main triggers of the operation was the March 27, 2002 horrific terrorist attack at the Park Hotel in Netanya during the Jewish holiday of Passover, in which 30 Jews were killed while celebrating the Passover Seder. This was looked upon with shock and horror by most Israelis. The resulting military campaign took place in cities and towns all over the West Bank for one month. By the time it was over, the number of terror attacks against Israelis had greatly decreased, enormous quantities of weapons were seized from the Palestinian Authority, and Chairman Arafat's movements were restricted to his headquarters in Ramallah, which had been partially destroyed. This was a decisive turning point in the struggle to quell the uprising and return the region to some sort of normalcy.

It took until February 2005 for the Second *Intifada* to end. At a summit at Sharm El Sheikh, in the Sinai desert of Egypt, the leaders of Israel and the Palestinian Authority finally agreed that all Palestinian factions would stop their acts of violence against Israel and that the Israeli army would similarly stop attacking the Palestinians. Instead of peace and normalization, which were the goals of the Oslo Accords of the early 1990s, now it seemed that the best that could be achieved was an armistice or what became known as the separation policy. The main symbol of this new policy was the new security fence/separation wall, which was built to divide the Palestinians from the Israelis, with the hope that each group could live on its side of the wall, without disturbing the group on the other side.

The Building of the Security Fence/Separation Wall

The decision to build what Israel called a security fence came as a result of mounting pressure by Israeli civilians on their government to do something conclusive to end the massive wave of terror attacks against them in 2002. Prime Minister Sharon was eager to do something to alleviate the pain and suffering of the citizens in Israel. Accordingly, he called in his military advisors and asked them for solutions. Their answer was the building of a long fence (which would be partly a wall), mostly along the borders from before the War of 1967. The purpose of the fence/wall was to end incursions by Palestinian terrorists into Israel. The Israelis saw it as essentially a security measure, and argued that it was very effective (and they continue to argue that it works). Between October 2000 and July 2003, there were 73 suicide bombings carried out from the West Bank. By the end of 2006, the number had fallen to 12.

I went to see the fence/wall on a study tour in 2002, to learn from one of the military architects of the project. He said at the time that the project would be mostly (95%) fence and only 5% wall, and that when there would be a peace agreement, it would be taken down. It sounded good then, but 20 years have passed and the fence/wall is still standing, and there is no peace agreement.

The Palestinians see this ugly grey concrete wall or barrier very differently than the Israelis. They call it the *separation wall* or sometimes even the *apartheid wall*. They point out that in some places it deviates from the pre-1967 border effectively annexing territory to Israel, which they view as essentially a land grab. Also, they complain rightfully that the wall divides many of their communities, severely restricting travel and freedom of movement, and it has become a symbol of Israeli oppression against them. They would like to see the wall disappear. But it certainly will not happen until there is a comprehensive peace accord.

The Disengagement from Gaza, August-September 2005

After crushing the *intifada* and building the security fence or barrier, Prime Minister Ariel Sharon gradually went through a transformation vis-a-vis his overall view of the Palestinian issue. In order to confront the continuing violence and counter-violence, he and his colleagues came up with a bold and daring move of unilateral disengagement – withdrawal of all Israeli Jewish settlers and all of the Israel Defense Forces from the Gaza Strip. He did not believe that he could reach an agreement with the Palestinian leadership about Gaza via negotiations. Instead, he felt that the only way to get Israel's citizens and soldiers out of the mire of Gaza was through a one-sided move.

Sharon had already begun to make surprising statements about Palestinian rights at the beginning of his term as prime minister in 2001. As a responsible elected leader, he began to envision possible solutions to the Palestinian-Israeli conflict that had been inconceivable to him previously. For example, already in September 2001, he was quoted in the media as saying that the Palestinians have the right to establish their own state west of the Jordan River. Also, in May, 2003, he endorsed a new peace plan proposed by the USA, the European Union and Russia, which was known as the *Road Map*. This led to discussions with Palestinian President Mahmud Abbas. Sharon was beginning to consider the possibility of peace which was a great surprise to many people in Israel and the world, given his military and right-wing background. Becoming prime minister suddenly made him more mature and pragmatic, and perhaps he wanted to change his legacy in history from a man of war to one of peace. However, tragedy struck Israel once again. In January 2006, Sharon suffered a severe stroke, and he was incapacitated and could no longer function as prime minister.

He was replaced by Ehud Olmert, who continued Sharon's policies. According to official Israeli policy, the plan was to continue to disengage from more settlements in the West Bank. This was what was said, but it was never clear if this was the real intention of the government. At any rate, the unilateral disengagement from Gaza turned out to be a disaster for Israel's security in the south, and no more settlers or settlements were withdrawn from the West Bank. This eventually led to a total rethinking on the Israeli side about the wisdom of unilateral withdrawals, instead of negotiated peace agreements.

Despite massive opposition by the right-wing in Israel to this plan, it was actually carried out in August 2005. All Israeli army installations in Gaza were taken down and more than 9000 Israeli settlers who were living in 25 settlements were forced to return to live in Israel. In addition, four settlements in the northern West Bank were removed, signaling that this could also be the beginning of a process of withdrawal from the West Bank, if the Gaza experiment went well, which it did not.

Within Israel, the citizenry was deeply divided about the disengagement from Gaza. It was clear that the majority of Israelis actually supported the plan, as evidenced from opinion polls. Those who supported the disengagement argued that it was a necessary move to protect Israel in the long term. They felt strongly that the cost of protecting Israeli settlers who were living in the midst of the densely populated Gaza Strip was detrimental to Israel's economy. In addition, some of the supporters argued that the disengagement would allow the security forces to be better able to protect Israeli citizens in West Bank settlements. They claimed that the presence of Israeli settlers in the Gaza strip was always meant to be temporary and therefore Israel would give up control of Gaza as part of any final agreement with the Palestinians for peace.

Opponents of the plan argued that Israel was retreating from Gaza under fire. They believed that the decision to leave Gaza was a form of capitulation to Palestinian terrorism, and that therefore Israel would be perceived as weak by the Palestinians and the Arab world. Some of the more fundamentalist opponents to the withdrawal also thought that the Gaza strip was important to Israel because of historic Jewish ties to the region. Also, they felt strongly that displacing Jews from Gaza would therefore set a bad precedent for the future.

The actual withdrawal from the Gaza strip took place very quickly. The army evacuated all the settlers during a five-day period in August, 2005, as well as evacuating four settlements from the northern West Bank. By September 12, 2005, the IDF had completed their withdrawal from Gaza.

The Palestinian reaction to the disengagement was swift and shocking. Very soon after the Israeli withdrawal, Palestinians entered the former Israeli settlements and burned buildings, including synagogues, to the ground. In addition, they looted materials from buildings and greenhouses that had been left behind. If there had been some hope that the PLO would take over the Gaza strip with a smooth transition and create a situation of peaceful coexistence with Israel, in gratitude for the withdrawal, this hope was quickly dashed. On the contrary, the disengagement proved to be a great disappointment to Israel from almost every point of view for many years to come.

The New Emerging Reality in the Gaza Strip, from 2006 and Onward

In the aftermath of the controversial unilateral withdrawal of all Israeli set-tlers and soldiers from Gaza, the reality in the Gaza Strip began to change. Officially Gaza was now under Palestinian rule, but its border crossings were supervised by Egypt to the south and by Israel to the east. Both Egypt and Israel supervised Gaza from the outside, from the point of view of security (although at the beginning, the Palestinian Authority controlled the Rafah land crossing to Egypt at the southern end of the Gaza Strip.) In fact, the Israeli army maintained a siege on the Gaza Strip, to prevent the smuggling of weapons and materials for armaments, which caused an ongoing human-itarian crisis among the poverty-stricken Gaza region.

Internally, the situation was different. At first the Palestinian Authority was in charge of the territory handed over to them, but this did not last long. In January 2006, the more extreme *Hamas* movement won the majority in the elections for the Palestinian parliament. *Hamas*, which is an Arabic acronym for the Islamic Resistance Movement, is a Palestinian Muslim organization, founded in 1987 by Sheikh Ahmad Yassin. It began as part of the Muslim Brotherhood, an international Islamic ideological stream which was founded in Egypt in 1928 as an Islamic revivalist movement.

From its establishment, *Hamas* was virulently anti-Israel and did not recog-nize the existence of the State of Israel, despite the fact that the PLO had done so in 1988 and again as part of the Oslo Accords in the early 1990s. According to the *Hamas* charter of 1988, Hamas sought to raise the banner of Allah over every inch of Palestine. They advocated for holy war, *jihad*, against Israel. They did not–and they still do not–believe in the idea of com-promise or relinquishing any territory that they feel is part of Palestine.

Israel and much of the western world was shocked by the victory of *Hamas* in the elections in early 2006. Indeed, following the elections, the interna-tional coalition known as the Quartet–comprised of the US, Russia, the UN and the EU–put some severe restrictions on the *Hamas*-led Palestinian government in Gaza. They said that if this government wanted to continue to receive foreign aid that they must recognize the State of Israel, end ter-rorism against Israel, and adhere to all previous agreements that the Palestinians had made with the governments of Israel. In retrospect, it was

27

a very curious set of demands, since the Quartet undoubtedly knew that the *Hamas* leadership in Gaza had absolutely no intention of accepting any of them.

There was a brief period in 2006 during which *Hamas* tried to cooperate with *Fatah*, their political rival. *Fatah*, led by President Mahmoud Abbas (previously led by Yasser Arafat), is mostly a secular movement of Palestinians—Christians as well as Muslims—which officially seeks to have a secular democratic Palestinian state in the West Bank and Gaza, although once they won power, they became less democratic, and more corrupt and autocratic. It was the *Fatah* leaders who negotiated the Oslo Accords with Israel in the previous decade, not the Islamic leaders of *Hamas*. This fundamental split within Palestinian society was to haunt the Palestinians and the peace process for a long time.

In 2006, there was a short-lived attempt at a unity government in Gaza, led by *Hamas* Prime Minister Ismail Haniyeh, with representatives from *Hamas* and from *Fatah* sharing power. But this unity government did not last long and *Hamas* won a victory over *Fatah* which resulted in an intractable division within Palestinian society. It totally destroyed any façade of Palestinian unity. Instead, it created a distinct divide between the Gaza Strip controlled by Islamic fundamentalists and the West Bank which was led by *Fatah* secularists, which included Muslims and Christians. Not only did this harm Palestinian society by creating a long-lasting and deleterious rift geographically, socially, religiously and psychologically between major parts of the Palestinian people but this also greatly diminished any hopes for a renewed peace process.

Not only did the *Hamas* movement deeply divide the Palestinian people, but it soon became a major source of violence against Israel. Rather than accepting the unilateral withdrawal from Gaza as a peace move, following which the leaders of the Palestinian people could have tried to move towards normalization of relations with Israel, the *Hamas* government in Gaza continued to see Israel as its enemy. In particular, its armed wing, known as the *Izz ad-Din-al-Qassam Brigades*, which had been formed in 1991 in opposition to the Oslo Peace Accords, played more of a role in convincing the government to launch attacks against innocent Israeli citizens in the south of Israel, using rockets (known as *kassam* rockets) to constantly bombard Israeli towns, villages and kibbutzim near the Gaza strip. This policy of armed resistance rather than peace negotiations characterized the *Hamas* government in Gaza. Moreover, it led to a situation in which Israel was forced to launch several military operations which it regarded as defensive wars in an attempt to stop the disruptive missile attacks from the Gaza Strip into southern Israel.

The Gaza Wars: 2007-2021

During the next 14 years, there were to be four wars between the IDF and the Hamas military wing, often in cooperation with other resistance groups in the Gaza Strip, such as the Islamic Jihad, and always funded by Iran. In each of these wars there was great disruption and destruction of property and loss of life on both sides, but always much more on the Palestinian side. As a result, critics called the response to missiles fired into Israel disproportional. On the other hand, Israel argued that they needed to use force to stop the rockets coming from the Gaza strip, which were fired in ever larger numbers in each round of violence, targeting and terrorizing innocent civilians in growing portions of the south and center of Israel.

The four wars took place during the following periods:

1. Operation Cast Lead began on December 27, 2007 (22 days)
2. Operation Pillar of Defense, November, 2012 (8 days)
3. Operation Protective Edge, July-August 2014 (50 days)
4. Operation Guardian of the Walls, May 2021 (1 week)

After each war, there was talk about some kind of long-term settlement of the problem but the talk was never translated into any serious negotiations. Every now and then, some ideas for peace have been floated. The Palestinian leadership in Gaza from time to time talked about a long-term truce which they called in Arabic a *hudna*. But the Israelis and Americans always rejected these ideas as nothing but propaganda. In fact, the Israeli government and the American government both continued to refer to the *Hamas*-led Palestinian government in the Gaza Strip as a terrorist organization, and did not negotiate or talk with them directly. They would only negotiate with the leadership of the Palestinian Authority in Ramallah, whose responsibility it was to arrange a reconciliation agreement with their brothers and sisters in the Gaza Strip, so that they could be brought back into the fold of a peace agreement were it ever to be actually negotiated again. Or they would negotiate through third parties, like Egypt, to obtain cease-fire agreements after each war.

Real attempts by the peacemakers–diplomats and politicians–to negotiate with Ramallah were few and far between during this period. Instead, periodic violence and counter-violence between Israel and *Hamas*-ruled Gaza became the new norm for the region. Also, the intractable rift between *Hamas* and *Fatah* continued unabated, despite periodic attempts to reconcile their differences, usually moderated by Egypt. Thus, *Hamas* continued to rule with its rejectionist policies in Gaza, and the Israel-Gaza front became the main military arena from the time that *Hamas* took control of Gaza in 2007 onward. Yet, the *Hamas*-Israel wars were not the only ones during this period. There was also trouble in the north with Lebanon once again.

The Second Lebanon War, Summer 2006

The Second Lebanon War is the official name given by Israel to the military operation which took place from July 12 until August 14, 2006. It was ultimately ended by diplomacy, via a UN brokered ceasefire agreement but not until much killing and destruction had taken place. During this period, Israel Defense Forces entered Lebanese territory to engage with *Hizbollah* militants, who had fired thousands of rockets into communities in northern Israel.

Hizbollah is a Shi'ite organization based in Lebanon, headed by Secretary-General *Hassan Nasrallah*, which has been waging a guerilla campaign against Israel since the 1980s. The group, which has both a military and a political wing, has been designated as a terrorist organization by the United States, Israel, Canada, the Arab League, many of the Gulf states, the UK, Australia and the EU. *Hizbollah* has also planned and carried out major terrorist attacks on Israeli citizens and infrastructure both within and outside of Israel.

The immediate cause of this war was the kidnapping of two Israeli soldiers–Ehud Goldwasser and Eldad Regev–by *Hizbollah* militants on July 12, 2006. This was part of a terrorist incursion into northern Israel, during which the *Hizbollah* organization launched *katyusha* rockets against Israeli communities in the Upper Galilee. As part of this highly provocative attack, eight Israel Defense Forces soldiers were killed.

This catalyzed Israel to launch a massive attack on *Hizbollah* posts close to the border with Israel. In addition, an armored force invaded southern Lebanon in an attempt to retrieve the abducted soldiers, but this force ran over a land mine, which killed four IDF soldiers in one tank. Attempts to extricate the tank and bring it back to Israel did not succeed. Instead, this led to another Israeli soldier being killed. After this incident, the government of Israel unanimously authorized a full-scale military operation inside Lebanon.

This second Lebanese war was an unfortunate continuation of the violence and counter-violence that has characterized so much of the Israeli-Palestinian conflict. Like so much of the previous violence, it was motivated by a policy of reprisal, and by fear of more kidnappings. It was also part of an ongoing mindset which believed that military force was the best conflict resolution modality. Israel therefore sought to destroy the *Hizbollah* infra-structure, despite the lessons of 18 years in the mud of Lebanon, from 1982–2000, in which it was demonstrated that a guerilla war is far more difficult to win than conventional wars.

The conflict was eventually brought to a stop by diplomatic means. American Secretary of State Condoleezza Rice came to Israel later in July for several days and met with Israeli leaders, but the conflict continued for more than four weeks. In addition, two days before the UN ordered a cease-fire, Uri Grossman, the son of the famous Israeli author and peace activist, David Grossman, was killed when a missile struck his tank in southern Lebanon. The death of this one soldier caused many in Israel to stand up and take note of the carnage around them. (A few years later, Grossman wrote an intense novel, *To the End of the Land*, which was about the mother of a young Israeli soldier about to complete his military service when a war breaks out.)

Since that war mutual deterrence has prevented another outbreak of hostil-ities between Israel and *Hizbollah*. But in the absence of a comprehensive peace agreement with the Palestinians, and in the absence of any peace agreement with Syria, the danger of another war with Lebanon (i.e., with *Hizbollah* militias) is always present. In addition, the continuing instability in the region caused by Iran's funding of the *Hizbollah* militias as their proxy in Lebanon–and Iran's continued attempts to establish forward bases in Syria–all make the military situation in the north of Israel very worrisome and explosive. The feeling in Israel is that a war in the north could break out once again at any moment with a well-armed, fortified *Hizbollah*.

Nevertheless, despite tensions in the north and south, attempts at peace-making continued to take place.

The Annapolis International Peace Conference and Talks between Prime Minister Olmert and President Abbas

Following the Second Lebanese War, there was another serious attempt to restart the Israeli-Palestinian peace process. At the end of November 2007, the US Administration led by President George Bush convened an international conference in Annapolis, Maryland, not far from Washington DC. At this conference, the Israeli Prime Minister Ehud Olmert, decided to make some bold moves towards peace, in the spirit of his predecessor. This led to a positive response from Palestinian President Mahmoud Abbas (Abu Mazen), who reached a joint understanding with Prime Minister Olmert to launch continuous bilateral negotiations towards achieving the goal of concluding a peace treaty by the end of 2008. Simultaneously they agreed that they would implement what was known as the *Road Map* (the Performance-Based Road Map to a Permanent Solution to the Israeli-Palestinian Conflict). It seemed at the time that these two leaders were serious about making real progress towards a peace agreement.

In fact, Prime Minister Olmert and President Abbas met many times, and Tzipi Livni, also of the *Kadima* party, who was the Foreign Minister of Israel at the time, met many times with Abu Ala, who was the number two person within the PA. According to a recent research report published by the Institute of National Security Studies of Tel Aviv University, Olmert, Livni and others from their teams, met over 300 times with Palestinian representatives as part of these talks. There was much trust and good relationship-building and it looked like a miracle might happen. President Abbas was talking a great deal about renouncing terror and using non-violence—which was music to many Israeli ears, including mine—after five long years of a very violent uprising and the counter-terrorism used by Israel to crush the *intifada*. Moreover, Prime Minister Olmert welcomed President Abbas warmly to his residence in West Jerusalem, with Palestinian flags flying as a symbol of good will. By many accounts, both sides were very close to reaching an agreement, but due to several factors–especially the corruption trial of Olmert, which led him to become a lame duck prime minister and eventually resign–such an agreement never took place. Yet, it was the closest both sides have ever come to reaching a comprehensive Israeli-Palestinian peace agreement.

In the end, however, despite all the good intentions and intensive talks, it was another peacemaking failure, which did not lead to a resolution of this seemingly intractable conflict. The politicians and diplomats on both sides were incapable of reaching an agreement that would have been for the mutual benefit of their peoples. Instead, the war process continued with the operations against Gaza in 2012, 2014, and 2021.

The Obama Years: Unsuccessful Peacemaking Initiatives

After President Barak Obama was elected in November 2008, he announced that he was interested in continuing the peace process with Israel. One of the first things that he did, on January 22, 2009, together with Secretary of State Hilary Clinton, was to appoint Senator George Mitchell as the Special Envoy for the Middle East. Senator Mitchell had become well-known for successfully negotiating the end of the "troubles" in Northern Ireland in what was known as the "Good Friday Agreement" in April 1998. From 2010 to 2011, Mitchell spent a year and a half attempting to resolve this conflict, but gave up after he saw that his efforts were futile. On May 13, 2011, he resigned.

Many years later, I had occasion to meet Senator Mitchell in New York at a lecture that I gave at St. Bartholomew's Church in Manhattan, followed a few months later by a conversation in his office. When I asked him why he found these negotiations so difficult, he told me clearly that the leaders on both sides of the Israeli-Palestinian Conflict were at fault, that neither one was prepared to make the necessary compromises to make any significant progress towards peace. Indeed, both Prime Minister Netanyahu, who served as Prime Minister from 1996-1999 and then again from 2009 until 2021, and President Mahmoud Abbas, who had replaced Arafat as President after he died in 2004, were stubborn and intransigent leaders, who made life quite difficult for any mediator who tried to help them and their peoples achieve peace.

The last attempt at getting the sides to the table was the one carried out by President Obama's second Secretary of State, John Kerry, between July 2013 and April 2014. Over the nine months Kerry met with Palestinian President Abbas on 34 occasions, and Israeli Prime Minister Netanyahu roughly twice as many times. After a tremendous effort, Kerry finally gave up, realizing, as Senator Mitchell had done, that the leaders were not ready for serious negotiations for peace. After another diplomatic failure, both sides blamed each other for being intransigent, when in fact neither side was ready to come to the table with honorable intentions to end the conflict.

The Trump Administration Puts the Israeli-Palestinian Peace Process on hold

Shortly after Donald Trump became president of the USA in January 2017, he announced that he and his team were going to develop "the deal of the century" to end the Palestinian-Israeli conflict. However, during his four disastrous years as president, he and his partner in Jerusalem, Prime Minister Netanyahu, did everything they could to bury the Israeli-Palestinian peace track. Trump recognized Jerusalem as the capital of Israel and moved the American Embassy there–a one-sided move that was designed to please the Israeli right-wing and the evangelical Christians in America, and to anger and humiliate the Palestinians, which it did.

Trump not only moved the American embassy from Tel Aviv to West Jerusalem, but he also defunded programs that promoted peaceful understanding and cooperation between Israelis and Palestinians, which was harmful to both sides. Moreover, he announced American recognition of the annexation of the Golan Heights, an issue that was to be left to final status peace negotiations. He disbanded the PLO office in Washington DC and he constantly issued anti-Palestinian statements. The Palestinian leadership was infuriated and humiliated. They refused to engage with the Trump Administration in any way since they viewed his intention to solve the conflict as insincere and unfair. In short, the Trump presidency–in full cooperation with the right-wing government of Benjamin Netanyahu–did everything it could to make sure that there were no negotiations for peace between Israelis and Palestinians.

Instead, it developed an end-run so-called peace process with some Muslim countries in the region–the United Arab Emirates, Bahrain, Sudan and Morocco–which became known as "the Abraham Accords." The Palestinians were completely left out of this process. These accords were made with countries with which Israel had not been at war. They were essentially normalization arrangements, or economic accords, with countries with which Israel already had positive relations. They had nothing to do with actually trying to resolve the Palestinian-Israel Conflict. On the contrary, these agreements—which were crafted in close cooperation with the Israel government and in total isolation from the Palestinian administration–assiduously avoided the Israeli-Palestinian question, even though the parties to these agreements did express some vague commitment to resolving that conflict. In this way, they allowed creeping annexation to continue in the West Bank and the continuation of the oppressive occupation of the

Palestinian people, even though formal annexation of the West Bank was temporarily taken off the table.

In November 2020., the American people elected the Democratic team of Joe Biden and Kamala Harris, who were known for their commitment to a two-state solution of the Israeli-Palestinian conflict. This new presidential administration began working to restore trust with the Palestinian government, which the previous administration had completely destroyed. Accordingly, there was once again some modicum of hope that the peace process could somehow be re-started.

Conclusion: From Political Despair to Hope through Peacebuilding

The peace process has been in a state of stagnation for most of the first two decades of the twenty-first century. Despite the many attempts of outside mediation to rekindle it, it has been stalled for a long time. Political leaders on both sides of the conflict have not been able to develop effective ideas to break and end the deadlock.

For the future, much depends on the local leaders of Israel and Palestine. In order for a serious political-diplomatic peace process to be renewed, they both would have to cease and desist from presenting impossible, inflexible, unrealistic, non-negotiable demands, which prevent negotiations from even beginning. Both sides would need to rediscover the importance of compromise and pragmatism in order for there to be genuine progress towards a peace agreement. This would require, of course, courageous and forward-thinking political leadership, which unfortunately was not the kind of leadership that either Palestinian or Israeli society has been blessed with in recent years.

The bottom line is that the political-diplomatic peace process is in the deep freeze. Even the fragile coalition formed after the 2021 elections, led by Naftali Bennett and Yair Lapid, which only lasted one year, was based on an agreement *not* to do anything on the peace process. On the Palestinian side, the rift between *Hamas* in Gaza and the Palestinian Authority in Ramallah has continued, so that there have been no Palestinian initiatives for peace for a long time.

I call this situation *political despair*. The citizens on both sides of the conflict have chosen leaders with no real interest in the peace process. They keep electing such leaders in Israel, and in Palestine, they allow one man to continue to rule for many years, without elections. Thus, it seems, the people

on both sides see no way out. They see their leaders as managing the conflict, not trying to resolve it.

Therefore, it has become clear that the only people who have been promoting peaceful relations between the two peoples during the first two decades
of the twenty-first century have been the peacebuilders, working in civil society, not in politics. Peacebuilders include rabbis, imams, kadis, ministers,
educators, youth workers, social workers, psychologists and peace activists
who volunteer in a wide variety of non-governmental organizations. Despite
the political despair all around them, peacebuilders have continued to envision and to act for a better future for their peoples. The underlying
assumption of these peacebuilders is that only by changing hearts and
minds can the two peoples rise up to choose leaders who will be peacemakers. The rest of this book will focus on the work of six leading peacebuilders in Israeli and Palestinian societies.

Timeline–Important Dates in the History of War and Peace in Israel and Palestine

1947-49	War of Independence/*Nakbah* (the Great Catastrophe)
1948, May 15	Establishment of the State of Israel–Declaration of Independence
1956, Oct 29-Nov. 7	Sinai Campaign/Suez Crisis
1967, June 5-11	Six Day War
1973, Oct	Yom Kippur War
1977, Nov 19	Pres Anwar Sadat makes historic visit to Jerusalem
1978, Sept 17-29	Camp David Summit with Pres Carter, Pres Sadat and PM Begin
1978, Mar 26	Signing of the Peace Agreement between Israel and Egypt
1982, June – 1985	First Lebanon War (from 1985 until 2000, Israel continues its presence in a security zone in southern Lebanon.)
1982, Sept 16-18	Massacre at the Sabra and Shatilla refugee camps in Beirut
1982, Sept 25	Demonstration organized by Peace Now in Tel Aviv. 400,000 Israelis protest against the war in Lebanon and against the massacre at the Sabra and Shatilla refugee camps.

1987, Dec 7	Beginning of First *Intifada* (uprising), which lasts until Sept 1993
1988, Nov 15	PLO announces recognition of the State of Israel, and declares a Palestinian state
1991, Oct 30-Nov 1	International peace conference in Madrid, including Palestinians
1992-93	Oslo back-channel peace talks in Norway, with Israelis and Palestinians
1993, Sept 13	Signing of Oslo Accord, the Declaration of Principles, signed by PM Rabin, Chairman Arafat, Foreign Minister Peres, in the presence of Pres Clinton, at the White House in Wash DC
1994, Oct 26	Signing of Peace Accord between Israel and Jordan, signed by PM Rabin and Chairman Arafat, in the presence of Pres Clinton
1991-1995	Negotiations between Israel and Syria but no agreements reached
1994, May 4	Agreement on the Gaza Strip and the Jericho Area, also known as 1994 Cairo

	Agreement. The Palestinian Authority is established.
1995, Jan 21-27	Oslo Peace Accord II, signed at the Taba Summit
1996, Jan 20	General elections held for the Palestinian Legislative Council
1995, Nov 4	Assassination of Israeli PM Yitzhak Rabin in Tel Aviv, by a Jewish extremist. Shimon Peres becomes Acting PM of Israel, continues the peace process.
1996, May 29	Benjamin Netanyahu elected as PM, continues the peace process with the Palestinians
1998, Oct 23	Wye River Memorandum, signed by PM Netanyahu and Chairman Arafat, near Wash DC, continues the peace process between the Israelis and the Palestinians
1999, May 17	Ehud Barak elected as PM of Israel, pledges to continue the peace process
2000, July 11-15	Camp David II, Summit with Barak, Arafat, and Clinton, fails to reach an agreement
2000, Sept 28	MK Ariel Sharon walks on the Temple Mount/*Harem El Sharif*
2000, Sept 29	Second *Intifada* (lasts 5 years)

2002	Building of the Security Fence/ Separation Wall
2004, Nov 11	Death of Yasser Arafat, former Chairman of the PLO and Pres of the State of Palestine
2005, May 8	Mahmoud Abbas, known as *Abu Mazen*, becomes president of Palestine and the Palestine National Authority (PNA). He has been chairman of the Palestinian Liberation Organization (PLO) since Nov. 2004, president of the PNA since Jan. 2005 and president of the state of Palestine since May 2005.
2005, Aug	Israel unilaterally disengages from the Gaza Strip, removing all settlers and soldiers
2006	Hamas wins elections in the Gaza Strip.
2006, July – Aug	Second Lebanon War
2007, Nov	Annapolis International Peace Conference in the USA–setting the Road Map for Israeli-Palestinian Peace
2007, Dec 27	First Gaza War, Operation Cast Lead (lasted 22 days)
2009, Jan-May 2011	Special Envoy to the Middle East, Sen George Mitchell, appointed by Pres Obama and

	Sec of State Hilary Clinton, tries to mediate an Israeli-Palestinian peace agreement but does not succeed.
2012, Nov	Second Gaza War, Operation Pillar of Defense (lasted 8 days)
2013, July	Pres Obama's second Sec of State, John Kerry, spends nine months trying to negotiate Israeli-Palestinian Peace but also does not succeed.
2014, July	Third Gaza War, Operation Protective Edge (lasted 50 days)
2020, Aug 13	Abraham Accords are concluded between Israel and the United Arab Emirates, later to include also Bahrain, Morocco and Sudan.
2021, Jan 20	Newly-elected Pres Joe Biden pledges to try to restore the peace process towards a two-state solution for the Israeli-Palestinian conflict.
2021, May	Fourth Gaza War, Operation Guardian of the Walls (lasted 1 week)
2021, May 4	Benjamin Netanyahu fails to form a coalition government in Israel and leaves office as PM after 12 years (2009-2021)

2021, June 13   Naftali Bennett (*Yemina-*
Rightwards) and Yair Lapid
(*Yesh Atid-*A New Future) form
a unity government in Israel,
with 8 political parties from the
left, right and center. They
agree to freeze the peace
process between Israel and the
Palestinian government. This
government lasted one year, till
the end of June 2022, when
Bennet and Lapid called for the
dissolution of Parliament and
new elections were set for
November 1, 2022.

Part Two

Profiles

Profiles in Peace

Palestinian Peacebuilders

Huda Abuarquob: A Feminist Muslim Palestinian Perspective on Peacebuilding

Photo courtesy of the Alliance for Middle East Peace (ALLMEP)

Huda Abuarquob is a leading Palestinian Arab peacebuilder in the West Bank. As someone who grew up under Israeli military occupation she embarked on a long journey of remarkable transformation from a victim of the oppression and humiliation of the Israeli army to a serious, sensitive and systematic peacebuilder. She is a Muslim feminist who believes fervently in the importance of publicly sharing her story and those of other peace activists, without fear. She went through a long process of growth and change, from someone who saw Israelis as only one-dimensional soldiers and settlers, to a mature person who has learned their narrative and engaged with them in programs and projects for peace over many years, and continues to do so with passion and professionalism.

Abuarquob comes from a Palestinian Muslim family with deep roots in Palestine. She is the oldest of twelve children, the daughter of respected Palestinian educators, and an aunt to 22 young nieces and nephews. After growing up in Palestine, she traveled extensively in Europe and the Middle East, lived for six years in the U.S., and now resides with her family in a village near Hebron, in the southern part of the West Bank.

The Impact of the *Nakbah* on her family and on her identity

During her formative years, as a child and teenager, she and her family suffered through many difficult experiences with the Israeli army as part of the oppressive military occupation which made life quite difficult for them in their village in the West Bank. Like many Palestinians, they lived with the trauma of the *nakbah* (the Arabic word for the great catastrophe that befell the Palestinians after they lost the 1948 war with Israel) and became refugees within their own land. Born in Jerusalem, her family moved to Bethlehem when she was very young. Then, after a year in Saudi Arabia, they came back to Palestine and moved to the village of Dura, where she grew up. Her memories of this shaped her identity as a Palestinian for the rest of her life.

> The *nakbah* defines our trauma, stripping us of every right, treating us as if we did not exist, denying us a connection to the only home we know, stripping us of our dignity, narrative, land, making us refugees. Also, there was a great shame that was experienced by the generations of my grandparents and my parents since Arab leaders had virtually denied our existence before 1948. I and my generation have been left with an unanswered question 'why us?' We understand the tragedy the Jewish people went through in Europe during the period of the Holocaust, but have never understood

why we as Palestinians had to pay the price for this by being expelled from our land.

Abuarquob recalled how the *Nakbah* was experienced by her family.

> I have been told by my parents that they were land owners, but they had to leave everything behind. They both lost their lands in the area south west of Hebron, in the village *Omm Eshugaf (Deir Mheisen)*. [This village became part of the state of Israel after 1948.] In addition, the Arabs in the neighboring Arab countries deceived them by selling them false notions of liberation. They told them that in a few days they will be able to go back to their lands, but it was not true. My grandparents died hoping one day they will get back their land. For them, their land was more than just a property, it was social status. After they lost their land, their social status was reduced to almost nothing. Both sides of my family refused to register themselves as refugees since with it came a great deal of shame.

For Abuarquob, the personal experiences of her parents and grandparents during the 1948 war and thereafter left an indelible impression on her for all of her life.

The Trials and Tribulations of Living Under Military Occupation

After the *nakbah*, the next main trauma for Abuarquob and her family was the Six Day War of 1967, during which Israel occupied the West Bank (of the Jordan River) which used to belong to Jordan. For several decades, the Israeli military occupation in that area – and in the Gaza Strip–became deeply entrenched. Palestinians were forced to live in a new reality under military control in which their freedom of movement and expression was severely limited. In addition, in response to terrorist attacks by Palestinians on innocent civilians in Israel, the military in the West Bank often clamped down on Palestinian towns and villages in harsh ways, which embittered the lives of innocent Palestinians living under occupation.

Abuarquob, recalled the repressive and demeaning conditions that she and others in her family had to endure for a long time in her village after the occupation of the West Bank following 1967:

> As I grew up, I and my family had been on the receiving end of many violent actions by the occupation. Once, when I was trying to go to *Al Maqasssed* hospital to visit my mom, my younger

brother was with me. The Israeli soldiers wanted him to get out of the car so they could search him. He did not even have an identity card with him. He was only 13 years old but he looked older. The soldiers wanted to arrest him. I had to struggle against them with bare hands until they let him go.

Another time, when the soldiers raided our home during the day—which did not happen as often as with the nighttime raids— they wanted to force my father to clear the street from stones which the *shebab* [Arabic for youth] had put there. My father was old and fragile then. The soldiers insulted him and were mean to him. I and my sisters had to fight them to get them off my dad. Eventually they took him to clear the street. We were fearful that he would not be able to do it. We were also worried that he would get angry since his dignity was harmed, and that he might react badly to the violent and rude behavior of these young soldiers.

I could go on and on. During my school years, the Israeli army raided our school, beat us up, searched our classrooms and took our male teachers away in their jeeps. Later we were told that they were taken for interrogation at an army base for several hours. In another incident, I was shot by a rubber bullet during one of the school raids. There was also tear gas, which was minor compared to seeing classmates being shot with live bullets, which happened more than once.

Later when Abuarquob became a teacher, she was stopped by so-called flying checkpoints and held as hostage by the army. She was used as a human shield by the soldiers against kids from a refugee camp who were throwing stones at them. All of these experiences helped to shape her identity as a Palestinian who grew up under military occupation by the Israeli army.

The Positive Impact of the Oslo Accords

An abrupt change took place when Abuarquob was just a teenager—the unexpected peace agreement known as the Oslo Accord was signed in September 1993. This event was to change her life in many ways. It gave her some hope that peace for her and her people might actually be possible. Based in her home in the West Bank, she vividly remembers the mood in her community when the famous Declaration of Principles was signed in Washington DC, on the lawn of the White House.

I was home in Palestine, teaching at that time in my small village in the South Hebron Hills, full of hope, excitement, anticipation, dreaming of a state, imagining the potential of being an active member of a state built on norms of freedom, justice and equality. I was in tears every time I remember my friends who lost their lives or are still in prison saying to myself, it paid off, finally we will have a state and we will honor their legacy by being the citizens of a free, viable and strong state. Finally, we will have a status, finally, we will be recognized as equals, finally, we will get the freedom we fought for. Even if Palestine is not from the sea to the river, we still can enjoy visiting and honoring the history, culture and heritage we once had; we will still have access to the sea we sang about, the mountains we took power from; we will walk in the streets that Ghassan Kanafani and Mahmood Darwish described in their stories and poems. Finally, we will unite with our identity and have closure for our long struggle for recognition. There is no doubt that the signing of this document was one of the main motivators for me to become involved with peace work in the years ahead.

Abuarquob–who was living in Dura, near Hebron, but travelled throughout the West Bank–was also witness to the spontaneous celebrations of Palestinians in the streets of Bethlehem, one of the major Palestinian cities, just south of Jerusalem. These experiences and memories were to stay with her for a long time. They influenced her view of the conflict, and became a basis for her peace activism in the 1990s and the decades thereafter.

Becoming a teacher for the Palestinian Authority and getting involved in joint projects with Israeli educators

After high school, Abuarquob spent a year studying English in Jordan, and then returned to Jerusalem, where she studied for a BA in teaching English as a second language, which she received in 1997 from the Al-Quds Open University in Jerusalem. Soon after, she was noticed by people in the Palestinian Authority's Ministry of Education as a promising young educator, whom they felt that they should recruit for becoming engaged with helping to establish educational systems in the newly emerging Palestinian government in the West Bank and Gaza.

The Palestinian Authority encouraged Abuarquob to join projects that promoted dialogue between Israelis and Palestinians, in the spirit of the Oslo Peace Accords of the early 1990s. Accordingly, she began to participate in many projects and programs that promoted dialogue and mutual understanding with Israeli Jews, such as a program with educators from Palestine and Israel which took place in Vienna in 1997 at the invitation of the Austrian government. This was clearly a transformative educational experience for her. She recalls it as a game-changer in her life.

> It was in 1997 when the Palestinian Ministry of Education—for whom I was working as a teacher of English—sent me to Vienna, at the invitation of the Austrian Ministry of Education, to attend a seminar on developing educational systems in Palestine and in Israel. We knew at that time that there would be Israeli teachers there, but this was OK, since we had the 'kosher stamp' of the government of Palestine. Attending these people-to-people programs was part of the Oslo process then. This was totally official, on behalf of the PA. The Ministry of Education of Palestine was brand new—it was only one year old. It had just taken over from the Civil Administration of the Israeli Army. I was part of it because I was a teacher of English, and I could speak English well. Of course, the PA had its own agenda at that time–promoting the narrative of the Palestinian people–which included the desire for peace with Israel, via a two-state solution.

In addition to formally representing the Palestinian Ministry of Education, Abuarquob had her own agenda. After all, this was the first time that she was meeting Israelis who were not soldiers at checkpoints or "security" forces coming into her village to wreak havoc. She was very curious about meeting Israelis and discovering first-hand, through dialogue, what they were really thinking and feeling.

> The thing that I was looking for in this experience was whether the Israelis were monsters or not. This is the image that we Palestinians had of Israelis. These images were based upon experiences that I grew up with in my village, which was always under Israeli military occupation. I wanted to see if Israelis are also human beings. This was very important to me. In my brain, it couldn't be true that Israelis were only monsters. So, when I met Israelis via the facilitated dialogue in Vienna (we had Israeli and Palestinian facilitators) I discovered that this seminar was not just about formal education in schools but it was also about meeting the other for the first time, what was called 'the contact theory' by scholars. When the Palestinians and the Israelis were in the room–

guided by trained facilitators—we talked about everything, not just about education! Outside of the formal dialogue process, we had many occasions for small talk (over coffee and at meals and during breaks) and it worked! We clicked immediately—as human beings, we got along right away! The Austrians were amazed that we were able to talk about everything with so much respect and acceptance.

However, there were limitations to the dialogue in a highly controlled situation, in which the hosts did not want to get into political issues with the participants. As she would do throughout her peacebuilding career, Abuarquob would try to overcome the obstacles and make the best of it, and focus on the topic of education.

But we did not get into a place where we could talk about narratives—who did what, when did it start. This would have been too difficult. Also, the Austrians were keen that we focus on the agenda of education in the official meeting rooms. We tried to develop educational systems, to focus on what we want the kids to learn. Based on our learning there, we were able to take ideas back to the Ministry of Education in Palestine. We developed new ways to relate to students—they were no longer to be only banks into which we deposited knowledge. We needed to relate to them as human beings. We were definitely able to improve Palestinian education.

In Austria, we did not talk about political issues like final status, or maps. It was a highly monitored process. It was under a lot of scrutiny. It had to follow the Oslo guidelines. We did focus on developing an educational curriculum, including giving attention to the psychology of the kids.

Since this was her first experience in dialogue with Israelis, much of the encounter dealt not only with professional educational strategies and methods but also with basic issues such as mutual respect and learning about each other's religions and cultures. Both aspects of this seminar were to become important in Abuarquob's personal and professional life.

We also promoted the notion of respecting the other—people of other religions and colors. In so doing, we included civics education in the English curriculum. There were also debates among the Palestinian teachers as to what are we teaching our kids, who is the other, what do we mean by democracy.

When I came back, I was hired by the Ministry of Education to be part of a national team to develop the Palestinian curriculum for the teaching of English. The Norwegians were funding it and the British were involved in everything that we did as well, through the British Council, which is the educational office of the British government here.

Why was this seminar so important in her life? Abuarquob's response to this was straightforward:

This was my first experience in meeting Israelis. It was amazing for me to meet them for the first time, not as soldiers or settlers, but as human beings, and as people who expressed interest in living in peace with me.

After this experience, there were many more to follow. For example, she was instrumental in helping Palestinian high school students to be accepted to the renowned Seeds of Peace program where, in its prestigious camp in Maine, young Palestinians and young Israelis would meet in a beautiful pastoral setting and get to know each other –and their narratives—for the first time.

During these years [late 1990s], I helped as a teacher to nominate Palestinian students to participate in the Seeds of Peace camp in the USA. This was authorized by the Palestinian Ministry of Education. It was important for Palestinians to be able to speak good English to attend this program.

Abuarquob recalls the mood of the late 1990s concerning the importance and the possibility of dialogue between Israelis and Palestinians:

It was legitimate to engage with Israelis during the 1990s! It was encouraged by the PA! And there were benefits. It was like a Fulbright scholarship. These programs were topic focused, not conflict focused, but we talked about the conflict outside the formal meetings! From 1997-2000, I was involved in 'kosher' [government authorized] meetings between Israelis and Palestinians, which were encouraged by both governments. This was all about Oslo—we were cooperating in building peace! The atmosphere was amazing. It was totally different from the way it is now. We even gained a lot of power for being there at that time—power from our society, from our families, from our circles of friends, from our teachers. This was a cool thing to do. It was fine with most people.

Her experience in Vienna and with Seeds of Peace led to more encounters with Israeli Jews who were involved in peace activism in the years ahead.

Additional Encounters with Israeli and American Jews in the USA

During the summers, from 2002-2006, Abuarquob participated in the University of the Middle East Project at Boston College, first as a participant and then for three years as a staff person. This was a unique program with peacebuilders from all over the world, including Israel and Palestine, which greatly enriched her skills and knowledge in the field of conflict resolution and transformation.

> This was a great program. They brought professors from Harvard University, Boston University and Boston College to teach us for four weeks at Boston College. We learned many educational theories, like Paulo Freire's *The Pedagogy of the Oppressed*. They brought a professor from George Mason University in Virginia whose specialty was Conflict Transformation and Peace Education. While we were there, we engaged with educators from all over the Middle East, including Moroccans, Algerians, Israelis, Palestinians, Qataris, and Jordanians.

Her participation in the University of the Middle East Project took place in the middle of the Second *Intifada* (Palestinian uprising). It was a time of much violence and counter-violence in Israel and Palestine, a very dark time. Yet, peacebuilders like Abuarquob—and others in this book—persisted in their peace activism, even though it became more and more complicated and less popular. She remembers the mood clearly:

> The atmosphere was totally different. The Palestinian Ministry of Education did not want to publicize this. People who were chosen had to keep it a secret. It was difficult to travel. There were no visas, due to the violence of the *Intifada*. Because Hala Taweel [the sister of the wife of Yasser Arafat] was involved, the Palestinian Authority did succeed in getting us permits to travel in 2002. This was the first time that I received a visa to the USA in my life! It was very difficult to leave during the *Intifada* but we succeeded somehow.

> Despite all these difficulties, I attended this program for four years, from 2002-2006. I persevered in this because I felt that this was the only way forward, even though my government and my society frowned upon the idea of my meeting Israelis!

> We were in the middle of a lot of violence. Also, we began to recognize the fact that the Palestinian Authority was completely fragmented and crippled. Everything that we believed in during the 1990s came crashing down! Yet, we were left with all the connections we had made, with all the many possibilities–we had found partners on the other side! We discovered that the partners could be in civil society, not in governments.

During her studies and her staff work with this project, Abuarquob continued to learn a great deal about conflict resolution and about some of the new ideas that might bring about genuine change, especially methods and strategies of action that could lead to greater impact. As she did this, she gradually began to develop her own voice and her own philosophy as a peace activist, one that would grow and become more eloquent during the next two decades.

> At that time, many theories of change and new methods started developing—interfaith dialogue, dialogue based on topics of mutual interest, focused on certain projects, including technology as a way for Israelis and Palestinians to meet, which is happening more and more lately. I was in this middle road, where I knew what was possible, through non-violence, where I felt so much more powerful than the Palestinian who sees herself or himself as a victim and just receives hand-outs [from various NGO's]. I claimed some parts of the power through my voice, and I believe that this is the only way.

Abuarquob wanted to continue to learn more and to become a more knowledgeable and enlightened peace activist. As a person who knew English well, she applied for and was granted a prestigious Fulbright scholarship to study in the USA for two years, from 2004-2006. She did her studies on Conflict Resolution at the Eastern Mennonite University in Virginia with one of the leading professors in this field, John Paul Lederach (who wrote many books on conflict resolution and later went on to teach at Notre Dame University), from whom she learned much and with whom she served as a teaching fellow one summer. This program strengthened her expertise and knowledge in the field, which became very useful for her in the years ahead.

> I was one of 15 students [studying Conflict Resolution at the Eastern Mennonite University] from all over the Middle East, including one Israeli Jew, and there were another ten students from all over Africa, a few Irish students, and a few American Christians

from different denominations. While I was there, I was also an activist, from day one. I partnered with Odelia, an Israeli woman, from the beginning. The university-and the Fulbright program-wanted us to do projects together-to raise the awareness of the American people about Israel and Palestine to counter the image that Israel and Palestine were only about blood and violence. We visited schools and universities together. The Fulbright people saw this as our service to America and the university saw this as my practicum. Odelia was working for the Peres Center for Peace [one of Israel's most prominent peacebuilding institutions], and she worked directly with Shimon Peres himself. I partnered with this Israeli woman for two years. At some point, some of the Arabs who were part of the program encouraged me and my relationship with Odelia, but they didn't think that it was wise for me to stand with Odelia on an equal basis, because she represented the occupier. There I started learning the notion of asymmetry in power relationships. I believe that we are powerful. We are not coming from a place of fear or collective trauma that is controlling our life.

While Abuarquob was in Viginia, she was constantly learning new ideas and engaging in productive conversations, which introduced her to new stories and new people all the time.

I was learning the ABCs of the dialogue—trauma healing and its importance in resolving conflict, the promise of reconciliation, and the need to engage in interreligious conversations. Theories of change that the Mennonites introduced made so much sense to me because they were not coming from a place of powerlessness; rather, they were coming from a place of power. I totally bought it. I was empowered, and I believed in it. I developed my own theories of change, based on what I learned there. I also strengthened my skills, especially with regard to speaking to the public.

It was during this time that Abuarquob also began to explore and learn much more about the Jewish narrative-how Jews think and feel about their religion, their history, and about the Israeli-Palestinian conflict.

I learned more about the Jewish narrative. I was addicted. I wanted to hear more from Odelia. She was a lefty, but she introduced me to other stories other than hers. I was changing as I went along. Learning the Jewish Israeli narrative was totally new for me. I wanted to know why-the question for me was always 'why us?'

Why were we, the Palestinians, paying the price of the Holocaust? This was a key question for me, and I wanted to know the answer. I wanted to know more about it, even though I grew up with stories about the Holocaust, because my parents were both educators, as was my grandfather, who was very lefty in his mindset.

Learning about the other was one way that I grew up with the desire to reverse the relationship of a foe to a friend. In order for this to happen, we need to learn more about them. This became a mission for me. I need to understand what is going on with their minds.

Ironically, it was during her studies at Eastern Mennonite University that Abuarquob began to learn the Jewish narrative in depth. Not only did she meet many American Jews there–and on her many visits to Washington DC, only two hours away–but she also embarked on a journey to learn more about Judaism. At the same time that she did this, she got involved with studies on comparative religion at the university, and wrote a master's thesis, which was another major building block in her becoming an interreligious peacebuilder. She was constantly growing in her inclusive and effervescent personality and in her professionalism. In addition, she was growing as a Muslim, and developing her spirituality.

A surprise for me was the identification of the stories of the Jews, including the religious ones. At the time, I was reading the Koran, using the lens of the peacemaker. I was looking for peace in the Koran. Where is the call for peace? The issue that I was grappling with at the moment was why we [the Palestinians] were denying the Jewish narrative, when it is there in the Koran! I began learning how religious institutions are sometimes working together and sometimes working against each other. I also learned how the religious institutions were helping the politicians to keep us divided, preventing us from connecting with each other as human beings. I discovered that the Koran teaches us that we are born with that instinct to connect. Even my understanding of Islam at that time changed. And my spiritual journey towards realizing who I am, as a Muslim, was on a new trajectory.

Abuarquob's studies helped her strengthen and develop both her Muslim and her Palestinian identities. While she does not like the terms "religious" or "secular," she considers herself a full Muslim, with deep family roots in the mystical traditions of Muslim Sufism.

I am a religious Muslim. But, I drink, I don't find God in a mosque or a church. Or in a synagogue. I tried. I went to many of these institutions when I was in the States, and when I came back home. When I go to shrines in search of God, I don't find Him or Her there. I consider myself a spiritual Muslim, because I come from a Sufi origin. I have Sufi traditions in my family. We are still keeping some of it. There are some parts of my family who still remember how to do the *zikr* [Sufi spiritual dance]. My great-grandfathers were Sufis, seven generations back–they had a *tikiyeh* [a charitable institution] near Ashkelon. They came from a town near Gaza, near the Gaza border. There is a myth about the story about our family name, Abuarquob. Originally, we were called Omari. The family name was Omar, going way back to one of the caliphs. But we are Abuarquob because of a spiritual leader who came to Palestine through Egypt. He stopped by Ashkelon and there was a siege and he hit the wall and cracked it. But he hit it with a bone from the leg of a camel, and that's what Abuarquob in Arabic means. So, we became the Abuarquob family from *Askelan*.

I would refer to myself as a full Muslim who embraces inclusivity, which I believe is at the heart of Islam. This is where I find myself in the text of the Koran. I have found that everyone has the same rights and are equal to each other. In my view, the differences have to do with the number of good deeds that they do. By the way, the Jewish story in the Koran is the prevailing story, from Abraham to Moses, until Mohammad. I got in touch with the Sufi part of myself when I was doing comparative studies for my Master's degree. I was writing my thesis about how peace was seen in the Koran and about fundamentalist Islam today. I wanted to find that notion of peace in the three religions, and to defy the theories of fundamentalism. Through this process, I experienced liberation. I am not giving in to those fundamentalist institutions that say Islam says this or that. This is because I found a way to be connected to the text, spiritually and intellectually, through my studies, without needing the institutions.

When the program was over, Abuarquob returned to the West Bank for two years, but then was invited to return to the USA. She lived for five years in the San Francisco Bay area, during which time she co-directed (with Professor Aaron Hahn Tapper of San Francisco State University) an organization called Abraham's Vision. This was a conflict transformation organization that planned and implemented educational programs within and between Muslim, Jewish, Palestinian and Israeli communities. The organization, which was founded by Professor Tapper, operated for ten years, from 2003-2013. Abuarquob worked with Tapper from 2008 to 2013, where she gained extensive experience in program development and management.

I first met her on a speaking tour to Northern California during this period. We spoke on a panel together at the University of California at Berkeley on approaches to peacebuilding in Israel and Palestine. I was impressed then by her intelligence, knowledge, communications skills, and her positive energy. It was clear that she was deeply committed to the work of peace through dialogue and action.

One of the major programs that she directed was a special summer program in Conflict Resolution for Jewish and Palestinian students who were studying at universities throughout the USA, which was held for five weeks in the Balkans from 2008-2012, with Palestinian and Israeli facilitators. In addition, she was a co-founder, with Professor Tapper, of the Center for Transformative Education, where she taught and trained students in new ways of thinking and in the importance of activism in the field. With this knowledge and experience, she would become a teacher and a trainer of many other peace activists as her career in this field developed.

Returning to Palestine and Getting Involved with the Alliance for Middle East Peace

Abuarquob returned to Palestine in 2013 and since then resides with her family in the village of Dura, near Hebron, where she grew up, in the southern part of the West Bank. After her return, she was recruited to serve as the regional director of the Alliance for Middle East Peace (ALLMEP), an international organization devoted to promoting peaceful relations among Israelis and Palestinians. This umbrella organization comprises over 150 international and local (Palestinian and Israeli) organizations which work for peaceful coexistence in Israel and Palestine in a great variety of ways, from dialogue to demonstrations. ALLMEP was founded in 2004. I was one of the initial members of the alliance, when I was serving as director of the Interreligious Coordinating Council in Israel (ICCI). I attended several meetings in Washington DC in those years, during which I also joined other peacebuilders from Israel and Palestine in lobbying members of the US Congress to create funding mechanisms to support peace work in Israel and Palestine, which (as you will see below) have become very important for peacebuilding organizations in Israel and Palestine.

In her position as Regional Director of the Alliance for Middle East Peace, Abuarquob has interacted with many Israeli and Palestinian peacebuilding organizations. In particular, she has devoted much time and energy to helping Palestinian peacebuilders and their organizations in extremely difficult situations under Israeli military occupation. In so doing, she has faced many challenges and obstacles, including anti-normalization attitudes in Palestinian civil society as well as the ongoing oppression and humiliation inherent in the military occupation by Israel of the West Bank. Despite all these problems, she has devoted herself to peacebuilding in our region with all her heart, soul and mind during the past seven years, and she feels proud of four major accomplishments that she has achieved with her groundbreaking initiatives with ALLMEP.

> The first major achievement has been involving more women in the peacebuilding processes. I wanted to involve more women in the peacebuilding world. I want them to be active, not only to be counted as numbers. This has already begun to happen. Almost every organization that I work with, including Combatants for Peace with Galia Golan [one of the peace activists featured in this book] has been including women more and more in their organizations. I was very humbled to work with her on women' programs in that organization – with someone of her caliber sitting in the room, as I was training them in strategizing how to have greater involvement of women in the organization. I focused on how women can take a leadership role rather than just following men's initiatives, within the peacebuilding community, and I know that Galia has taken a leadership role in Combatants for Peace in forming a women's Israeli-Palestinian group. I have also helped women in organizations create partnerships between organizations, because men didn't like doing it so much.

Abuarquob was particularly gratified by her pioneering work with an important new women's peacebuilding organization called Women Wage Peace, which was founded in 2014, after one of the wars between Israel and Gaza. This organization has become the largest peacebuilding group in Israel. Even though it is an Israeli NGO, it has persistently reached out to Palestinians within Israel and in the West Bank. With Abuarquob's help, they also have reached out to many new segments of the Israeli Jewish citizenry, who are not usually involved in the peace camp.

As the regional coordinator of the Alliance for Middle East Peace, and as a feminist with a great deal of peacebuilding knowledge and experience, Abuarquob met with the leaders of Women Wage Peace early on and helped them develop important strategies regarding target groups for their outreach. She remembers her meetings and her activities with them vividly.

> When they came here [to the American Colony Hotel] to meet with me, I realized that they were a bunch of lefty women and it was going to be another lefty organization. I wanted to help them change this, because I felt that the left in Israel was losing its voice and its presence. I helped them realize that what they wanted was to form an Israeli organization which could reach new pockets of Israeli society, the men and women who kiss Netanyahu's hand. So, I went with them to Ofakim [a development town in the Negev], to many kibbutzim, and all kinds of other places. I helped them strategize and I also spoke to many of these controversial audiences. For me, it was amazing to speak with Arab-Jews [Jews whose families have immigrated to Israel from Arab countries] and to identify with their issues and to try to understand why they need to be affiliated with the powerful party. I learned that they are coming from displacement and fear, and that violence and discrimination was practiced against them. The fact was that they could connect with me.

A second major achievement for her was her ability to reach out to Jewish Israeli settlers in the Occupied Territories, especially in the West Bank. This was a controversial move, which not everyone in the peacebuilding community agreed with, but for Abuarquob it was a major strategic success.

> I worked with the organization known as Roots/Shorashim/Judor in Gush Etzion [which brings together Jewish Israeli settlers and Palestinian Arabs], south of Jerusalem, in the West Bank. I fought for Roots. This was controversial because some people in the peace community thought we can't talk to the 'devil' and I said, because they are the devil, we must talk to them. At least let's start at a place where the Israelis in the peace community can talk to them. I got to know Hadassah Froman [one of the other peacebuilders in this book, who is involved with Roots/Shorashim/Judor] and that has been an important relationship for me. The fact that she

and the other people involved with this Jewish-Palestinian peace-building organization were helping in easing the violence at checkpoints, was an important step towards creating a space for peace negotiations. They–Jewish women from Gush Etzion–helped immensely; they would go to demonstrations in front of the Ministry of the Interior, and they would argue for the release of the bodies of Palestinian martyrs. This was very important.

Abuarquob and others in ALLMEP are also involved in a third major initiative–creating programs for many of people in Israel and Palestine who are graduates of peacebuilding programs and have not raised their voices for peace in a significant way. She very much wants to change this and is enthusiastically doing it herself. She is constantly being interviewed by peacebuilding groups abroad and locally–on podcasts and in seminars and conferences–where she speaks up eloquently and passionately about the importance of being a peacebuilder. In addition, she is encouraging others to do the same and is succeeding in doing so.

> We have thousands of peacebuilding alumni, Israeli and Palestinian, from many of the programs, who don't speak about their experiences, for many different reasons. The Israeli kids go into the army and the Palestinians experience violence, and they are all afraid to speak up. So, in 2018, ALLMEP wanted to respond to that. We received a small grant and hired someone to create an alumni leadership forum. This group created the Middle East Storyteller's project, which is in its second year, and we just gave out awards to the best storytellers in the second cohort. People are coming forward, defying the notion that we should only work under the radar. They are now prepared and willing to be visible, which is one of the needs that we are working on, and they are not ashamed of naming themselves as peacebuilders. These are very powerful stories.

I personally can attest to the power of these stories, since I heard three of them at an inspiring event sponsored by ALLMEP in October 2021 at the American House (a branch of the American Embassy in Israel, which quietly serves Palestinians in Jerusalem and the West Bank) in downtown East Jerusalem. The event was opened enthusiastically by Abuarquob, who applauded the courage and honesty of all the peacebuilders who came forward to tell their stories.

> There is no shame in being a peacebuilder. We have been invisible
> for too long. We need to speak from the heart, to speak publicly,
> and to constantly reaffirm our belief in our work for peace.

In addition, Avi Meyerstein (an American Jewish lawyer from Washington
DC, the president and founder of ALLMEP, who was spending a year in
Israel on a Fulbright scholarship to help develop the work of the peacebuilding community in Israel and Palestine) welcomed everyone in attendance
by stressing the growing impact of this kind of work:

> Tonight's program shows just how much even one person's story
> can open our minds, inspire us, and move us to act for change.
> Now imagine them multiplying. Imagine if there were thousands
> of people who not only had these kinds of stories but also had a
> platform to tell them. They could reach millions of people.

In my own work with youth and young adults who graduated from dialogue
and action programs of the Interreligious Coordinating Council in Israel
(which I directed for 24 years), it was often very difficult to get graduates of
our programs to raise their voices within their own families and communities. Many of the Palestinians reported that they couldn't even talk about
being part of a Palestinian-Israeli dialogue group in their schools and universities, for fear of what other Palestinians would think about them. And
Jewish young adults were also fearful about speaking up because of the growing anti-Palestinian attitudes after the Second *Intifada* (2000-2005).
Accordingly, the fact that both Israeli Jews and Palestinian Arabs are now
proud to be peacebuilders–and are telling their stories loudly, clearly and
poignantly–is a sign of great progress and hope for the future.

The Alliance for Middle East Peace has become a significant player in the
peacebuilding community in Israel and Palestine through Abuarquob's continuous and committed work with many of the member organizations in
the coalition. She has built up a small staff who are implementing impactful
programs and projects like the ones mentioned above. In addition, she has
helped the ALLMEP team in the US lobby for several years for significantly
more funding for peacebuilding organizations in Israel and Palestine. In
2020, they achieved a major success with the passage by the US Congress of
MEPPA, the Nita Lowey Middle East Partnership for Peace Act. This new
fund will deliver $250 million over a period of five years to projects that
support peacebuilding and Palestinian economic development and partner-
ships. It represents the largest investment ever in the region's peacebuilders.

The legislation grew out of ALLMEP's 12-year campaign to establish an International Fund for Israeli-Palestinian Peace, a long-term project which continues to gain momentum among other governments interested in leveraging this innovative US government investment. Until now, most strategies toward peace have focused on diplomats negotiating a final solution and failed to engage with peacebuilders working on a people-to-people level every day. The Lowey Fund recognizes that sustainable and lasting peace must be built from the ground up to create a broad base of support. The fund is being administered through two different US government agencies: USAID for people-to-people programs and the US International Development Finance Corporation for economic projects.

In order to help local Palestinian and Israeli organizations get ready to apply for significant funding from these new funds–and then to plan and implement more substantive and sustainable programs and projects in peacebuilding settings–Abuarquob and her regional staff in Israel and Palestine have been engaging in a fourth major initiative, which they call *capacity-building*. According to another staff member who works with her (who preferred to remain anonymous), this term is a very broad one, with manifold implications.

> A capacity-building program includes any activity which assists in scaling whatever capacities organizations have or need. From project management, human resource management, to negotiations skills, to mediation skills, it can be the hard skills or soft skills. It is whatever an organization has and wants more and better, or what they are lacking and therefore need to develop. It's a very broad term. It can mean a number of things. It depends on how the trainer and the organization define it in each particular case.

According to Abuarquob, all this capacity-building work that they are doing, and that they will continue to do in the years ahead, is to help their members in the growing peacebuilding community in Israel and Palestine to apply for these funds in a professional way. That is why they are trying to scale up the organizations so that they can apply for larger grants and increase their impact. As she has said many times: "Our success is the success of everybody."

Conclusion

The main lesson that we can learn from Abuarquob's professional growth as a peacebuilder is one of determination and the power of transformation. From her life as a child and teenager who suffered the humiliations of the military occupation of the West Bank, to her emergence in recent years as a profound peacebuilder who is having significant impact in the peacebuilding community in both Israel and Palestine, we can bear witness to her personal and professional life of resilience and resolve. Her many important learning and growth experiences—both at home and abroad—have enriched her life greatly, and they have helped her develop a sound ideology and vision which informs the lives of many other peace activists on the ground, both in Israel and Palestine, as well as internationally. Moreover, her extensive knowledge of the field and her unwavering commitment to the work of peacebuilding in civil society has become a burning drive and intensive passion in her life, which she radiates with great determination and faith. She does so with all the people she encounters, within the context of the growing diversity of peacebuilding organizations in the region.

Abuarquob's story is one of trajectory and movement. It is apparent that she developed a true passion for peace and adjusted her actions to the changing times. She serves as a model for many people, proving through perseverance that spirituality can be found in the search for peace and in the act of peacebuilding. Her personal journey can serve as a guide for her own people and for all the people living in this land. She keeps the flicker of hope for peace alive, under very difficult circumstances.

Professor Mohammed Dajani Daoudi: A Muslim Philosophy and Practice of Moderation

Photo by Sari Kronish

Mohammed Dajani Daoudi is undoubtedly the most well-known and outspoken Palestinian Muslim professor and peacebuilder in Palestine. For a long time, he has promoted the concept of *wasatia*, the middle way: the notion that Islam is a religion of moderation, peace, tolerance, justice, love, and reconciliation. Throughout his career, he has emphasized that this basic idea in Islam is in stark contrast to distorted interpretations by extremist radical Islamic groups. These extremists get a lot of media attention by promulgating violence and hatred in the name of Islam and, in so doing, misinterpreting fundamental texts and taking them out of context.

Dajani has developed unique methods and models of conflict resolution, based on his views of Islam as an ethical and peaceful religion and culture, and he has spoken about these ideas at conferences, seminars, workshops and panels all over the world. (In fact, we have attended some of these events together, and wrote one joint paper together, with other scholars; see the bibliography). Moreover, he showed unusual courage and commitment–which cost him his job at a Palestinian university in Jerusalem–by taking Palestinian students to the death camp at Auschwitz on a unique journey to learn the narrative of the Jewish people vis a vis the Holocaust. While recognizing the asymmetry concerning two historical tragedies–the Holocaust and the *Nakba*–he took Israeli Jews to a Palestinian refugee camp in the West Bank so that they could learn the narrative of the Palestinian people. In these two extraordinary actions, he demonstrated the idea that people from both sides of the conflict need to learn and recognize the historical narrative and suffering of the other, even if that recognition is difficult and not yet acceptable in each society.

Background and Early Years

Dajani's formal name ends in *Daoudi*, which is derived from the Arabic *Daoud* meaning David. The last name is in reference to the part of the family who were residing in the *Navi Daoud* neighborhood where they served as caretakers of Prophet David's tomb. *Nabi Daoud* is a Muslim Prophet, according to the Koran. In 1524 Sultan Suleiman the Magnificent appointed Sheikh Ahmed Dajani and his family to be the custodian of the King David Tomb on Mt. Zion in Jerusalem. Despite the fact that his formal last name is Daoudi, he goes by the last name of Dajani in daily life.

Mohammed Dajani was born in 1946 in what was known as the Dajani neighborhood in West Jerusalem, into a prominent Palestinian family which has long been associated with opposition movements. In the 1920s and '30s, the Dajanis joined with other leading Palestinian families to oppose policies of the Grand Mufti of the time, Haj Amin al Husseini, since they felt that his policies were separatist. One of the members of their family, Hasan Sidqi Dajani, who was considered to be part of this opposition group, was assassinated in 1938. Moreover, some of his ancestors played important roles in the history of Jerusalem: Abdelrahman Dajani was mayor of Jerusalem from 1863-82; Aref Dajani was mayor from 1917-18; and his grandfather was a city councilor. In short, the Dajani family has a long and distinguished history in Jerusalem.

While growing up in divided Jerusalem, Dajani was very close to his extended family, many of whom shared stories of Jerusalem life with him. In particular, he remembers poignantly how the experiences of the 1948 war affected people in his life, particularly his grandmother, with whom he was very close, even though he ultimately chose a very different path than she did.

The 1948 *Nakba* left a deep scar on my grandmother from my mother's side. Already she was burdened with a heavy responsibility following her husband's sudden death by a heart attack leaving her in charge of a big family of three sons and four young daughters. His work as a judge did not pay much salary so she had to bear the responsibilities of a single parent. The traumatizing effect of being forced to leave her cozy home in West Jerusalem to take refuge in East Jerusalem left her bitter. To add to her grief, one son of her husband from a previous wife was shot by mistake by the Palestinian *mujahideen* [guerilla fighters] as he was traveling from Nablus to Jerusalem due to mistaken identity. They assumed he was British since he was blonde. She never forgot her lost paradise and made sure that we do not forget as well. She would curse the Jews on any occasion that reminded her of the past. To her, Jews were the enemies of God and man. We loved her very much and thus her views left much impact on the way we felt. It affected the way we [my brother and I] felt when studying for ten years in the United States where our socialization circle with Jews was very limited.

As a young Palestinian who lived in Jerusalem during the 1948 war, Dajani heard many stories during and after the war from other family members, especially his mother, who also had a strong influence on his life. Her focus on education would be a central pillar in Dajani's personal and professional life.

My mother used to tell us about her life before the *Nakba*. Her house was in the German Colony, and she went to *Almamuniah* Girls School, next to Salah El-Din Street. On her way, she and her sister would drop by her brother's law office in Mamilla, who used to give them candy and spending money. She was not bitter about the past, nor did she harbor any enmity for those who forced her to leave her home. She was a social butterfly who was very busy with her women's circle of friends. She saw education as the most important life goal. She instilled in us the love of learning. She discouraged me from reading detective novels thinking they would spoil the mind. I don't remember her saying anything wrong about Jews. She felt my grandmother's suffering but never shared her anger and bitterness. She used to say: 'I would not have minded someone coming to live as a neighbor, but when someone, even your brother, evicts you and throws you out, it pains you.'

The influences of his grandmother and his mother reflect a certain tension in Dajani's life. This would lead him to join the Palestinian struggle as a young man but as he grew older and matured, he would change direction, to focus more on education, to refrain from anger and bitterness and to engage in dialogue towards reconciliation.

Joining the Palestinian Struggle

As a young man, Dajani left Jerusalem to study abroad. In the late 1960s and early '70s, he became a political activist with the PLO during his student years at the American University in Beirut. At that time, he believed in the armed struggle by Palestinians to reclaim their lost land, although he did not carry arms or engage in violence but mostly engaged in public relations. He remembers what motivated him to get involved in Palestinian nationalism during that period.

In the aftermath of the Six Day War of 1967, Palestinian and Arab youth joined the Palestinian resistance movement, myself included, believing in armed struggle to liberate the homeland. No politician or scholar dared speak of peace, reconciliation, negotiations, normalization, and recognition back then. As a Palestinian, I viewed the Six Day War as a devastating defeat for the Arab armies but not for the Palestinians [who were not involved]. Following the Six Day War, the word peace was deleted from the Arab and the Palestinian dictionary. Those who called for peace were vilified as traitors to the Arab cause. At the time, I did not believe in peace, dialogue, and negotiations with the Israelis. Egyptian president Abdel Nasser developed the slogan, 'What has been taken by force, would only be regained by force,' and that became our motto. The *Fatah* motto 'Revolution till victory' was our inspiration and the liberation of our homeland was our goal. We opposed any peace plan short of that. We opposed the 1967 UN Resolution calling for Israeli withdrawal from the Occupied Territories. We opposed the 1968 American Middle East peace plan, proposed by US Secretary of State William Rogers, to break the deadlock in Israeli-Arab relations although it called upon Israel to withdraw from the territories it occupied in 1967.

Dajani's identification with the Palestinian national cause led him to study and live in Beirut from 1964-75. These were formative years in his life. During that period, he also lived for a year in Cairo in 1969-70 after he was elected as vice president of the General Union of Palestinian Students (GUPS), which had its headquarters in Egypt. But he was soon to become disappointed and disillusioned by some of the goals and methods of the movement, especially of its leadership.

My idealistic dream made me join *Fatah*, but realism awakened me from the dream and led me to leave *Fatah*. In the beginning, I was very dedicated to the cause, but little by little, the disillusionment crept in. The idealists found they do not belong with the opportunists who moved from the lowest echelons to the top of the ladder by deceit and conspiracy. Though corruption was growing, the leadership did not stop it. As the struggle for leadership posts heightened, corruption became a necessary political tool to move up. In 1975, I decided to move on with my life and focus on my educational career.

Dajani left Lebanon in March 1975 to go to the United Kingdom, where he attended Loughborough University to work on a doctoral program in politics. However, later that year he decided to change direction and join his younger brother, Munther, in the United States. He went to study at Eastern Michigan University, where in December 1976, he earned a master's in the social sciences. After this, he moved to the University of South Carolina in Columbia, where he earned his first doctorate in political science. He was not able to go back to Jerusalem, where his family still resided, due to restrictions imposed on Palestinians by the government of Israel. Instead, he applied to the University of Texas in Austin, where his brother was studying. At this university he did a second doctorate in political economy. By the time he graduated, his family had succeeded in having King Hussein of Jordan grant him permission to return to Jordan and retrieve his Jordanian passport. He moved to Jordan in 1985, where he lived for ten years. During the first five years, he worked for a private company, and during the second five years, he served as the chairman of Political Science and Diplomatic Studies Department at the Applied University in Amman, from 1990 to 1995.

In September, 1993, while he was in Jordan, Dajani heard about the Oslo Accords. As a Palestinian who had lived in the USA for a long time, and now was closer to home, he was following events in Israel and Palestine very closely. He remembers his excitement about the signing of this historic peace agreement.

> Before the Oslo Declaration of Principles of 1993, I would have never imagined that peace can be achieved. I was living in Jordan. People there were shocked that a peace agreement between the PLO and Israel was signed.

Even though Dajani was positively inspired by the Oslo Accords–the first time that the Palestinians were not only negotiating with the Israelis but actually coming to an agreement–he kept away from politics while in Jordan and focused on building his academic career. According to a biography written by one of his students, Zeina M. Barakat, entitled *From Heart of Stone to Heart of Flesh: Evolutionary Journey from Extremism to Moderation*: "Teaching conflict resolution, pluralism, ethics and political philosophy courses helped widen his horizon and put him on the right track to later form his *Wasatia* movement."

An Awakening About "The Enemy" Through Transformative Experiences

During this period, in 1993, Dajani's father, who was suffering from cancer, succeeded in getting him a family reunion permit to return to Jerusalem. Once he was back in Jerusalem, his father, who shunned politics and believed in dialogue, encouraged him to meet Jewish friends in order to know the other. His grandfather and father worked in the tourism industry. They owned souvenir shops and were the protected tenants of the New Imperial Hotel in Jaffa Gate (which the family still rents). In the late '50s until the mid-'60s, they held the license for catering to airlines and were in charge of hospitality at the Jerusalem Airport in Qalandia. Dajani began to follow his father's suggestion to meet Jews in Jerusalem, but for a long time he continued to hold onto the view that Jewish Israelis were his enemies.

> I had this negative attitude towards them [the Jews] at the time. I felt that they had usurped my land and were my occupiers. I didn't want to harm them, but I didn't want to have anything to do with them.

However, this attitude changed dramatically after his father brought him along to some of his chemotherapy appointments at Hadassah Hospital in Jerusalem. There he witnessed doctors and nurses who treated his father as a human being and this affected him deeply.

> I was expecting that they would be treating him differently—with discrimination—as a Palestinian Arab Muslim. I found that this was not the case. They were treating him like a patient. At the same time, I looked around the hospital and found that there were many Palestinian patients with Israeli doctors treating them. This helped me to see the human side of my enemy. It helped change some of my views with regard to Jews and Israelis. This was a life-changing experience for me which motivated me to become a different person–from being a bystander to an active peacebuilder.

Dajani's father died in 1995 but soon after he had another medical episode in his family that was similarly transformative regarding his views about Israeli Jews. On the way home from a family outing in Tel Aviv, his mother suffered a heart attack in the car. When they got off the highway near Ben Gurion airport, he did not believe that anyone would help his mother since at the airport Israelis are very conscious of security and often do not act kindly to Palestinians, to say the least. However, to his surprise and that of his family, the security guards at the airport immediately called for help and paramedics arrived quickly. They applied electric shock treatment and a massage in attempts to save his mother. When this did not succeed, they transported her to the closest medical facility–a military hospital! – where doctors tried to revive her but did not succeed. On his way back to Jerusalem that night, Dajani thought deeply about what had happened.

> I was looking at her empty seat and I was thinking about her loss, and how in the morning she wasn't sick and then suddenly during the day she died. But at the same time, I was thinking about my enemy who tried to save her. That had a great impact on me in

helping me think in terms of us and them, and trying to see a peaceful solution to our conflict with the Israelis.

These experiences changed his life profoundly and catalyzed him to turn towards peace and to reach out to the other side.

Since then, Dajani has been active in dialogue with Jewish Israelis, like myself, who have reached out to Palestinians to learn about their identity, their narrative and their hopes for peace. I have spoken on many panels and on public dialogues with him in Israel and abroad over the years for Jewish, Christian, Muslim and interreligious audiences, and we have written articles together, such as the monograph which we wrote with other scholars after attending a seminar at the Peace Research Institute in Frankfurt, Germany in 2014, entitled *The Practice and Promise of Interfaith Dialogue and Peacebuilding in the Israeli-Palestinian Conflict* (see bibliography). In addition, I have taken groups to his beautiful *Wasatia* center (founded in 2006), where he sits surrounded by thousands of books and pamphlets, on the fourth floor in his historic home in *Bet Hanina*, a large Palestinian neighborhood in north Jerusalem, and he has been in my home in West Jerusalem on many occasions.

Joining the Struggle for Peace: The Big Dream and the Small Hope

After having returned successfully to Jerusalem in 1995, Dajani was recruited to work with the United Nations Development Program (UNDP) in Jerusalem as Chief Technical Advisor for the emerging Palestinian Authority, based on his extensive experience in the USA and in Jordan. He quickly became active in the civil service of the new Palestinian National Authority which was developing as a result of the signing of the Oslo Accords in 1993 and 1994. Having been a member of *Fatah* in the past actually helped him to build good working relations with the new administration, and to cooperate with them in their endeavors to create the institutional foundations for the new Palestinian government. His political background paved the way for him to work as Chief Consultant for the Palestinian Authority's Ministry of International Cooperation and to be appointed Director of the Department of Technical Assistance and Training at the Palestinian Economic Council for Development and Reconstruction (PECDAR).

During the years 1995-97, he set up the structure for several government ministries of the new Palestinian government and he was active in training Palestinian civil servants. Following this he became intensely involved in

Palestinian affairs locally in Jerusalem. He prepared and implemented many training workshops for Palestinians who were just beginning to become civil servants. Many of those workshops also dealt with issues of ethics in government. This prepared him well for planning and implementing training workshops in the areas of peace and reconciliation, which would become his main focus of peace activism in the decades ahead.

In addition, in the late 1990s, his work was noticed by other peacebuilding organizations, who began to invite him to many workshops, seminars and conferences abroad, as part of the post-Oslo pro-dialogue atmosphere of that period in which many Palestinian Arabs and Israeli Jews began to meet regularly to get to know each other. One of the most important conferences that he attended was one in Turkey in 1999, which was organized by the Israel-Palestine Center for Research and Information (IPCRI), which brought together 30 teachers of religion–15 from each side–from Israel and Palestine.

> The idea was to have teachers of religion from the West Bank and teachers of religion from Israel, e.g., from Bar Ilan University [a university outside of Tel Aviv, under the auspices of Modern Jewish Orthodoxy], to meet and talk. But in the first session it was difficult to have a reasonable discussion because no one was listening to the other. Rather, everyone was involved with his or her own narrative and was not willing to listen to the narrative of the other. There was a lot of tension between the Palestinians and Israelis in attendance.

At this conference, he began to develop some ideas about conflict resolution which would mushroom into a full-blown model for the field. He gave the model a beautiful name "Big Dream, Small Hope," which he fully delineated later in a long article, *Big Dream/Small Hope: Peace and Reconciliation Vision*, which implied that both sides need to come down from their high trees and their all-or-nothing ideologies and adopt practical ideas that could give their peoples real hope. He developed a power point presentation which he used in many lectures at conferences, seminars and workshops in the 1990s and in subsequent decades at universities and other settings – in many parts of the world, including from Hong Kong to Japan, from Europe to the US.

Dajani also presented his model at a conference in the Former Soviet Union, in the countries of Georgia and Armenia in 2005, which was organized by Seeds of Peace. In addition, he presented his model for two years to young emerging peacebuilders from Israel, Palestine, and other countries, at the Seeds of Peace camp in Maine in the early years of the new millenium. He also presented his model in a peace education conference in Anatolia, Turkey and he took students from Al Quds University to this conference. His model has been shared in many settings and is being used in many places in the world. His work has also appeared in books and articles in several languages. He also shared it with his students in the years during which he taught at Al Quds University in Jerusalem.

Dajani credits the renowned Palestinian poet Mahmoud Darwish with the invention of the phrase "Big Dream/Small Hope." According to Dajani, the poet once asked this question, "What is more important—a small hope or a big dream?" Dajani answered the question:

> In my view, the Oslo Accords brought an essential change: From now on it is not Palestinians against Israelis and Israelis against Palestinians; but it is Palestinians and Israelis who believe in the big dream, and similarly Israelis and Palestinians who believe in the small hope.

In his article, Dajani explained what he meant by "the big dream" and "the small hope."

> For the Israelis, the 'big dream' is to wake up one morning and find that Palestinians have disappeared in the desert and that only Jews live in the promised land of Israel in a purely Jewish state with the river and the sea as its borders and unified Jerusalem as its capital. For the Palestinians, the 'big dream' is to wake up one morning and find that all Israelis have departed and only Palestinians live in the Holy Land in an Arab state from the river to the sea as its borders and Al-Quds el-Sherif [Jerusalem] as its capital.

> Advocates of 'the big dream' are those, at present, in the majority, who struggle for the eventual triumph of their perception of good over evil as resembled by the other, and as a result seek to establish their state exclusively on the historic land of Israel/Palestine. In their effort to achieve their goal, the 'big dream' camp demonizes the other and implements a highly nationalistic curriculum in its educational system that delegitimizes and demonizes the other. It promotes conflict education, which teaches the new generation the war philosophy of the old generation. It appeals to the

emotional bondage of the people to the land and focuses on historical ties to the past. It denies the narrative of the other and ignores their history, literature and traditions.

For Dajani, both the majority of Israelis and the majority of Palestinians unfortunately advocate "the big dream." They are the mirror image of each other. In stark contrast, Dajani advocated the "small hope" theory, which he believed was more pragmatic and held out more chances for peace.

> The 'small hope' advocates are those—at present, in the minority—who believe in peaceful coexistence between the two people and call for the establishment of a two-state solution, living next to each other in harmony, peace and security, with Jerusalem as a shared capital for both. The 'small hope' advocates teach Israel/Palestine as two independent neighboring states, with Palestine as the West Bank and Gaza Strip, while Israel's boundaries would reflect the 1967 borders with minor modifications; refugees would exercise their 'right of return' to the State of Palestine in addition to being compensated. In the world of the 'small hope,' Jerusalem would become the international City of Peace, reflecting the multicultural, multiethnic, multireligious and peaceful nature of the city... In educating about the 'small hope,' both Israeli and Palestinian text-books would not include negative images of the other. Rather, they would include the narrative of the other, which would include positive features and traits of the other, stories about friendship and cooperation between Israelis and Palestinians, and a human multi-dimensional, individual approach.

In addition to this broad vision of what he would like to see happen as part of the unfolding political peace process, Dajani–always the educator–also developed a strategy for what he called "Peace Education," which is an essential methodology in peacebuilding:

The 'small hope' educational peace strategy aims at being:

- Democratic–fostering independent and creative thinking

- Peace-oriented–focusing on the acceptance of the other and embodying mutual respect for the other

- Non-authoritarian–making manifest that truth is not absolute

- Rational–teaching students to think in a rational way, avoiding emotional decision-making

- Tolerant–teaching students to be tolerant of each other.

Clearly, Dajani's ten years at American universities had a great impact on him. He brought the values and the methods of the best of American education back with him to Jordan and then to Palestine. These goals, objectives and methods would guide him in his career, as a professor at Al Quds university in Jerusalem in the years ahead, and as an informal educator in the non-governmental organization which he would establish in Jerusalem to educate religious leaders, youth and women in Palestine.

As an educator myself, I discovered that my views about peacebuilding, and my work in the field, also focused on educational philosophies and methodologies. In particular, the concepts of dialogue—which involved getting to know the other deeply—and the notion of learning each other's religious and historical narratives, became central to my own peace work. This is why Dajani and I have been able to cooperate and collaborate over the years, in written and oral presentations of our work, both in theory and in practice.

In 2001, Dajani joined the faculty of the Palestinian Al Quds University in Jerusalem, where he founded the program in American Studies. Since he had two doctorates from American universities and had spent ten years in the USA, he was uniquely qualified for this job. He taught many courses in this program and mentored many students. He also taught courses about peace and reconciliation. In 2002, he was also appointed director of the libraries of the university.

Wasatia: finding the middle way

In 2006, while he was at the university, he founded an NGO called *Wasatia*, Arabic for "the Middle Way" or "Moderation." The idea to establish this organization came to him after an incident which occurred near his home in the Palestinian neighborhood of Bet Hanina in northern Jerusalem.

One Friday morning in 2006, he was standing on a balcony in his home, which overlooked an Israeli military checkpoint. He watched as a long line of Palestinians gathered there, waiting to enter Jerusalem, to go to pray at the Al Aksa Mosque on the Temple Mount (known to the Muslims as *Harem El-Sharif*). Apparently, the Israeli army personnel at the checkpoint were not letting the Palestinians through because they did not have permits. At first, there was an attempt to push the crowd back, and the soldiers even used tear gas. As Dajani was observing the situation, he was sure that the violence was about to escalate, but instead he witnessed something quite amazing. Suddenly a compromise was reached. The officers at the checkpoint arranged for busses to take the Palestinians to the mosque to pray, and, in return, the Palestinians agreed to leave their identification cards at the checkpoint.

Dajani remembers that as another critical transformative moment in his life.

> This was a win-win situation. The Israelis worried about security and made sure that nothing happened. And the Palestinians wanted to pray and did not want to plant a bomb. I realized that these were moderate Palestinians, not extremists, because if they were, they wouldn't have accepted the deal with the Israelis. My question was, who represents them?

This incident motivated Dajani to establish *Wasatia* to represent the Palestinians, who he believed were overwhelmingly moderate, but needed a philosophy and a movement to guide them. It was designed to be a moderate, sensible, intellectual and pragmatic organization. According to Dajani, the goals of *Wasatia* were established at that time.

> *Wasatia* was founded as an independent, nonpartisan, nongovernmental, nonprofit Palestinian Muslim initiative dedicated to the promotion of moderate religious, political, and social values and culture within the Palestinian community. It carries out its mission by implementing special programs and activities aimed at disseminating temperate ideas and thought, particularly among the youth and future leaders of society. In addition, *Wasatia* supports a publishing agenda that fosters independent research on the topics of centrism, dialogue, tolerance, coexistence, and acceptance of the other in order to enable religious leaders, government officials, scholars, academicians, journalists, educators, students, and other interested citizens to design and produce policies, speeches, sermons, articles, books, and other works that reflect a balanced middle-ground, rational, and objective perspective.

Dajani has distributed many of the Wasatia publications at conferences, seminars, lectures and workshops in Palestine, Israel and abroad, for many years.

In its initial years (2006-2014), Dajani introduced many groundbreaking programs. In March 2006, the first annual conference for *Wasatia* took place. After that, they held an annual conference every year, until 2016 (when Dajani left for the USA for two years). Moreover, for nine years, *Wasatia* held an annual conference with religious leaders in Ramallah, such as Sheikh Taseer Tamimi, who was the chief Muslim kadi [religious judge] and other kadis and imams. The first one took place in March 2007 in Ramallah. Stories about these conferences appeared in Arabic newspapers, so that many people in Palestine knew about these activities. They used different teacher–sheikhs, professors, imams–to teach their ideas of Islam as a moderate, tolerant, peaceful, conciliatory religion. They would write papers and present them on different aspects of the main ideas of *Wasatia*. Also, during these years, they held workshops for speakers in mosques in Palestine, for youth, and for women. These workshops took place in different parts of Palestine—Ramallah, Bethlehem and Hebron. The conferences were large meetings, with over 50 people in attendance at each one. The workshops were smaller, for 20 people, in which they focused on a particular topic in a more interactive fashion.

These educational programs had a major impact in Palestine on the religious leaders, youth and women who attended them. They introduced the main concepts of *Wasatia*. They taught them that there is such a thing as moderation in Islam.

> We challenged the version of Quranic interpretation that is being presented by the radicals. Instead, we offered a moderate version! We explained both the Koran and the *Hadith* in a moderate way. This was in great contrast to what was usually taught in Palestine.

He partnered in the first years of his new NGO with the Konrad Adenauer Foundation in Ramallah in sponsoring the initial conferences and workshops. During these years, Dajani exposed thousands of Palestinians to the ideas of *wasatia*, through conferences and workshops and via books, pamphlets and brochures that he published and distributed in Arabic. In addition, he acquired publications about *wasatia* from the Arab world and re-published and distributed them in Palestine. The idea was to bring to Palestinians the literature about ideas of moderation in Islam from other places in the world.

In the Heart of the Other's Narrative

In 2014, Dajani's remarkable work was abruptly halted. In March 2014, Dajani and his colleagues embarked on a groundbreaking new program, which they believed would develop empathy and mutual understanding for each other's narrative, for both Palestinian Arab and Israeli Jewish students. He and his staff took 27 Palestinian Arab students from *Al Quds* University on a study tour to Auschwitz. In the same month they took Israeli Jewish students separately to a Palestinian refugee camp in the Bethlehem area, just south of Jerusalem.

> All of this changed in 2014, after I took Palestinians to Auschwitz, due to all the media reports in the press. Until then, we were a 'rising star'—we were 'kosher'—we were legitimate, we were moving up. Our success was part of the background of what happened to us after the trip to Auschwitz. The Palestinian Authority —and people with other ideas about Islam—used the trip to fight us and to delegitimize us. The radicals, the extremists, did not like what we were doing and used the negative media reports about us to make life very difficult for us.

This historic study tour—which received much media coverage in Palestine, Israel and abroad—was a courageous move, and perhaps also overly idealistic. Dajani believed that educating about the pain and suffering of the other should be a normal part of peacebuilding and reconciliation work.

Dajani had visited Auschwitz himself three years earlier on a special pilgrimage organized for Jews, Christians and Muslims from around the world. Two hundred people from 40 countries stood united against Holocaust denial and racism, and they launched an appeal for peace and intercultural rapprochement. On February 1, 2011, they braved sub-zero temperatures to pay their respects to the victims of the Holocaust at the Nazi death camp of Auschwitz-Birkenau in a visit organized by the Aladdin Project in partnership with UNESCO and the City of Paris. The members of this international delegation declared that this act of intercultural and interfaith solidarity was intended to recall the dramatic consequences of Nazism and fascism, reject Holocaust denial and trivialization, and call on political and religious leaders and intellectuals across the world to counter the old and new forms of hatred, anti-Semitism, racism and intolerance. Dajani recalls this as a life-changing experience for him.

> In 2011, I was invited by a French organization to visit Auschwitz. That was an eye-opening experience for me. We were invited to go

with over 150 religious leaders. It was in February and it was extremely cold, and that helped us to see how the prisoners there
were living under extremely harsh conditions. It was a great educational experience. My impression of the Holocaust, like that of
other Arabs, had been framed in terms of denial, or that the
Holocaust was exploited to create Israel and generate sympathy for
Israel. There was a very strong link in our minds between the
Nakbah [the great catastrophe] and the Holocaust, and at that time,
we felt that the Holocaust issue was an exaggerated narrative by
Israel.

This was the beginning of Dajani's journey to learn more about the Holocaust. Having grown up in Jerusalem under the Jordanians, he had not
learned anything about it in school. As he began to learn more, he felt that
it was important for other Palestinian Arabs to know more about this too.

It was not part of my education and not part of my schooling. It
was more hearing it in the public area, in the political discourse.
The first time I heard about the Holocaust was at the American
University in Beirut, and that, written in Arabic, was the denial
narrative. My encounter with the term Holocaust was that it didn't
happen or was part of the atrocities of World War II, but not
something that was uniquely Jewish or aimed at the annihilation
of the Jews. Eventually, I co-authored a book about the Holocaust
in Arabic, because I couldn't find a text that documented it in
terms of what really happened. We had to fill in that gap.

In addition, in 2011, Dajani co-authored an important op-ed on the topic
in the *New York Times* (along with his friend and colleague Robert Satloff,
Executive Director of the Washington Institute for Near East Policy where
Professor Dajani has served as a researcher) entitled "Why Palestinians
should learn about the Holocaust." Among other things, they asked and
answered an important question:

Should Palestinians (and other Arabs) learn about the Holocaust?
Should this historical tragedy be included in the Arab curriculum?
We—a Muslim-Palestinian social scientist and a Jewish-American
historian—believe that the answer is yes. Indeed, there are many
reasons why it's important, even essential that Arabs learn about
the Holocaust.

Palestinians, and Arabs more generally, know little about the Holocaust and what they do know is often skewed by the perverted prism of Arab popular culture, from the ranting of religious extremists to the distortions of certain satellite television channels to the many ill-informed authors... Arabs have nothing to fear from opening their eyes to this chapter of human history. As the Koran says: 'And say: My Lord, advance me in knowledge.' If Arabs knew more about the Holocaust in particular and genocide in general, perhaps Arab voices would be more forceful in trying to stop similar atrocities.

Palestinians have more specific reasons to learn about the Holocaust. We do not urge Holocaust education just so Palestinians can understand more sympathetically the legacy of Jewish suffering and its impact on the psyche of the Jewish people. While it is important for both Palestinians and Israelis to appreciate the historical legacies that have shaped their strategic outlook and national identities, teaching Palestinians about the Holocaust for this reason alone runs the risk of feeding the facile equation that 'the Jews have the Holocaust and the Palestinians have the *Nakba*.' We urge Palestinians to learn about the Holocaust so they can be armed with knowledge to reject the comparison because, if it were broadly avoided, peace would be even more attainable than it is today.

It is evident that Holocaust education for Palestinians, as part of their learning the narrative of the Jewish other and as part of their coming to grips with suffering in the world, had been very much on Dajani's mind for many years. In addition, he wanted Israeli Jewish students to learn about the *Nakbah*–even though he acknowledged clearly that this is very different from the Holocaust–which is why he wanted them to visit Palestinian refugee camps in the West Bank.

Taking students to Auschwitz in March 2014 was part of a project which he and his colleagues called *Hearts of Flesh–Not Stone* (based on a verse in Ezekiel, "I will give you a new heart and put a new spirit in you; I will remove from you your heart of stone and give you a heart of flesh." Ezekiel 36:26). This radically innovative program, which was funded by the German Research Foundation, was not a program of Al Quds University, although the Palestinians in the program, who were Dajani's students, came from this university. The fact that Professor Dajani led this study tour to the death camp in Poland, undoubtedly the greatest symbol of Jewish suffering in modern history, earned him much notoriety. Palestinians from the university and from outside vehemently protested his taking Palestinians to Auschwitz. This hostile response led him to resign from his positions as Professor of American Studies and Librarian at *Al Quds* University later that year.

Yet, Dajani does not regret that he took his students on this important study tour.

> Most of them were students of mine from Al Quds University, students who had been studying with me, especially in the American Studies program, which I founded. We selected 30 students to go on the program (which was funded by a German institute, not by Al Quds University), out of many more students who applied. The program which we developed called for taking 30 Israeli Jewish students to the *Dahaishe* refugee camp near Bethlehem and 30 Palestinian Arab students to Auschwitz, with all the major differences between them. The Israelis went separately to the Palestinian refugee camp in March 2014, before the Palestinians went to Auschwitz at the end of that month. After the trip, we published a book entitled *Teaching Empathy and Reconciliation in the Midst of Conflict* which included important essays by students, faculty and journalists, who gave many moving testimonies of the importance of this journey.

In one of these essays entitled *Encountering the Suffering of the Other*, co-authored by Dajani and Marin O'Malley, a professor at Fredrick Schiller University in Germany, which was a partner in this project, they wrote:

> We are part of an international team of academics that organized in late March 2014 a trip of 27 Palestinian students to Auschwitz in Poland, the first trip for Palestinian students to that memorial of Nazi crimes against humanity. (A parallel trip was also organized for 30 Israeli students to visit two refugee camps in the West Bank, established as a result of the 1948 Palestinian *Nakbah*.) As scholars, we are interested in the dynamics involved in 'experiencing the suffering of the other' within existing conflict situations and how such experiences impact feelings of empathy, and ultimately, reconciliation.

The Palestinian participants experience Auschwitz with an ever-present reminder of their own conflict. All of our student participants live in Palestine and as such are subject to the daily encounters and hassles of the Israeli occupation. Some participants had spent years in Israeli jails. Travelling to Auschwitz involved crossing multiple checkpoints to get to the Allenby bridge in order to cross to Jordan and fly from Amman airport to Poland...Nevertheless, those students who found in themselves the courage to participate were capable of learning about the Holocaust with deep attention, and yes, empathy, and later shared their reflections on Facebook.

These scholars who studied the effect of the trip on these students found some profound changes among the students. These significant transformations were totally overlooked in the media storm over the trip, which is very unfortunate. Nevertheless, these academics discovered that the students were able to empathize with the Jewish victims of the Holocaust, which was one of the goals of the trip—to put yourselves in the shoes of the other, to try to understand the experience of the other. This should not have been such a surprising finding but apparently, according to these scholars, that was the case.

Perhaps it should not be radical for Palestinians to recognize the Holocaust and express their empathy for its victims. And yet acting in a moderate way when people are suffering can seem radical. Such courageous moderation is necessary for moving in the direction of more dignity and more peace for people that desperately need dignity and peace. Whatever happens in the political process, Palestinians and Israelis share a future as neighbors in one form or another. Though it may be easy to lose heart, we prefer to recognize the hopeful signs and counsel support of movements, scholarly projects and political acts that can contribute to peace and reconciliation.

I love this term, *courageous moderation*. It is a good summation of Dajani's approach to this trip as well as his overall approach to searching for possibilities for peaceful coexistence among Palestinians and Israelis, which was what this project was really all about. He and his colleagues were able to focus on hopeful signs that they saw arise from this process. The focus on hope—and the insistence on the positive, even in the midst of great despair—were not only the hallmarks of this potentially groundbreaking program,

83

but are also central to Dajani's entire *Wasatia* philosophy and movement, with its constant emphasis on learning the other's narrative towards the goal of reconciliation between the parties to the conflict.

The Struggle Against Rejectionism and the Anti-Normalizers: Promoting Moderate Islam

Following the trip to Auschwitz, the project came to a halt. There were many attacks from the Palestinian public against it, and public pressure was intense. This made people afraid to continue to participate in the project. The students stopped attending the follow-up meetings. In Dajani's view, all of this was very unfortunate, since in the original plan for this project there was an idea to do a follow-up trip with both the Israelis and Palestinians to Auschwitz.

Dajani's courage and refusal to go along with "the Palestinian street" by continuing to deny the existence of the Holocaust, or by accusing Israelis of using it as a political weapon in the propaganda war against Palestinians, earned him great respect among Israeli and Diaspora Jews, and among people of good will around the world. But large segments of Palestinian society continued to reject learning about this seminal event in Jewish and general history as part of "anti-normalization." For most Palestinians, learning about the Jewish narrative, meeting with Jews, and empathizing with their suffering was considered part of "normalization" with the enemy who was occupying them, and was therefore frowned upon. Dajani was accused of being a "normalizer" not just because he took Palestinian students to Poland but because he continued to insist on the importance of dialogue with Israeli Jews, which included learning their narrative. Just as he wanted Israeli Jews to learn the narrative of the Palestinian people, which included learning about the great catastrophe, the *Nakbah*, that led to 700,000 refugees and hundreds of villages destroyed, so too he insisted that it was vital for Palestinian Arabs to learn the Jewish Israeli narrative, which includes the centrality of the Holocaust in contemporary Jewish history.

Following this disruptive episode in his personal and professional life and despite the fact that he received death threats and his car was torched near his home, he has energetically devoted himself to peacebuilding via his NGO, *Wasatia*. He has given many lectures, appeared on many panels—in Israel and abroad—with me and with other Jewish Israeli peacebuilders. In addition, he has been interviewed in many magazines and newspapers. Furthermore, he has published many pamphlets in English and in Arabic about the central concepts related to *Wasatia* via the publishing program of his organization. In so doing, he has outlined the vision of *Wasatia* and how it relates to the future of Palestine.

> The doctrine of *wasatia*, or 'centrism' lays out a middle ground between secularism and fundamentalism in the Islamic world. Generally speaking, it represents the mainstream of the Muslim masses. *Wasatia* in Palestine supports the peaceful democratic aspirations of Palestinians. For *Wasatia*, an Islamic movement guided by the Quran and Prophetic traditions, should avoid being too radical, too political, or too rejecting of the peace process. It should practice diplomacy, creativity and brilliance in dealing with the international community. Although secular parties in Palestine are clearly distinct from religious parties, they are not uniformly homogenous from within. *Wasatia* identifies a 'gray zone' of young moderate leaders in both camps urging them to promote these values within their own ranks.

Dajani has promoted a moderate vision of Islam. As a professor, publicist and activist he has developed a comprehensive secular-cultural philosophy of Islam. Not only has he studied the Quran carefully, but he has put the ethical principles related to peace and reconciliation, which he views as central to Islam, into practice. Moreover, he has served as a guide for other Muslims, perhaps the large Muslim middle ground in Palestine and elsewhere, who are looking for a way in the world other than that of extremist fundamentalist Islam, which is often portrayed in the media as the real Islam. Indeed, Dajani has spent much of his time and energy combating Islamic extremism and offering a reasonable alternative. He has stated clearly:

> Rather than remaining bystanders, moderate Muslims need to join forces in recognition that their religion and its central texts have been hijacked by a small group of minorities for political ends. Furthermore, moderation would erode the occupation's *raison d'être* by helping Palestinians and Israelis see their overlapping goals. A good starting point would be mutual recognition.

Dajani's promotion of the doctrine of *Wasatia*—a moderate, tolerant, peaceful, conciliatory philosophy and practice of Islam—is one of his greatest contributions to contemporary Palestinian and Islamic culture, not only in Palestine, but around the world.

The Wasatia Graduate School for Peace and Reconciliation

In recent years, Dajani has devoted much time and energy to establish the *Wasatia* Graduate School for Peace and Conflict Resolution program at the European University in Flensburg, Germany. This new program aims to respond to the growing demand for academic skills and knowledge and professional training that addresses the complex issues of moderation, peace, and conflict resolution. Students will receive a PhD from this university after studying in a rigorous three-year academic program, which will build on experiences that they have acquired at various institutions. In their studies, they will focus on key concepts such as peace, moderation, conflict resolution, mediation, justice, empathy, interreligious understanding, dialogue, tolerance, and other related topics.

According to Dajani, this program will provide the unique opportunity to prepare skilled individuals, educators, and professionals from the Middle East, Europe, and the international community to create an environment of moderation, tolerance, balance, temperance, pluralism, diversity, and peaceful coexistence. The target groups are postgraduate students from different disciplines and conflicts as well post-conflict regions interested in learning why it is important to achieve peace and maintain it. Students who will graduate from this program will be future leaders in their communities, guiding their people to improve their lives and challenge traditional thinking.

The learning process in this program will be implemented both locally, in Palestine, and in Germany via seminars and lectures conducted through video conferences. Both regular lecturers and visiting professors will serve as research advisors to students as they develop their research work. The program envisions a future in which people living in conflict areas will achieve a significant stage of cooperation, understanding, and open-mindedness, to facilitate living in a healthy environment free of enmity, bigotry, racism, hatred, and violence.

By setting up this unique graduate program, Dajani is looking towards the future. His vision of a healthier environment for everyone in the region—Israeli Jews and Palestinian Arabs alike—keeps him going. This is what makes his life meaningful each day.

Conclusion

The lesson that we learn from Mohammed Dajani is the importance of education towards moderation and reconciliation today, for his own people, and for others as well. This comes out of his understanding of Islam, based on years of studying the core texts of the religion—the *Quran* and the *Hadith* (the Sayings of the Prophets). From his comprehensive study of the main sources of Islam, he has concluded that Islam is a moderate religion, one of the *middle way* (*wasatia*), one that shares the core universalistic values of peace, justice, tolerance, and reconciliation with the other two monotheistic religions—Judaism and Christianity. Moreover, his method is one of openness and inclusivity, which he accomplishes through interreligious and intercultural dialogue with Jews and Christians. He has used dialogue as a way to practice peacebuilding, which, for him, includes intensive learning about the other's religion and narrative. In the case of Palestinian Arabs and Israeli Jews, this meant that he needed to take Palestinians to Auschwitz and Israelis to *Dahaishe* (a Palestinian refugee camp near Bethlehem), while recognizing and acknowledging the asymmetry involved with these two study tours. In doing this, he has stressed both the particularity as well as the universalism inherent in studying both about the Holocaust and the *Nakbah*. At the heart of his philosophy is the need for each side to learn about and empathize with the pain and suffering of the other.

To sum up his legacy in two words, I would suggest **courageous moderation**. He has demonstrated the courage to speak up and educate the younger generation, even at the risk of threats on his life, and he has displayed constant commitment to his values of moderation, to *wasatia*, through his writing and lecturing, and even his frequent posts on social media, as a means of outreach to the younger generation.

Bishop Munib Younan: A Christian Theology and Life of Peacebuilding

Photo courtesy of Lutheran World Federation

Bishop Munib Younan is without doubt the leading religious Christian peacebuilder in Jerusalem. He has been involved in many interreligious peacebuilding programs and institutions–both locally, in Jerusalem, and internationally–for several decades. The Jonah Group, co-facilitated by Bishop Younan and myself for many years, was comprised of Jewish Israeli clergy and educators, together with Palestinian Christian clergy and educators. He has also been deeply involved–as one of the founders and core members–with the Council of Religious Institutions of the Holy Land, which has included many of the leaders of the Jewish, Christian and Muslim religious establishments in Israel and Palestine. In these activities he has always approached the issue of peace from his deeply rooted Christian perspective, based on his foundational faith in the possibilities and the promises of peace, justice and reconciliation for Palestinian Arabs and Israeli Jews. Indeed, he has been and continues to be a witness for peace—in Israel, Palestine and internationally.

I have known Bishop Younan for a long time as a professional colleague and personal friend. I was present at his installation as bishop in 1998 at the beautiful Church of the Redeemer in the Old City of Jerusalem. As one of the few Jewish guests present, I was seated in the front row. At this occasion, I will never forget how he talked about the need for peace, both for Palestinian Arabs and for Israeli Jews, a theme that he reiterated throughout his career. I have travelled with him to lecture together in the United States and have spoken with him on panels for visiting groups to Israel over the years. Moreover, we have visited each other in our homes, churches, and synagogues, and have frequently discussed contemporary issues over breakfast at Jerusalem coffee houses.

Born in Jerusalem in 1950 and raised in the Old City, Bishop Younan was educated in Palestine and Finland. Since his ordination as a Lutheran minister in 1976, he has served Lutheran congregations in the West Bank—in Ramallah and Bet Jalla—and in East Jerusalem, at the Church of the Redeemer. Moreover, he served as the Bishop of the Evangelical Lutheran Church in Jordan and the Holy Land for 20 years, from 1998-2018. In this position, he was in charge of Lutheran communities in Israel, Palestine and Jordan. Since 2018, he is officially retired, with the title of Bishop Emeritus, but remains very involved in interreligious dialogue and activism for peaceful coexistence.

Bishop Younan is also the President Emeritus of the Lutheran World Federation, the first Palestinian Christian to hold this post. His term as president lasted for seven years (from 2010 to 2017) during which time, he spoke up for peace and reconciliation all over the world. Among other things, he was instrumental in enabling a historic reconciliation between the Lutheran Church and the Catholic Church as part of the historic commemorations marking 500 years since the Reformation. He has received recognition for his interfaith work for peace and has been the recipient of several awards and prizes, the most recent one being the Sunhak Peace Prize in 2019.

Bishop Younan is married to Suad Younan who grew up in Haifa but whose family on her father's side originated from the Christian village of Biram in the Upper Galilee. She served as the principal and the director for the Helen Keller School for the Visually Impaired in East Jerusalem for many years (1995-2018) and later pursued a Masters of Arts degree in Education, Educational Leadership and Policies of Education at the Hebrew University of Jerusalem which she completed in 2017. Together they have three children and seven grandchildren, and all of them live in Israel. They live in the neighborhood of Beit Safafa, a Palestinian village that has become part of Jerusalem.

In addition, Bishop Younan is the author of two books of essays which are collections of his writings, speeches and sermons (see the bibliography). Also, he is a passionate and persuasive lecturer—via zoom and in-person— and has been a scholar-in-residence for the network of Lutheran colleges and universities in North America.

The Influence of the 1948 War/The *Nakbah* on Bishop Younan's Identity

Bishop Younan comes from a family with deep roots in Palestine, but with origins in Greece. According to stories that he heard from his father when he was a child, the Younan family was once a well-to-do family with landholdings and olive groves near Athens. At some point—Younan doesn't know the exact century—one of his ancestors visited the Holy Land as a pilgrim and arrived in Gaza. When this man's sister died in Gaza, he did not want to return to Greece. Instead, he remained in the Gaza strip, ultimately marrying a Palestinian woman, and moving to Beersheba in southern Palestine. As a result, Bishop Younan still has relatives in Gaza to this day.

According to family stories, Bishop Younan learned at a young age that his grandfather was a wealthy merchant who sold goods to the Turkish army during the rule of the Ottoman Empire in Palestine. His grandfather was educated in the Evangelical Alliance school in Beersheba, which no longer exists. He was a very religious Christian, and an avid reader, from whom Bishop Younan inherited many theological books in Arabic.

Bishop Younan's mother's family was from the western part of Jerusalem. His mother studied in the *Talitha Kumi* School when it was located on King George Street in central Jerusalem. (Today it is located in the Palestinian village of Beit Jalla, next to Bethlehem in the West Bank.) She received an excellent education in this Lutheran school, as did Bishop Younan as a child. She also developed a strong evangelical faith, which she shared with Bishop Younan's father, who came to Jerusalem from Beersheba.

The background of Bishop Younan's family strongly shaped his own identity, especially the fact that they were refugees in their own land.

> We are a family of refugees. All sides of my family and my wife's family were affected drastically by the Catastrophe of 1948. My father was a refugee from Beersheba who came to Jerusalem for safety during that period, just before the armistice, when the *Haganah* [the pre-state Jewish army] was attacking Arab communities to expand Jewish landholdings... As for my mother, her home was in the western part of Jerusalem. Her family assumed, as did many Christian families, that Jerusalem was to be an international city with protection guaranteed by the world community. But by April 30, 1948, two weeks before the declaration of independence of the State of Israel, and before the entry of Arab armies into the war, all Palestinian neighborhoods in west Jerusalem had been militarily occupied, and all Arab residents had been driven out.

Bishop Younan remembers vividly how these experiences affected both his mother and his father profoundly. They both passed along their memories of this period to him throughout his childhood. In particular, he recalled how his father described his experience:

> My father comes from Beersheba where his family had lived for a long time. He moved from Beersheba to Jerusalem during the *Nakbah*, in 1948. I visited the house a few times over the years from the outside but the new inhabitants did not let me come inside. The first time I visited that house was with my father in 1968. We went to that house, in the old city of Beersheba. He recognized it from the tall pine tree in front of the house, rang the bell, and a woman came out and said, 'What do you want?' And my father

said, 'this is our original family home, can we just look at it?' She slammed the door and said, 'Get out! I received this house from the government.'

For Bishop Younan, the experience of the *Nakbah* was not just personal; it was also collective. He sees himself both as part of the Palestinian people and as part of the Christian minority within Palestine:

> We Palestinians refer to the 1948 war as *The Nakba*, which in Arabic means 'the great catastrophe.' We remember this as the time when we were expelled from our homes, and we felt that the world was against us since they did not come to our aid, including the British who gave so much power to the *Haganah* and to other Jewish groups to do what they have done. We remember well that 750,000 Palestinians were expelled out of their homes. Also, for me it is important to remember that 50,000 of them were Christians, a fact that is largely unknown to the outside world. Our family is one of the 50,000 who were expelled from their homes–my parents and their siblings had to leave their homes and find another place to live within Israel, or to leave the country.

For Bishop Younan, both his Christian identity and his Palestinian identity were shaped by his family's narratives. He has become a well-known and respected leader of the Palestinian Christian community in Israel and Palestine.

Growing up in Jerusalem

After Israel took over western Jerusalem in early 1948, Bishop Younan's mother's family fled to the Old City of Jerusalem. Along with 15 other families, they found shelter in the compound of the Greek Orthodox convent of John the Baptist, very close to the Lutheran Church of the Redeemer, in the Christian Quarter. At first, they thought that this would be a temporary situation, but it became permanent. This was to be their home for many years. Shortly after this, his parents married in the Greek Orthodox church. They lived in a small apartment, up some stairs, bordering on David Street, one of the main shopping streets in the Old City of Jerusalem. They were a poor family. In those early years of the state of Israel, the whole country was very poor, and there was often not much to eat.

His parents baptized all of their five children in the Greek Orthodox Church, but at an early stage, they decided that they wanted their children to grow up in the Lutheran tradition. Therefore, even though the parents were Orthodox, the children were raised as Lutherans. Bishop Younan attended the Martin Luther School in the Old City, near their home. This is where he began his education. At the age of 11, he was sent to study in Bet Jalla at the *Talitha Kumi* school, which used to be in downtown Jerusalem. One of Bishop Younan's most distinct memories is how much he and his classmates hiked as teenagers in the area near Bet Jalla and Bethlehem:

> I got to know every inch of the hills throughout the region south of Jerusalem. As I grew up, I fell in love with the land.

It seems to me that attachment to the land, as a Palestinian, was very similar to many Israeli Jews' connectedness to the Land of Israel. Clearly this is something they share. Both Palestinian Arabs and Israeli Jews are deeply attached to the land that one calls Palestine and the other calls Israel.

In addition to formal schooling, at a young age Bishop Younan received a good deal of Christian education at home. On Tuesday afternoons, the Younan home in the Christian Quarter of the Old City was a place for Bible study for anyone who wanted to come. Bishop Younan was deeply impacted by this Bible study and by the age of eleven he already began to talk with his parents about the idea of studying theology.

Bishop Younan grew up in the 1950s and 1960s in Jerusalem. The Six Day War of 1967 was another watershed moment in his life. When the war began his family once again sought shelter in the basement of the Greek Orthodox Church in the compound where they were living. After Jerusalem was conquered, his family adjusted to the new situation of living under Israeli occupation in Jerusalem. But it was not easy. They were living in difficult circumstances which raised serious questions for the young Younan:

> We were living in an atmosphere of fear. We were losers. We should be quiet. Yet, faced with occupation, I needed to make theological sense of this situation. Does God allow injustice? Is God only a God of Power? Is this the end for us?

It was during this period that Bishop Younan began to study Hebrew. Among other things, he learned from his teachers of Hebrew that Jews studied the Bible very differently than Christians. This prompted him to develop an interest in studying the Old Testament. He was later to write his master's thesis on Isaiah, one of the most important classical prophets of the Hebrew Bible.

At the same time, as a teenager, he began to think about going abroad to further his education, not only because he wanted to study theology, but for other existential reasons:

> I wanted to find a way out of the occupation. An outlet–what do you call it in psychology–a kind of escapism. You cannot bear it. Everything is closed. Everything is blocked, unclear. You are powerless. This is what life was like for Palestinians, including myself.

This serious crisis in his life would lead Bishop Younan to study in Finland for several years.

After the Six Day War of 1967

Following the Six Day War some Palestinians who lived in Jerusalem, like the Younan family, visited relatives in the Galilee and had conversations with them raising their awareness of their new reality. Bishop Younan recalled what this was like at the time:

> I want to tell you something which you have maybe never heard. We were happy that the borders were open and we could see our relatives throughout Israel–in Haifa, in Ramleh, in Jaffa, in Nazareth. Some were happy! But still our relatives in the Galilee told us to be careful. 'It's still the honeymoon stage,' they said. The Israelis had just lifted the military restrictions on the Arabs of the Galilee [in 1966]. So, our families told us to wait a minute and you will see how the Israelis will treat you. Some people did not believe these predictions. But later on, we started to understand that what they had warned us about was true–that Arab Palestinians would never be equal, no matter what we do.

This was a bitter lesson that Bishop Younan learned early in his life. It was to accompany him throughout his life as a Palestinian living in Jerusalem, where Palestinians continued to be discriminated against in many ways, and where the small and diminishing Christian communities are desperately trying to maintain their identity.

In addition, after the 1967 War, Bishop Younan had his first encounter with fundamentalist evangelical Christian theology. An American Protestant pastor from West Jerusalem came to the door of his family's home with the following message: 'Thank God that Israel has liberated the Old City.' He quoted many passages from the Bible to prove that this was the fulfillment of Biblical prophecy. Bishop Younan began to question this approach to Christianity. He was bothered by these uses–or misuses–of passages from the Bible. This troubled him greatly and was one of the motivational factors in his deciding to study the Old Testament in a serious way.

Theological Studies and Development of Palestinian Christian Identity in Finland

In April 1969, Bishop Younan was granted a scholarship to study theology in Finland. At the age of 18, he began his studies there, which were to last for seven years. During these years of studying and living in Finland, he received both a bachelor's degree and a master's degree. All of these studies helped to shape both his Christian and his Palestinian identity.

> Finland helped to shape my national identity as a Palestinian. Some said to me 'Get your PhD.' I said 'No. I am called to serve my people. I can get my PhD later.'

As an expatriate in Finland, he began to become involved in Palestinian politics for the first time. At first, he resisted it, since it was contrary to his family upbringing. But later on, he became more and more involved in what he called "constructive nationalism," which he saw as something very positive:

> When I speak of nationalism, I mean in a positive, not in a negative way. First of all, I am a Christian. So, what is Christian? I'm Arab. Yet, it is not enough simply to be lumped together with those from other Arab countries. I'm a Palestinian. That's distinctive. The more I climbed the nationalist mountain, the more I was conscious of my Christian identity. The more that I was conscious of my Christian identity, the more I became conscious of my Palestinian identity. They grew along parallel tracks, increasing to the same degree. Had I not been in Finland, I would not have gained that identity.

Undoubtedly, his years of study and living in Finland had a great impact on Bishop Younan theologically and personally. It shaped his identity for many decades to follow.

While he was in Finland, he studied contextual theology, among many other topics. Finnish theology had been greatly influenced by their own revival movements. The gospel had been adapted by local preachers to fit the Scandinavian environment. Later, when he was a pastor in Ramallah, Bet

Jalla and Jerusalem, Younan would adapt his theology to the Palestinian context. This impacted his work as a peacebuilder. For example, in a dialogue group, which he and I co-facilitated for many years, we both made an effort to make our dialogue highly contextual by bringing indigenous Palestinian Christians and local Israeli Jews into the dialogue. Until then, much of the Jewish-Christian dialogue in Jerusalem had involved mostly Western Christians and Western Jews who were living in Israel at the time, which was the norm in interfaith circles in the early '90s in this field. In doing so, we were able to focus the dialogue on our local situation, including existential issues that had to do with the Israeli-Palestinian conflict and the search for peace.

As someone who studied contextual theology, the changing political and security situation in Israel and Palestine would always be important to Bishop Younan. For him, theology—the word of God, as it has come down through the Bible, via the Old and New Testaments and in later Christian teachings—must be relevant for the contemporary situation of Jews, Muslims and Christians who are living together in the Holy Land. The basic teachings of Christianity—which can be found in the Gospels—and in particular in some foundational texts, such as the Sermon on the Mount have guided him throughout his life.

Bishop Younan was to develop a full and deep Protestant Christian Theology over time, based on his studies of both the Hebrew Bible and the New Testament.

> For me, you cannot understand the Old Testament without the New Testament nor the New Testament without the Old Testament. This is very significant and essential inner Lutheran understanding. We take both Testaments as the book of the Church.

> There are many foundational texts in both Testaments. The message of all the prophets in the Old Testament are messages of metanoia or repentance or *tshuva* to God. It is a message that does not prophesy the other nations but one's own nation as well. For example, Prophet Isaiah presents a theology of universalism. He opens the boundaries of faith to all nations. God's liberation is for every human being. Prophet Amos concentrates on social justice. Micah and Hosea and others concentrate on justice, doing mercy and following the commandments of God. The Old Testament culture is closer to the Palestinian culture in many respects. This

is the reason we concentrate on liberation and justice which we believe is what God wants in our world.

Moreover, Bishop Younan's education in Finland, as well as his practice over several decades back in Palestine, have led him to develop a unique Palestinian Christian theology:

> For me, Palestinian Christian theology is based on understanding the central message of the Old and New Testaments. It is based on the fulfillment of prophecies in the birth and crucifixion and resurrection of Jesus Christ. As the Exodus story was a pilgrimage of liberation, so we consider that the crucifixion and resurrection are the Second Exodus of liberation for all human beings. This liberation on the cross is for every human being and reflects on all the world. God hears the cries of the oppressed. God is not partial but loves every human being and God wants them to live in justice, dignity, equality and freedom reconciled with God and with their neighbors.

In addition, Bishop Younan has developed a profound theology of reconciliation, which he has applied to the reconnecting of the Lutheran Church with the Catholic Church, after 500 years since the Reformation, as well as to his approach concerning the importance of reconciling differences between Israeli Jews and Palestinian Arabs:

> St Paul also admonishes every Christian in his second letter to the Corinthians (5:18-20): 'All this is from God, who reconciled us to Himself through Christ, and He has given us the ministry of reconciliation.' So, being a Christian for me, a believer in Christ, as my savior and redeemer, I am called to be a minister of reconciliation. This is the basis of my theology which is solid and clear. As God through Christ reconciled the whole world not only for the Christians, so it is my call as a follower of Christ to be a minister of reconciliation wherever I am needed in this world.

During his decades of service, to his church and to humanity, Bishop Younan developed his own, contextual theological approach, which meant that he would constantly be adapting his belief system to confront the situation of conflict and the struggle for freedom and reconciliation between Israelis and Palestinians in the Holy Land. By the time he returned from Finland, in 1976, the situation was quite different from when he had left in the late 1960s, since the Israeli occupation in the West Bank and

Jerusalem had become more entrenched. Even though Bishop Younan was able to witness the peace with Egypt in 1979, the growing violence–especially the uprising by the Palestinians and the rapid responses of the Israeli army during the First *Intifada* from December 1987 until 1991–was very disturbing. However, in the early 1990s there was a great change for peace in the region which motivated Bishop Younan to increase his involvement in programs for peace and reconciliation with Israeli Jews in the wake of these historic changes.

Dialogue Programs in the wake of the Oslo Accords of 1993

Bishop Younan had been in dialogue with Jews and Muslims before the Oslo Accords, including with myself and other rabbis and Jewish educators in Israel. Yet, the Oslo Accords in the early 1990s represented a major new opportunity for peace and reconciliation. He recalled the historic moment of the signing of the Declaration of Principles:

> These accords were really a major breakthrough between Palestinians and Israelis. The Declaration of Principles of September 1993 between the Israeli government and the Palestine Liberation Organization recognized that a Palestinian people exists which deserves its own rights and that the State of Israel has a right to exist. There was mutual recognition. This process spurred me to be more involved in peacebuilding with other religious leaders.

Bishop Younan built on relationships he had forged earlier to become more involved in interreligious dialogue for peace at the beginning of the 1990s. In his memoir *Witnessing for Peace*, he described his first trialogue with Jews, Muslims and Christians in Sweden in 1990–followed by trialogues in Switzerland (1993) and Thessaloniki (1997)–as well as his initial encounters with rabbis (including myself) in Jerusalem in those years. After these important experiences abroad, he participated in a series of five trialogues funded by the Norwegian Lutheran Church in Jerusalem in 1998. It was important for him to engage in dialogue locally, not just internationally. The international trialogues catalyzed him to bring the concept of trialogue-dialogue with Jews, Christians and Muslims–back to Jerusalem for the sake of peace.

> We agreed to continue the trialogue back home in Israel and Palestine, under two conditions. First the discussions should be

local. This should not be something manipulated by European and American religious leaders. Second, we should be discrete. The more open we were at this stage, the more danger there was of misunderstanding by uninformed parties and of misinterpretation by those with political motives.

It was important at the beginning for this dialogue to be off-the-record, beneath the radar, to build trust and confidence among the participants. Bishop Younan felt that it was necessary to meet on a regular basis in dialogue with his Jewish partners. In 1991, during the Gulf War, he discovered how important this was:

> At a meeting at the Hebrew Union College in Jerusalem [the headquarters of Reform Judaism in Israel], questions and accusations were raised. 'Why are Palestinians standing on the rooftops cheering when scud missiles are launched against Israel?' This was a very difficult question for those of us who had begun the dialogue process. We began to talk more about the years of occupation and the pent-up anger of the Palestinian people. Many of our rabbi friends agreed. 'We need to speak out more strongly concerning an end to occupation.' In 1993, when Rabin and Arafat shook hands on the White House Lawn, these same rabbis telephoned to congratulate us on the major progress that had taken place.

I was involved in many of these dialogues with Bishop Younan and other Christian clergy and other rabbis at the time. The most important and long-lasting dialogue group that we were involved with together, "The Jonah Group," was comprised of local Christians from different denominations–Lutheran, Roman Catholic, Anglican, and Armenian–and local Jews, which included Reform, Conservative and Orthodox rabbis, as well as Jewish educators. We met at each other's churches and synagogues, studied together, ate together and discussed contemporary issues of mutual concern, especially problems relating to discrimination and the ills of the occupation. These were all meaningful occasions; personal and professional relationships were developed at that time that lasted for many years. According to one of the most consistent participants in these encounters, Rabbi Levi Weiman-Kelman, Rabbi Emeritus of Congregation *Kol Haneshama* (Reform) in Jerusalem, these dialogues were very important:

> More than the content of the meetings it was the interpersonal connections that made it worthwhile. The one meeting that really stands out for me was one around the High Holidays. I remember

we were sitting someplace in the Church of the Redeemer. We got into a discussion about forgiveness. One of the Christian clergy described how great the power of God's forgiveness was; even the greatest sinner if they turned to God, if they repented, God would forgive them. They would be forgiven. I remember the Jews sputtering, 'Do you mean that if Hitler repented on his deathbed, God would forgive him?!' And the Christian clergy (can't remember who) said, 'Yes.' I think most of the Jews were just horrified but I really felt that it was the first time that I really understood how different the Christian understanding of forgiveness is from the Jewish view. I also felt that the Christians could help the pathology of the Middle East if they could teach Jews and Moslems how to forgive each other. That has really stayed with me.

In addition to discussing theological issues like forgiveness and relating them to our contemporary reality in Israel/Palestine, we also studied Jewish and Christian texts together and visited each other's churches and synagogues in Jerusalem. I remember one year in which we held a model seder before Passover at Congregation *Kol Haneshama* in which we read portions from the *Hagaddah* together, as well as contemporary readings, which catalyzed us to discuss the importance of freedom for both peoples in our region–the Jewish Israeli people and the Palestinian Arab people.

The Jonah Group and other peacebuilding activities–some of which began in the early 1990s before the Oslo Accords–took on greater meaning and more intensity after the signing of these accords. After the signing of the first Oslo Accord on the White House lawn in September 1993, Bishop Younan remembered that the excitement he felt at the time was shared among Palestinians in Jerusalem, where he lived, and in the West Bank.

It was a euphoric moment. People were blowing their horns in their cars. I went out of my home in Ramallah, where I was serving as a pastor, and saw people honking their horns with happiness. And I saw soldiers who used to shoot young Palestinian boys who used to throw stones at them, and those Palestinian boys who used to throw the stones were distributing flowers! People were singing and rejoicing! And I thought to myself: 'Now we are starting a new period of justice and peace between Palestinians and Israelis.' This showed me and continues to show me that even if peace is very far away, it is possible. This is why I continue to work for peace to this very day.

Bishop Younan also recalls how the positive mood for peace after the signing of the Oslo Accords opened up new opportunities for encounters and dialogue among youth-and even for politicians-on both sides of the conflict.

> After the Oslo agreements there was a big change. During those years, we began twinning programs between Palestinian Lutheran Schools and Israeli schools in Tel Aviv. Our youth-and their young people-began to visit each other and by so doing, they started to understand each other, to see the humanity of the other. For the first time, Jewish youth saw Palestinian youth as human beings, not just as terrorists. Also, politicians began seeing others as human beings, not just as media stereotypes.

Yet, only two years after the Oslo Accord, the peace process suffered a major setback when a Jewish extremist assassinated the Prime Minister of Israel, Yitzhak Rabin, on November 4, 1995. This was an existential moment, both for Israelis and Palestinians, and for the world. Bishop Younan, who was involved in an interreligious dialogue for peace on the very night of the assassination, remembers vividly where he was and how he felt on that traumatic night.

> I was invited by the World Council of Churches to a dinner in Jerusalem with Israeli Jews on the night that Rabin was assassinated. We started to eat together—Palestinians and Israelis, who were in dialogue without fear. All of a sudden, we received the news that Rabin was shot! Can you imagine what we were thinking and feeling, Israelis and Palestinians sitting together. We all cried together. We had been moved by the fact that Rabin had moved from being a general in the Israeli army to become a warrior for peace.

Bishop Younan felt that the assassination dealt a very serious blow to the political-diplomatic peace process of the 1990s. At the same time, he felt determined to persist in working for peace. In the years ahead, Bishop Younan and other peacebuilders persisted in their work for peace, even though it became more difficult with each passing year.

The Impact of the Second *Intifada* (2000-2005)

Many pundits say that the assassination of Prime Minister Rabin dealt a death blow to the political peace process. I don't agree. I felt that it wounded the process severely but the peace process kept going throughout the 1990s, despite all the obstacles and challenges.

Instead, I would say that the Second *Intifada* —the violent uprising of the Palestinians, epitomized by many suicide bombs going off in Israeli cities, and the counter-violence of the Israel Defense Forces for five years, 2000-2005—had a much more deleterious effect on the peace process. It caused severe fear and trauma on both sides which remain to this day, grinding the process to a halt. It led to the total absence of trust between the two sides of the conflict, and to a situation of political despair, by which I mean that none of the major politicians on either side had any concrete ideas any more as to how to resolve the conflict and achieve peace. Nevertheless, this did not deter peacebuilders like Bishop Younan, who continued to persist for peace. He spoke out for peace with courage and conviction at every possible opportunity, in Israel, and Palestine, and even in the USA.

In January of 2002, Bishop Younan, Dr. Mohammed Hourani (a Muslim educator from Jerusalem) and I were invited to speak together in New York City at the largest Reform temple in the world, Temple Emanuel, at their annual clergy institute for Christian and Jewish clergy from New York City. We travelled to the USA and spoke in synagogues, churches and in academic settings for nine days, in New York City, Boston, Worcester and Chicago. In every place we spoke we were greeted warmly and our messages of peace and reconciliation were appreciated and applauded. At each forum, each one of us would begin with a 10–15-minute presentation, each one of us opening with our own unique perspective on the situation, including our analysis of the root causes of the conflict and our visions for a better future for both peoples, the Palestinian people and the Jewish people. At almost every session, Bishop Younan would include in his introductory remarks his view that the root cause of the conflict was the ongoing military Occupation of Palestinian lands by the state of Israel. Invariably, I would be asked in the question-and-answer session what I thought about that and I would reply that I felt that there were two root causes of the conflict—one was the Occupation and the other was the refusal of many Palestinians to recognize the right of the state of Israel to exist.

A few weeks later, in March of that year, I convened the same panel of the three of us to speak to a visiting delegation of American Reform rabbis who were in Israel to attend the annual convention of the Central Conference of American Rabbis (the national body of Reform/Progressive/Liberal rabbis in North America) which took place in Jerusalem. The panel took place in the ICCI Education Center, in the offices of the NGO that I founded and lead for nearly 25 years. Each of us gave a brief initial presentation, but this time Bishop Younan did not mention his view about the root cause of the conflict in his introduction. Instead, one of the rabbis asked him: "Bishop Younan, what do you think is the root cause of the Israeli-Palestinian Conflict?" His response was: "There are two root causes of the conflict..." Even though I knew from previous dialogues with him and from speeches that I heard him give, including the one at his ordination as Bishop which emphasized how peace was important both for the Israeli Jews and Palestinian Arabs, I was gratified by the results of our public dialogues together. As a public speaker, I have noticed that there is a tendency to fall back on your own narrative. But here, both of us had enhanced our public stance to include the narrative of the other. These dialogues had reinforced the notion that there are two overarching narratives to our conflict, each one with its own emphases and foci, and that listening carefully and consistently to each other helps us to realize this and to enunciate it.

The Alexandria Process and the Establishment of the Council of Religious Institutions of the Holy Land

As the violence of the intifada increased during 2000-2002, religious leaders who sought peace and reconciliation on the basis of their faiths did not stand idly by. On the contrary, throughout the year 2001, Rabbi Michael Melchior (who is one of the other peacebuilders profiled in this book) and others were deeply involved in preparing an interreligious peace initiative, which led to the signing of the famous Alexandria Declaration in Cairo in January 2002. This was a major statement for ending the violence and working towards peace by Jewish, Christian and Muslim religious leaders from Israel, Palestine, and Egypt, with the blessings of the Archbishop of Canterbury, from the UK.

Bishop Younan was also involved in some of the meetings and dialogues during 2001, which led to the signing of this important document. While he was not in Egypt personally when the declaration was signed, he took part in the meetings which were held in Jerusalem after the declaration was signed, as did I. I sat in these meetings as an observer for the international organization known as Religions for Peace, since the organization which I led, the Interreligious Coordinating Council in Israel was the Israel member of this international organization. These meetings–which took place discreetly and without publicity in a hotel in Jerusalem for several months following the signing of this historic interfaith document in Egypt-

attempted to deal with the implementation of the declaration, but not much was achieved, due to the ongoing violence of the Second *Intifada* during that very difficult year of 2002.

I found that year particularly difficult for dialogue and peace activism because of the high level of suicide bombings in Jerusalem. In fact, about two months after the signing of the Alexandria Declaration, I had a close call with death related to the violence of this period.

Following the panel discussion described above with the Central Conference of American Rabbis and Bishop Younan, I joined three rabbis and their wives for lunch at the popular Café Caffit, in the German Colony, one block from my office. As we were finishing our lunch, suddenly I heard someone yell for everyone to quickly vacate the restaurant. As a well-trained Israeli citizen, I followed the order immediately, and took my colleagues and their spouses with me in a hurry. After waiting around the corner for more than an hour, we learned that a Palestinian terrorist had approached the café with a bomb strapped to him under his winter coat. A fast-acting waiter had noticed him and tackled him, successfully disconnecting the wires from the bomb. The bomb and the terrorist were taken into custody by the police. A few weeks later, we learned that the detonator had been faulty, which is why the bomb didn't blow up. We were all saved by the quick action of an Israeli waiter and by luck!

So, with the help of God, I am still here to tell the story. It was a traumatic event for me. Yet, I was one of the lucky ones, since in my incident no bombs actually exploded and no one was killed. Serious suicide bombings continued in Jerusalem during that week. A bomb exploded the same week at the Moment Café in the heart of Jerusalem, killing 11 people, and injuring 54 and another one exploded at Café Hillel, on the same street where I worked, killing a father and a daughter on the eve of her wedding. It was a very difficult and scary period in Jerusalem. I was unable to return to Caffit for about a year. Yet, despite this incident, I did not remain in despair. Instead, like Bishop Younan, who also faced many obstacles and challenges along the way, I recommitted myself to peacebuilding through dialogue, education and action, as a way to deal with the ongoing conflict.

Bishop Younan and some of his colleagues felt that the implementation of the declaration from the Alexandria Process was not moving forward fast enough. In addition, he felt that the Christian voice was not being heard enough since the dialogue was mostly between Jews and Muslims. As a result, he and some of his colleagues started another organization, which was a spin-off from the Alexandria Process. They called it the Council of Religious Institutions of the Holy Land, which included the Heads of Churches in Jerusalem–the Latin Patriarch (Roman Catholic), the Anglican Bishop, the Lutheran Bishop (Younan), and Armenian Bishop–the Chief Rabbis of Israel and their representatives, and the Head of the Muslim (*shariyah*) Courts in Palestine. In addition, it had financial and personnel support from the Norwegian Church, who not only provided money for the new organization but sent a mediator to manage it by the name of Trond Bakkevig, who served as a neutral moderator of this new peacebuilding institution. Bishop Younan became intensely involved in this Council.

> We started at that time. It was very successful, because all the churches believed in it, including and especially the Orthodox churches. The Christian communities had a real voice. The Armenian, the Roman Catholic, the Greek Orthodox, the Lutheran and the Anglican bishops were all involved We had a core group and I was asked by the heads of the Christian churches to represent them in the core group. The representative from the Muslim community was Salah Suheika, who was the chief judge, and the deputy minister of the Wakf in Palestine. He was also a member of the core group.

The establishment of this council was another religious response to the violence of the second *intifada*. It was a way that religious leaders from the three major faith traditions in Israel and Palestine could play a role in trying to calm the violence of the ongoing uprising as well as in promoting new ways of understanding and cooperation. Bishop Younan, who has been involved with this council for many years, felt that the council chalked up some significant achievements, especially in the early years, after the end of the second *intifada*:

> We built trust among the institutions–with the Chief Rabbinate, with the Heads of the Churches and with the Muslim leadership. In addition, we wanted to respond to the growing wave of incitement in Palestine and in Israel. Accordingly, we hired two communication companies, one in Tel Aviv and one in Ramallah, to monitor what rabbis, imams and others were saying since we noticed that the problem often came from statements by rabbis, imams, and Christian clergy who did not depict the 'other' positively. We were disturbed by that. The communication companies brought a report to the Council which led us to discuss how we

can send messages to rabbis, imams, and clergy to use the scriptures positively to talk about the 'other.'

During the years 2005-2012, Bishop Younan and his colleagues in this new council continued to play a role as peacebuilders in Israel and Palestine. They believed that it was the right thing to do and because they felt that there was an expectation on the part of their peoples who were interested in a just settlement of the conflict for both sides. As their influence grew and developed, they were invited by the US State Department in 2007 to visit Washington DC, where they met with senators and congress-people and with then-Vice President Joe Biden. They also visited churches, synagogues and mosques in the Washington DC area together. In addition, they spent three days together, during which time they developed an important joint statement. According to Younan, the statement was an important milestone for the council.

> The statement said that we are against incitement, and we agreed that the occupation has to end and that the security of Israel has to be ensured. In addition, I raised the issue about some Jewish settlers who at the time wanted to enter the *Haram Al Sharif*, the *Al Aksa* Mosque, and the vicinity in the heart of the Holy Basin in the Old City of Jerusalem. We asked the chief rabbis to make a statement and they did so. They said very clearly that this a holy place for the Muslims and that they did not want any Jews to enter there at that time. They also said that they were not interested in building the third temple because the third temple will come in messianic times. This public statement by the rabbis helped to calm the Muslims in Jerusalem. I believe that this was an influential statement.

Moreover, the Council commissioned a major study of the textbooks used in Palestinian and Israeli schools. The study-which was undertaken by scholars from the United States, Israel and Palestine-issued a report with many recommendations for improvement. Unfortunately, the Israeli government did not accept the report at all. They refused to consider it since they felt that it was not balanced. The Palestinian government didn't do much better. They said that they would consider the recommendations but they just placed them in a drawer.

Nevertheless, Bishop Younan and his colleagues in Lutheran schools in Palestine did implement at least some of the recommended changes in their educational settings. Bishop Younan remembers this as a positive step forward.

> In the Lutheran schools, when I was the bishop, I asked my educational team to implement the recommendations of the report, and we have done so. At least we made some changes in my schools. That's very important. I believe that a just peace can begin from the actions of a small group. Then it is like throwing a stone in the water. It will make ripples. It will grow and grow and grow. This is what I still believe. We are still talking about a two-state solution and a shared Jerusalem, the capital for both peoples. People say to me that I am still thinking about an illusory peace but I don't agree with them. I still believe peace will come even though the pendulum is not on our side right now. One day it will come.

Bishop Younan saw his role as a peace educator clearly and decisively. Even if the Palestinian Authority did not make necessary changes in its curriculum, at least he was able to do so in educational institutions under his control.

Maintaining Peace Activism and Keeping Hope Alive Despite Many Obstacles.

Along with most Palestinians in Jerusalem and the West Bank, Bishop Younan faced many difficulties and challenges in the years during and after the Second *Intifada*. Particularly troubling was the building of the security fence/wall, which Israel began building in 2002, supposedly to keep terrorists from infiltrating and committing acts of terror inside Israel. Bishop Younan felt this was a serious problem, causing much hatred and division. Yet, he insisted that it is important to keep peacebuilding activities going since efforts to try to bring justice and peace to both sides should never stop.

First of all, the wall was unfortunate. For me, it was a hatred wall. It's not a barrier. It gave us the impression, as Palestinians, that these are the borders for the future. It has created indifference on both sides. The Israelis did not want to know what's behind the wall. And the Palestinians do not want to know what's on the other side of the wall. It created alienation and estrangement. After the first *intifada* and after the Oslo agreements in the early 1990s, we started to bring people together. However, the wall didn't stop our efforts to continue for justice and peace. Even though it was difficult for our Jewish partners to enter the West Bank, we kept going. Those of us who had permits could enter Israel. We–Rabbi Kronish and I–started initiatives to do dialogue in Jerusalem via the Jonah Group, which we co-moderated for many years, bringing Palestinian Christians into dialogue with Jewish Israelis. We studied together, discussed painful issues with each other, and engaged in common statements and actions whenever possible.

Bishop Younan believed that it was important to keep going, despite the difficulties. For him, it is a matter of religious belief, not one of political partisanship.

As time went on, Bishop Younan continued to face many obstacles along the way. Even the disengagement from Gaza in the summer of 2005, which was meant to be a step towards peace, turned out to be a huge disaster. The government of Israel decided to unilaterally disengage from the Gaza strip, without negotiating with the Palestinians with whom they had ceased to talk. All of the approximately 8000 Jewish settlers who were living in Gaza and all of their settlements were uprooted and destroyed, and all the Israeli soldiers who were there were brought back to Israel.

Bishop Younan felt that the disengagement from Gaza was a major mistake in the way that it was implemented. As part of his discreet peace activism as a religious leader, he and other Christian leaders sent a message to Israeli leaders at the time, urging them not to withdraw unilaterally. Instead of a one-sided move which did not include any discussion with the other side, they suggested that the method of dialogue and that principles of non-violence should be used.

> We said to the Israeli government: Do it in dialogue with your Palestinian partner. Otherwise, they [*Hamas*] will think they won. It sends the wrong message. Moreover, this policy sent a message to the Palestinians, especially the *Hamas* leaders, that only violence will work with Israel. This is unfortunate. This is against what we believe. I am a person of non-violence.

Nevertheless, much violence continued to take place between Israel and the Palestinians, especially with the Palestinians in Gaza ruled by the *Hamas* movement. Four mini-wars took place from 2006-2021, with no hope for a resolution to the conflict in sight. Instead of peace, there was just one cease-fire after another following each war.

As a result of these wars, a major split developed among the Palestinian people in the region. *Hamas* ruled in Gaza and *Fatah* reigned in the West Bank via the Palestinian Authority. This greatly bothered Bishop Younan, so he and other Palestinian Christian religious leaders engaged in quiet diplomacy. They contacted both sides, including *Hamas* leaders, and told them that this is not right, that they must accept the leadership of the Palestinian Authority, Mahmoud Abbas, known as Abu Mazen, and that it is important to find a way towards cooperation with the Palestinian Authority. As a deeply religious Christian, Bishop Younan felt that the concept of reconciliation was very important. Therefore, he and the Latin Patriarch at the time, Michel Sabbah, went to Gaza, where they met Ismail Haniya, the head of *Hamas*. This was an important act of back-channel peacebuilding. Bishop Younan recalls what Patriarch Sabbah told Haniya on this occasion.

> We came here as Lutherans and Catholics to tell you that for 500 years we fought each other and were divided, but now we have become allies and we are working together. We want you as the leader of *Hamas* to learn from us how you can reconcile with your Palestinian brothers and sisters in *Fatah*.

Patriarch Sabbah and Bishop Younan tried to bridge the rift between *Hamas* and *Fatah*. They even asked President Abu Mazen, to go to Gaza to try to engage in reconciliation with the *Hamas* leader. Unfortunately, both parties were stubborn and refused to cooperate.

For Bishop Younan, these acts of dialogue and reconciliation were not only important for Israeli Jews and Palestinian Arabs, but for the different factions within the Palestinian community. As a person of dialogue, he realized that internal discussion and cooperation were also essential in working for peace with the other side.

Conclusion: Being a Witness for Peace

Based on his seriously considered Christian religious faith, Bishop Younan has witnessed for peace for many decades—through his religious and inter-religious activism, his writings, his sermons and his lectures around the world. As a Protestant Christian religious leader and theologian, he has raised his voice consistently for peace and reconciliation, both in Israel and Palestine, as well as internationally. His leadership in the reconciliation process between the World Lutheran Federation and the Catholic Church in 2016 during this commemorative time of 500 years since the Reformation—at which time he and Pope Francis signed an historic declaration called "A Common Path"—was one of the seminal events in Christian ecumenical dialogue and internal peacebuilding in the contemporary period. As far as the Israeli-Palestinian conflict goes, he has consistently offered a Christian religious voice for sanity and sensibility, for dialogue and deliberation, for peaceful coexistence and reconciliation, and for a future without war and violence, which would be for the benefit of the Palestinian Arab people and the Jewish Israeli people. His deeply held religious faith is what has guided him along this path for decades, and it continues to inspire Palestinian Christians and Muslims, Israeli Jews, and people around the world.

Jewish Israeli Peacebuilders

Rabbi Michael Melchior: Pursuing Religious Peace

Photo by Ron Katzenelson

Rabbi Michael Melchior is without a doubt the leading interreligious Jewish pursuer of peace in Israel, where he has been promoting the idea of a religious peace between Israeli Jews and Palestinian Arabs for decades. He has established good relations with leading Muslims and Christians in Israel and abroad. In particular, he has done groundbreaking work in reaching out to Muslim religious leaders in Israel, Palestine and all over the Middle East, with whom he has met and engaged in dialogue about peace, based on their religious traditions, which urge them to pursue it with all their strength. Moreover, he has been instrumental not only in producing important historic declarations for peace on the regional and international levels–especially the historic Alexandria Declaration of January 2002–but he has also established important organizations to do the work of peace on the ground.

Rabbi Melchior is the guiding spirit behind many pioneering peacebuilding programs and projects, the foremost of which is the *Religious Peace Initiative*, an idea and a movement which he helped to co-found, which includes leading rabbis and Muslim and Christian clergy in Israel, the West Bank, Gaza, and other parts of the world. In this work, he has been engaged in many behind-the-scenes back-channel mediation efforts, which have saved lives and helped both the Israeli and Palestinian governments save face and prevent disasters.

In addition, Rabbi Melchior is a gifted speaker, communicator, sermonizer and story-teller. He has spoken to hundreds of groups who have come to visit him and hear from him about his religious peace initiative and he has spoken at countless international conferences, seminars and workshops on his work all over the world, whereby he is continually spreading his message that peace is possible and preferable to ongoing wars and violence. He has many amazing stories to tell about his peacebuilding initiatives, some of which will be shared with you in the pages ahead.

Childhood in Denmark and Early Years in Israel

A descendant of seven generations of rabbis in Denmark, Rabbi Melchior was born in Copenhagen in 1954 and grew up there. His father, Rabbi Brent Melchior (who passed away in 2021) was the Chief Rabbi of Denmark for many years, during which time he was active in interreligious affairs throughout Europe. I used to meet him at interreligious conferences which I attended. In addition, one of Rabbi Michael Melchior's sons, Jair, who is also a rabbi, grew up in Israel and is now the Chief Rabbi of Denmark, based in the Great Synagogue in Copenhagen, the same synagogue in which his grandfather served for many years. Another son, Yoav, is currently the chief rabbi of Norway. The Melchior family is deeply connected to Scandinavia as well as to Israel.

As a young man, Rabbi Melchior came to Israel from Denmark to study at *Yeshivat Hakotel* (a prestigious academy for higher Jewish learning in Jerusalem) from 1973-1980, and later received rabbinic ordination from the Chief Rabbinate of Israel and leading rabbinic authorities in Israel. In 1974, during this period, he married Hana, who became a physiotherapist and worked at Shaarei Tzedek hospital in Jerusalem for many years. After his years of studying at this yeshivah in Jerusalem, the family returned to Scandinavia in 1980 where Rabbi Melchior served as Rabbi of Oslo and later as the Chief Rabbi of Norway, where he was instrumental in helping to renew the Jewish community which had been shattered during the Holocaust. In 1986, he and his wife and family made *aliyah* (Hebrew for "moved up," i.e., immigrated to Israel), where they chose to live in Jerusalem. Rabbi Melchior serves until today as the rabbi of a dynamic Modern Orthodox synagogue in the *Talpiyot* neighborhood, while still holding the title of Chief Rabbi of Norway and of Scandinavia.

Recognizing the Two Narratives of the Conflict

Rabbi Melchior became involved in the religious peace movement in Israel as a young man while studying in Jerusalem. In 1975 he attended the first meeting of *Oz V'shalom*, the first religious Zionist Peace movement in Israel. According to interreligious scholar and activist Yehezkel Landau, this organization was founded in that year by a group of Orthodox or traditionalist academics from Bar-Ilan University, Hebrew University and Tel Aviv University, as well as members of the religious kibbutz movement. The leaders included Professors Joseph Walk, Uriel Simon, Avi Ravitzky, Mordecai Breuer, and Michael Rosenak, among others, including serving or former members of Knesset such as Moshe Unna and Avraham Melamed.

Attendance at this first meeting of this religious peace group in Israel made an indelible impression on Melchior as a young man.

> The meeting was a reaction to what was happening inside the movement known as Religious Zionism, which was going in a different direction. We wanted to show that Religious Zionism has many different facets and that not all the people involved with it believed that the direction of Rabbi Tzvi Yehuda Kook [one of the founders of *Gush Emunim*] and his students were correct. They

were saying that only by supporting the ideology of the Greater Land of Israel-which meant settling throughout the West Bank and Gaza-would we achieve redemption.

This movement, which I was a part of, was a religious peace movement which supported the political peace process. It was comprised of young religious Jews who were loyal to what I believe Religious Zionism was all about. From its beginning the ideology of Religious Zionism was not an extreme one. The people, like me, who joined *Oz V'Shalom* were loyal to values of this movement, which included the ideal of peace and the contemporary idea that we should make peace with our neighbors.

During this time, Rabbi Melchior began to learn about the Palestinian narrative concerning the Israeli-Palestinian Conflict and over the years his knowledge and sensitivity to this narrative would deepen. As he came to substantially understand the Palestinian narrative, he recognized the centrality of the *Nakbah* (the great catastrophe and the beginning of the refugee issue, after the 1948 war) in their narrative.

I can't tell you when was the first time that I heard this term but I can tell you that it was many years ago. By now, I can say that this term has become more and more used as a concept for the catastrophe which the Palestinians felt, which I can very much understand. We have to understand that this is part of their history, their narrative, their story, which we have to live with. There are different stories and we don't have to accept the other's narrative, but we have to listen to them. We have to be sensitive to their existence and we have to find ways of not repeating the sins of the past in order to find a way to live together here today.

At the same time, Rabbi Melchior learned about the Jewish Zionist narrative, especially about the 1948 War of Independence, from people in his family who fought in the war-very much like Palestinians who heard about the *Nakbah* from members of their own families.

As someone who was born six years after 1948, I only know what happened [at that time] from stories. The stories that we heard included stories from my family. My father was a volunteer in the '48 war-he came from Denmark and went back to Denmark after the war. His brother and sister fought in the war, which was an essential war. Their stories influenced my life. In addition, they are people who were very sensitive to the Palestinian cause, but they did not see at that time some of the wrongdoings which we did then.

Clearly the narratives that Rabbi Melchior heard from family members were very important to him as a child and as a young man. They were formative in his decision to ultimately come to live in Israel and make his unique contribution to Jewish and Palestinian societies here, which he has done with great distinction over several decades.

Rabbi Melchior is a fervent religious Zionist, even if his form of Zionism is different than the right-wing mainstream in Israel today. For him the existence of the State of Israel is central to his Jewish identity. Moreover, he feels strongly that Israel was founded on moral principles, as enunciated in its Declaration of Independence of May 14th, 1948, a foundational document which is still very important to him. In fact, he has elevated this declaration to the status of a religious document.

> The Declaration of Independence is a very relevant document for me. My teacher, Rabbi Amital, of blessed memory (who also founded my political movement *Meimad*) was one of the greatest leaders of *yeshivot* [higher Jewish academies of learning] in Israel. He saw the Declaration of Independence from a religious perspective, which I totally identify with. It is a religious document in the sense that it talks about the basis for the existence of the State of Israel. The principles which it lays out are both particularistic and universalistic. They are important principles for the existence of the State of Israel.

Israel's Declaration of Independence not only envisioned a society in which there would be equality for all of its citizens, but it also issued a clarion call for peace with Israel's Arab neighbors who were in preparation for an all-out attack to destroy the emerging Jewish state. Moreover, according to Rabbi Melchior and other religious Zionists, the foundation of the state not only had national significance as the fulfillment of the aspirations of the Jewish people, but also had deep religious and spiritual significance.

Experiencing The Six Day War of June 1967 as a Teenager

The State of Israel grew and developed in the 1950s and 1960s, but in 1967 it was faced with a threat from its neighboring countries—Syria, Egypt and Jordan—which led to a period in which the leaders of the state were deeply worried about a war that could be an existential threat to the young state.

Rabbi Melchior was not yet living in Israel in 1967 but he vividly remembered the fearful period that the Jewish state was facing with regard to its very existence during the weeks before the Six Day War.

> I think that in order to understand what happened during the Six Day War and what happened afterwards, you have to understand what transpired before. There was a great fear before the Six Day War, a fear which was also in Israel and around the Jewish world. At the time, I was a teenager in Denmark, a 13-year-old. I remember that my father, the rabbi of the community, helped to organize large demonstrations in Copenhagen. There was a feeling of real fear of what would be. We heard the threats from the President of Egypt, Nasser, who announced that he would destroy the State of Israel. There were many people who believed that this might be the end. Understanding this background will help you understand the belief that was felt by the people of Israel–and Jews around the world–after the Six Day War. It will help you realize why there was euphoria in Israel after the victory for survival after this war.

On the other hand, in retrospect, was there a chance for peace after this war? From an Israeli point of view, some of the leaders of Israel at that time extended their hand in an offer of land for peace but it was rejected by the Arab countries at the time. Rabbi Melchior remembered this well.

> This war did not lead to peace even though many of our leaders including Prime Minister Levi Eshkol expressed their desire to trade land for peace at the time, according to UN resolution 242, which became the basis for all later peace agreements. On the other hand, the leaders of the Arab countries at an Arab League Summit answered with the three no's of Khartoum [August 1967]: 'No to negotiations, no to recognition, no to peace.' Because of this, there was absolutely no possibility to do anything for peace at that time.

The Six Day War of June 1967 not only did not lead to peace, but it led to a new triumphalist spirit within Israel, since the victory was so swift and the conquest of territories—the entire West Bank, the Gaza Strip, the Sinai Peninsula, the Golan Heights and Jordanian Jerusalem—was so substantial. This catalyzed new movements for settlement and for exclusive control of these territories, which would haunt the Israeli-Palestinian conflict for many years to come.

116

The Rise of Jewish Messianism after the Six Day War

Following the Six Day War, there developed a new movement in Israel to settle all parts of the Land of Israel that had been captured from Egypt, Jordan and Syria. As a result, groups of Jewish settlers began to establish new settlements all over the occupied territories. Many of these settlers were religious Jews who were imbued with messianic fervor, which Rabbi Melchior saw as very dangerous for Israel. He recognized the deleterious influence of the settler movement from early on.

> The seeds of the settlement movement predate the '67 war. They can be found in Israeli religious society at the beginning of the 1960s in *Yeshivat Merkaz HaRav* [the higher academy for Jewish learning, named for Rabbi Kook, the Chief Rabbi of Israel in the pre-state period] in Jerusalem. The seeds of *Gush Emunim* started already at that time. There was a small group who since the 1948 War of Independence had not been satisfied with the borders that Israel had and wanted to expand them. Also, they felt that we were on the track to messianic times.

> After the Six Day War of June 1967, their views flourished and attracted more and more adherents. They believed that we were not only at the *beginning of the flowering of our redemption* [a concept in a prayer for the state of Israel], but that we were actually now near the end station of redemption [of the Jewish people and the land of Israel]. They saw that the whole land was already in their hands, and it was time for them to be pioneers again! They could feel the land, they could sow the land. The connection to the land was and is very strong.

For Rabbi Melchior, this new movement was to be an obstacle for peace for many years, even decades. He would oppose this movement and ultimately create his own alternative religious Zionist movement, based on Jewish humanistic values.

The Importance of the First Peace Accord with an Arab State

Despite the rejectionist settler movement, some amazing developments for peace took place in the 1970s. Foremost among them was the visit to Jerusalem of President Anwar Sadat of Egypt in 1977, followed by the Camp David Summit in 1978 and the signing of the Egyptian-Israeli Peace Accord in 1979. In particular, the historic visit of President Sadat to Jerusalem, especially his speech in the Knesset in 1977, was a game-changer to many of the citizens of Israel that has never been forgotten.

Rabbi Melchior recalled the importance of Sadat's visit to Jerusalem and how it greatly impacted the religious Zionist community in Israel. He has an amazing story to share from this period.

> That was a very special moment. When we heard Sadat speak in the Knesset there was great euphoria in Israel. I remember clearly that it was a Thursday evening. That Shabbat was the Sabbath of *Parshat Toldot* [the Torah portion in Genesis about the births of Jacob and Esau] and I was studying in the Old City of Jerusalem at *Yeshivat HaKotel*. I was already married at that time. I had begun to study at the yeshivah in 1973 and I got married in 1974. During these years I was already active in religious peace work via the religious peace movement called *Oz Ve'shalom* [Strength and Peace], which started before Peace Now [which began in 1978].

> When President Sadat stood in the Knesset, and said no more war, it was a special moment for us. His willingness to come here, to Jerusalem, and break that total wall of animosity reached deeply into the hearts of all Israelis. It was an amazing gesture that changed people here totally overnight. There was not an eye which was dry. Religious families baked challot [bread for the Sabbath] which were called Sadat challot for that Shabbat. They found clues for this idea in the Torah portion of that week, in which we find an Aramaic expression in the Torah, which they felt referred to Sadat, *Yagur Shaduta*. This referred to an agreement made between Jacob and Laban in the story in the Torah in which they reconnected with each other again and made peace. I remember it very clearly. In our synagogues there was a great outburst of joy. This was what people really wanted. People don't want to live here in war. Rather, the overwhelming majority here just want to live in peace.

The visit of Sadat to Jerusalem–and the ensuing peace negotiations and the historic peace agreement between Israel and Egypt–was an important milestone for peacebuilders like Rabbi Melchior. It was a watershed moment for him, which propelled him to become more active for peace in the decades ahead.

Another Religious Peace Movement is Formed in the 1980s

In the 1980s, following the beginning of the war in Lebanon in 1982, another religious peace movement called *Netivot Shalom* was formed, mainly to oppose this war from a religious point of view. This movement was formed by a group of young religious Zionist activists, who felt that a separate peace movement was necessary in order to appeal to a religious audience. Also, the main secular peace movement of the time often excluded them from participating since many of their events took place on the Jewish Sabbath, which they did not want to desecrate. To avoid duplication, this new group merged with the other religious peace movement which had been formed a decade earlier, and since then the movement goes by the name *Oz Veshalom/Netivot Shalom*. For a long time, the most prominent figure in this movement was Professor Avi Ravitsky, a professor of Jewish thought at the Hebrew University in Jerusalem, but as time progressed, they also gained the support of Rabbis Yehuda Amital and Aharon Lichtenstein, the heads of the prestigious higher academy of Jewish learning in *Gush Etzion* (south of Jerusalem) called *Yeshivat Har Etzion*.

This religious peace movement was the precursor to the religious peace movement and political party called *Meimad*, which became very important in the life of Rabbi Melchior in the late 1980s when he went into politics and joined the government of Israel.

> *Meimad* started as a political party, in the elections in 1988. I was involved, but I was quite new in Israel at the time. I was still commuting between Oslo and Jerusalem. I led the Jerusalem branch of *Meimad*, which was the biggest branch. Rabbi Amital was the leading force of *Meimad* since he had founded it. There was a large group of religious Zionist Jews who followed Rabbi Amital at that time.

This religious political party which has an explicit peace agenda was to catapult Rabbi Melchior into national politics a few years later. Rabbi Amital and the *Meimad* party ran for the Knesset in the elections of 1988 but they did not receive enough votes. After that it ceased functioning as a political party for some time. It was re-established as a movement, but not as a political party, around the time of the Oslo peace process in the early 1990s. As time progressed Rabbi Melchior became one of the leaders of this party. Rabbi Amital became a minister in the government of Shimon Peres in 1996 after the assassination of Prime Minister Rabin (November 1995). Rabbi Melchior was an assistant to Rabbi Amital at that time, who was the titular leader of the movement, but in practice, Rabbi Melchior took over the leadership of the party.

Later, Rabbi Melchior became a minister in the Prime Minister's Office, responsible for Diaspora and Social Affairs (August 1999 to March 2001) in Ehud Barak's government after *Meimad* merged with the Labor party. Following this, he also served as the Deputy Minister of Foreign Affairs in the unity government headed by Ariel Sharon (March 2001 to November 2002) and later as Deputy Minister of Education, Culture and Sports (January to June 2005). But we are getting ahead of ourselves here.

Engaging with Palestinians Before and After the Oslo Accords

It took another decade for some important developments in the peace process to occur. There was significant progress with the announcement by the PLO in 1988 in which they recognized the State of Israel and for the first time offered to engage in negotiations. This was a surprising development and also encouraging to some people like Rabbi Melchior. It was during this time, a few years before the Oslo Accords, that innovative opportunities for constructive dialogue among Israeli Jews and Palestinian Arabs emerged.

Rabbi Melchior began developing relationships and participating in encounters with Palestinians. He remembers how his involvement with Palestinians began, especially through his work with the Muslim community in Norway, from the beginning of his service as Chief Rabbi there.

> We began [establishing relationships] before Oslo. I had personally attended meetings with Palestinian representatives in the late 1980s and the beginning of the 1990s. I was always in favor of peace. I have always believed that peace is necessary for our future, it is part of Jewish destiny, part of our return to Zion, and it includes living and developing relations with our neighbors. At the end of the 1980s—especially after the Palestinian decision of 1988 to recognize Israel, which was a preamble to the Oslo Accords, since it was the first time the PLO actually recognized Israel—at that time, I began to establish relationships with Palestinians.

> I built on my good experience of creating relationships between Muslims and Jews in Norway. I learned that if you build good relationships and developed real trust between people on a personal basis, then the sky is the limit in terms of what you really can do, also in reaching agreements.

Rabbi Melchior's outreach to the Muslim community in Oslo was to be one of the highlights of his rabbinic career there. This early work with coalition-building with the Muslim community was to serve him in good stead when he came to Israel:

> From the first day that I was in Norway, I tried to reach out to the Muslim community, without much success, to have dialogues. It was before things like that were done anywhere. It was difficult because the Muslims didn't want it very much. Also, they were a small minority of Muslims and they were at that time very insecure. Eventually, we achieved many important breakthroughs. We developed a coalition, which was led by Jews and Muslims, but included other minorities, including the Humanists, those who are against all religion. We worked well together and we became good friends. We discovered that we had a common purpose.

It is important to state that Rabbi Melchior's work with Muslims in Norway was a groundbreaking experience, both for him personally and for the Jewish community in Norway, and for his later work with Muslims in Israel, Palestine, and internationally.

> In the coalition that we created with Jews and Muslims we eventually included the Norwegian church. But this was essentially a coalition of minorities, working on important social, ethical matters together in Norwegian society. As time progressed it became a very strong coalition of all minorities but it was very much led by Jews and Muslims. This whole process taught me a lot about how to build coalitions. The way you build a coalition is not just by inviting others to a dialogue, but by doing practical things together, achieving things together, working on issues. It was extremely successful.

> This is also what I brought with me here to the Middle East. First of all, we won in the end the campaign for fair treatment of minorities in Norway and we went to the European Human Rights court. But not only that. We established the first coalition of its kind in Europe which was copied in other countries in Europe and was institutionalized in the Norwegian public. It is now an important official body whose advice is sought by many groups in Norway.

All of this work in coalition building with Muslims in Norway would influence greatly the work of the religious peace initiative with Muslims, Christians and Jews in the years and decades ahead. However, in Israel and Palestine, the focus would be on dialogue between religious Jews and religious Muslim Palestinians, which would prove to be much more challenging and complicated, but no less worthwhile or productive.

> I started to talk to Palestinians about it and I started to talk to other rabbis about it in the early 1990s. Among the Palestinians that I talked to were people in Gaza. I spent time in Gaza during the beginning of the first intifada [January-February 1988]. I talked to people, I researched, I met with people. We started to talk about the role of religion and how religion can be a force for promoting peace. As time developed, I met more and more Palestinian leaders. For example, I met Faizal Husseini, with whom I developed a whole series of talks about the concept of Religious Peace.

Even though Rabbi Melchior had been involved in dialogues with leading Palestinians before the Oslo Accords of 1993-95, he nevertheless felt that they were a major breakthrough for peace. Moreover, he was engaged with many of the key players in the peace process during this time, on an unofficial level.

> And then came Oslo. I was not directly involved in the negotiations although many of the partners had talked with me at different stages. I also had several talks with the person who became the initiator of the Oslo talks, Larsen, from FAFO, who consulted with me before they became the secret talks. [The FAFO Institute for Labor and Social Research is an independent research foundation, which conducts social science research on a wide area of working life and welfare state issues.]

> When the Oslo Accords were signed, it was a time of great hope. Although, already at that time, I gave several interviews in which I warned that if the process does not include the traditional and religious populations, that it would be difficult to succeed. But I was part of the joy and the hope of the Oslo Accords.

Rabbi Melchior also became increasingly involved in more in-depth dialogue with Palestinians after the Oslo Accords. Some of his dialogues took place abroad, including in Oslo, since he was the Chief Rabbi of Norway at the time. Before and after the signing of the Oslo Accords, there was much opposition back in Israel by Israeli Jews on the religious and political right, who did not want to give up any parts of the Land of Israel. This became evident to Rabbi Melchior in some very special circumstances.

At the time of the awarding of the Nobel Peace Prize to Prime Minister Yitzhak Rabin, Foreign Minister Shimon Peres and PLO Chairman Yasser Arafat in September 1994, Melchior was intensely involved in some fascinating encounters between Israelis and Palestinians which took place in Oslo, where he lived at the time.

> In 1994, one of the most amazing things that happened was the Nobel Prize for Peace, which was given to Arafat, Rabin and Peres in Oslo, which was my domain at the time. We sponsored events around the Nobel Prize ceremony, which took place in September 1994. For example, we hosted Rabin and Peres as guests of the Jewish Community in Oslo on the *shabbat* of September 10th 1994. They were in the synagogue for *shabbat*, as were several hundred Israelis who came to demonstrate against the Nobel Prizes going to these three leaders at the time. They came with coffins to demonstrate in the streets of Oslo, and since they were religious Jews, they also came to the synagogue on *shabbat!* Everyone met in the synagogue amidst great tension.

Following the Nobel Prize for Peace award ceremony, Rabbi Melchior organized a high-profile program with Israelis and Palestinians in the Jewish community of Oslo, in which he was a leader. Afterwards, he initiated important contacts with the Foreign Ministry of the Norwegian government in Oslo which was very involved in supporting the diplomatic process as well as supporting civil society initiatives. Together they came up with the concept of starting a religious track to supplement the political peace process. This was the first such attempt to do this. Rabbi Melchior was able to get a representative of the Norwegian Foreign Ministry to mediate this process. Once this was all set, they began to reach out to important rabbis, as well as Christian and Muslim religious leaders, back in Israel and Palestine, to join the process.

> I went to meet with Rabbi Bakshi Doron, who was one of the Chief Rabbis of Israel at the time, and I asked him to be part of the group and to support such a process. Thus, we started a process back in Israel which included the most important church leaders, headed by Msgr. Michel Sabbah, the Latin Patriarch, and others, and it included Muslim leaders also. It was centered in *Passia*, in

East Jerusalem. The head of *Passia* was the head of the Muslim delegation. We also had a Jewish delegation, which I was leading, and it included two representatives who were sent by Rabbi Bakshi Dorron —Rabbi Yitzhak Ralbag, who was a member of the Chief Rabbinate Council, and Rabbi David Brodman, a *haredi* [ultraorthodox] rabbi of Dutch background.

We had conversations which were quite tough, starting from the mid-90s, for a period of several years. The problem was at the time that the Muslim partners were more politically oriented than religiously oriented, and therefore there were too many arguments about who was right and who was wrong, and I didn't see any point to this. This hadn't led us anywhere for 25 years before that! Therefore, I felt that these conversations could not bring us very far. Nevertheless, we did have a good dialogue and we did become friendly, there was a certain trust that was built up among us. However, I didn't feel that we were making real progress in bringing peace on the ground, which is what I believe in. I don't believe in dialogue for the sake of dialogue. I believe that we learn and we teach—as we say in our daily prayers —in order to practice, *lishmor ul'kayem*, to be effective, to have impact.

Rabbi Melchior involved Chief Rabbi Bakshi Doron in much of his work in the early years of religious peace activities. On one occasion, he was instrumental in helping to resolve a major conflict between Jews and Muslims in Israel and Palestine which could have sparked a major conflict.

For example, in 1997, we had a tremendous problem after some young Jews in Hebron, Russian immigrants, who had made some drawings of Mohammed as a pig. This quickly developed into a major scandal in the whole world. A major crisis occurred and it escalated very quickly. Condemnations were coming in from all over the world. Benjamin Netanyahu was then prime minister. He and the president of Israel condemned it. But it didn't help at all. So, I went to Chief Rabbi Bakshi Doron, and I said to him that you have to do something. He asked me 'what should I do?' I told him to go to the Mufti of Hebron. And he immediately went down to the car, and we went to the Mufti of Hebron, and without being invited he went into his office and he told him 'This is not Judaism. This is against everything we believe in and stand for.' The Mufti of Hebron nearly fell off his chair. He was so moved by this action that he immediately called all the leading imams of Hebron, who were preparing to declare war on Judaism on the coming Friday after their prayers in their mosques, and he told them: 'The leading religious Jew of Israel is sitting here in my office, and he just told me that this is not Judaism. You have to cancel everything.' Through this action of a religious Jew to a religious Muslim, no hateful sermons were given and violence was averted. It was amazing–the effect was immediate. I saw this in many other cases.

As we will see later, Rabbi Bakshi Doron, was also a partner with Rabbi Melchior in the historic Alexandria Declaration of 2002.

Was There a Partner for Peace?

The Oslo Accords were followed by a peace agreement with Jordan in 1994 and another peace agreement between Israel and the Palestinians in 1998. This was followed by a new opportunity for peace negotiations which appeared on the horizon at the beginning of the next century. In the last year of his eight years as the president of the USA, in July 2000, President Bill Clinton invited Prime Minister Ehud Barak and Chairman of the PLO Yasser Arafat to Camp David for a peace summit that was supposed to finally end the conflict. However, this summit failed miserably. Rabbi Melchior was serving in the government of Israel at that time and therefore was intimately knowledgeable about the inner workings of the peace process.

After the failure of this summit, both sides blamed each other for its dissolution. Most of the leaders of Israel blamed Chairman Arafat for this. However, Rabbi Melchior was also critical of the policies of Prime Minister Barak. He particularly did not like the "no-partner for peace" mantra. He felt that it was counterproductive to achieving peace. Rather, he felt that it was important to see Palestinians as potential partners for peace. In an important essay that he wrote, entitled *Establishing a Religious Peace*, he argued positively for the importance of seeing Palestinians as our partners:

> If we look at the other as a partner, and not as an enemy, and we don't work on a 'divide and conquer' attitude towards the other, then we might conclude that it would be good for all Palestinian parties to be involved in making peace with us. This would create a difference in our attitude and polices toward the Palestinians and vice versa.

After this summit, peacebuilders like Rabbi Melchior did not allow themselves to descend into despair. Rather, they continually sought new and creative ways to engage in peacebuilding.

The Alexandria Declaration of January 2002 in the Midst of the Second *Intifada*

The failure of the Camp David talks led to a major eruption in violence in Israel and the West Bank which become known as the Second *Intifada* (uprising), which broke out in late September 2000. For the rest of 2000 and all of 2001, violence between Israelis and Palestinians increased to unprecedented levels. Rabbi Melchior was deeply disturbed by these events, but felt that as a religious leader he must do something.

As a result, Rabbi Melchior took dramatic steps during the height of the violence. He made many attempts to try to reduce the enmity and mutual destruction that was going on between Palestinians and Israelis at the time. Specifically, he led an important interreligious initiative for peace, which was a substantive summit that culminated with an historic document called the *Alexandria Declaration*. The event took place in Alexandria, Egypt, in January 2002. Rabbi Melchior was able to pull this off as a result of his many years of encounters with Palestinian religious leaders as well as religious leaders from the region. This led him to believe that there are in fact partners on both the Jewish and Arab sides for peace, and this strengthened his resolve to seek to include religious dimensions in the peace process in the years ahead.

Rabbi Melchior and his Muslim counterpart, the late Sheikh Talal Sider, were the prime-movers behind this interreligious summit, co-sponsored by the Grand Mufti of Egypt, Grand Imam of *Al-Azhar* Mosque Sayyid Tantawi, the Archbishop of Canterbury George Carey, and one of the Chief Rabbis of Israel, Rabbi Eliyahu Bakshi-Doron. For a few months during the second half 2001, they met secretly to plan for this meeting in great detail, with much sensitivity to the feelings and ideas of each side of the process. Rabbi Melchior remembers this well.

> It wasn't so hard. I had an excellent partner, Sheikh Talal Sider, may he rest in peace. I had already been talking a long time with Sheikh Talal. Canon Andrew White from England was intensely involved, as the representative of the Archbishop of Canterbury. He was helpful with logistics and he was helpful with getting the leading sheikh from El Azar University in Cairo on board.

Canon Andrew White wrote about Rabbi Melchior and the Alexandria process in one of his memoirs. He recalled how he worked hard to bring all the parties together:

> Throughout all of the Middle Eastern conflict there had never been any serious engagement between opposing sides at the religious level, but I wanted to see the rabbis, priests and imams agreeing to work together for peace. Achieving this was, of course, an incredibly delicate, complex task.

One of the first persons that Canon White recruited to support this process was none other than Yasser Arafat, the President of Palestine and Chairman of the PLO. Since he had developed a personal relationship with Arafat, it was not actually that hard to get him on board. After speaking to Arafat, he went to the Foreign Ministry of Israel and met with Deputy Foreign Minister Rabbi Melchior. He was pleased to discover that "not only did Rabbi Melchior support the initiative, but it was clear that he wanted to be actively involved in every aspect of the event," which indeed became the case. Canon White and Rabbi Melchior worked hand in hand to bring about the proclamation at this significant international gathering.

The idea was to bring many of the important religious leaders from Israel and Palestine together, under the auspices of Egypt, the largest Arab country in the Muslim world, and under the sponsorship of *Al-Azhar* Mosque (associated with *Al-Azhar* University, the most important Muslim religious institution in the country and the region), in order to agree upon common principles for preventing violence. In addition, there was a desire to adopt a declaration that would express common goals of working together for peaceful solutions to the conflict, based on religious principles. Accordingly, the agreement, which became known as the *First Declaration of Alexandria of the Religious Leaders of the Holy Land*, pledged the faith leaders to use their religious and moral authority to work for an end to violence and the resumption of the peace process. In this statement, they declared:

> In the name of God who is Almighty, Merciful and Compassionate, we, who have gathered as religious leaders from the Muslim, Christian and Jewish communities, pray for true peace in Jerusalem and the Holy Land, and declare our commitment to ending the violence and bloodshed that denies the right to life and dignity.

According to our faith traditions, killing innocents in the name of God is a desecration of his Holy Name, and defames religion in the world. The violence in the Holy Land is an evil which must be opposed by all people of good faith. We seek to live together as neighbors, respecting the integrity of each other's historical and religious inheritance. We call upon all to oppose incitement, hatred, and the misrepresentation of the other.

The Alexandria Summit was hosted by His Eminence Sheikh Mohammed Sayed Tantawi, Grand Mufti of the Al-Azhar and His Grace, the then-Archbishop of Canterbury, Dr. George Carey, and was signed by 14 important religious leaders. In his essay *Establishing a Religious Peace*, Rabbi Melchior explained how the Alexandria Declaration was developed via strong personal relationships:

> At that time, I served as Deputy Minister of Foreign Affairs in the government of Israel. Sheikh Talal Sider, who was a minister in the Palestinian government, became a close friend and excellent partner. Our work took place during the peak of the Second *Intifada*, which made it very complicated since bombs were going off all the time and there was much counter-terrorism activity as well. Nevertheless, the process sent an important message and has had multiple effects within and outside the region. The Declaration of Principles which we wrote and signed in Alexandria has become, in our region and in other regions of the world, the foundation for understanding how to create the religious basis for peace. The idea is that religious peace should support the secular peace, which is negotiated by the elected leaders, rather than replacing it. The religious leaders would work on Track II diplomacy to legitimize the religious perspective toward peace. Everyone involved was in agreement with these principles.

After the success of the Alexandria Declaration, Rabbi Melchior and his colleagues were invited to meet the Pope at the Vatican, who voiced his support for the Alexandria Declaration in a speech which was part of his Easter message. They also received the support and endorsement of Kofi Anan, the Secretary-General of the UN at the time. In addition, Rabbi Melchior led a delegation to another meeting in Egypt, this time in Cairo, which included 70 religious Muslim judges from the West Bank, where they met with some of the leaders at *Al Azhar* University. In addition, he spoke at *Al Azhar* three times after the Alexandria Declaration.

Rabbi Melchior felt that the Alexandria Declaration was only the beginning. While it received major media attention for a few days, its seminal influence was to be felt in the years ahead when, together with his colleagues, Rabbi Melchior went back to the region, where they would implement the principles of this declaration in programs and projects over many years. Therefore, it was no accident that some of the most important peace-building developments took place back in Israel and Palestine after the conclusion of the Alexandria process.

> The most important thing for me personally was what happened in the relationship that I developed after the Alexandria Process with Sheikh Abdallah Nimer Darwish of *Kafar Kassem* [in central Israel], when we started a religious peace track. I had known Sheikh Abdallah before the Alexandria Process, sporadically, but not very closely. After that, we started to establish a relationship which was formalized through the Adam Centers and the *Mosaica* Center. We only formally called it the Religious Peace Initiative in 2007 because then there was what Bush called 'the Road Map.' Sheikh Abdullah said we will have a 'Religious Road Map.' We were able to agree immediately on all the elements for peace. We agreed that the religious leaders had to be at the head of this, that we would do what was lacking in Alexandria, namely we would include in the tent the so-called extremists as well as the moderates.

Rabbi Melchior felt that his religious peace process had major impact both in the Arab world in general and in Israel in particular.

> I believe that the path we have taken has changed history. We have seen revolutionary developments in the new approach to a religious peace process in the Muslim world, and we continue to see this happening before our eyes right now. More and more Muslims are joining the religious peace process and accepting Israel's existence, on the condition that the Palestinians will have a state and will have a future. I'm not talking about just the leadership of the Arab world, but I am talking about additional Muslim leaders who have influence on hundreds of millions of Muslims.

> In addition, we see progress here in Israel as well. It's been remarkable with the *Ra'am* party which is now led by one of the students of Sheikh Abdullah-the founder of the Islamic Movement in Israel, with whom I worked closely for many years-and his

protégés, including Mansour Abbas, the head of *Ra'am* [the Islamic political party connected to the Southern branch of the Islamic movement in Israel], who has been active in the religious peace process with us for a long time [and who became part of the government in the coalition set up by Naftali Bennet and Yair Lapid, with eight political parties, which lasted one year from 2021 to 2022]. I believe that our religious peace process has already changed the relationship between Arabs and Jews within Israel, more than anything in the last 73 years.

Rabbi Melchior is justifiably proud of his groundbreaking work with Arabs and Jews in Israel over many years. He has clearly seen the fruits of his labors.

Increasing Religious Peace Activism after the Gaza Wars

The periodic wars between Israel and Gaza, from 2006-2021, caused peace-builders like Rabbi Melchior much consternation. Indeed, he thought that these wars were a major obstacle to the peace process. Ongoing wars with Gaza and ignoring the Gaza leadership because of their hardline positions were mistakes that made a genuine peace between Israel and the Palestinians much more difficult.

Gaza is a key element in the whole peace process. There are a lot of people living there, more than two million. And they are Palestinians. They are part of the Palestinian people. They are part of the equation. There won't be a comprehensive peace agreement without a solution that includes Gaza. We believe a totally divided Palestinian leadership is not good for peace. We need peace with all the Palestinians, at least the vast majority. This will be the best guarantee for true peace, for true security.

During the fighting in Gaza, Rabbi Melchior and his colleagues in the Religious Peace Initiative were not inactive. Rather, along with one of his partners, Sheikh Imad Faluji, they set up a center for dialogue and reconciliation in Gaza, called the Adam Center. They became *inside negotiators*, a term they used to describe their mediation work with various groups within each society. This is now a term that Rabbi Melchior—and the new director of the Religious Peace Initiative, Rabbi Daniel Roth—have adopted from the language of conflict resolution methodology to describe what they do.

A lot of essential players in the religious peace track have become what we call *inside negotiators*, bridge-builders, negotiators, because of their background, their religious identity and because of their contact network. This is a big part of what we do. Sheikh Imad Faluji is doing that on several levels, both in his Center for Dialogue and Civilizations in Gaza, and in our center in Ramallah. He has secured the trust with the *Hamas* leaders and with the Fatah–and with different parts of the *Fatah*–so he can often be someone who can interact and negotiate and mediate between different factions.

Rabbi Melchior regards his work with Sheikh Faluji as very important, especially in the midst of the ongoing violence between Israel and the Palestinians in Gaza. He has developed a vital personal relationship with him which has lasted many years and has led to some very positive results.

Sheikh Faluji is still very active with us in the religious peace process. I am in touch with him by phone. He comes to Jerusalem sometimes and gives us a full report of what is going on in Gaza. We try to help him get humanitarian support for the people in Gaza, because the situation is so difficult. It is part of my strategy to keep up contacts with people in Gaza even in times of war. I believe in change. I believe one of the biggest *mitzvot* [commandments] in the *Torah* is how you turn your enemy into your friend. I've seen how many times we have done this by creating good relations together. It is something which goes very deep. It comes from the same belief in one God and in creation, and the desire to create happiness, trust and a future for our children.

Despite several wars with the Palestinians in Gaza, Rabbi Melchior remains passionate about the potential for peace.

We have had too many wars with Gaza. I am an Israeli patriot and I want also my children to come back alive and well. At the same time, during the wars, we have all these friends inside Gaza who are sitting in a miserable situation, and we were calling each other very often to see how they were doing. And even when my children were serving in the IDF, I kept up my relationship with Imad Faluji.

We have had too many wars and I believe that we need a finish to this conflict! There is no reason why it should not be possible to end it. We have no vested interest in Gaza today, except for them to stop all the violence inside Israel. Gradually, I think that many of the people within *Hamas* are realizing this. More and more of them want to find the right way to end the conflict, such as a long truce which they call a *hudna,* and we need to help them do this, for our sake as well.

While some people feel that the conflict can somehow be resolved only in Ramallah with the leadership of the PA (*Fatah*), while leaving the people in Gaza out of it, Rabbi Melchior believes that they are mistaken. In addition, the problem of the division in Palestinian society is detrimental to peace. A divided Palestinian leadership is not good for peace. Rather, Rabbi Melchior believes that peace must be achieved with all the Palestinians.

> This will be the best guarantee for true peace, for true security. On the other hand, if there is such a strong in-fighting among the Palestinians, such big disagreements and nothing is functioning, and people are frustrated and in despair, those who believe in the Israel government's divide and rule policy, like the infighting. But I don't think it serves us. On the contrary, I think it is very harmful to us.

Rabbi Melchior has remained a believer in the importance and the possibility of establishing peace with the Palestinians, both political peace and religious peace. He has continued to work towards these goals through many periods of war and peace in Israel and Palestine, and he does not give up. He is a persistent pursuer of peace.

Building Upon the Abraham Accords

In the fall of 2020, in the last few months of the Trump administration in the USA, some agreements known as the Abraham Accords were announced with two Arab countries—the United Arab Emirates and Bahrain—which led to normalization of relations between Israel and these countries (not peace agreements per se, because there had not been a situation of war). At the beginning, this was mostly public relations and bombast without much substance. Much work needed to be done to make them effective.

Some peacebuilders have been trying to build on the Abraham Accords, to make them more effective in real life. Rabbi Melchior has been one of those people. He feels that much improvement can be made to these agreements, especially with regard to relating to the Palestinians as the essence of the conflict with Israel.

We are involved behind the scenes in the Abraham Accords and follow-up. The partners have asked us to be involved. Our goal of involvement is to ensure that there will be good results. The accords should be promoting not only political peace between us and the Emirates, Bahrain, and Morocco. We are very much involved with all these countries. But we believe they should promote peace where the real problem is – between the Palestinians and Israel. This is where we can, under the radar, try to amend what wasn't done at the first stage of the accords. On the one hand, you can say the whole concept of the Abraham Accords does take into consideration what I have been talking about all along, i.e., religious peace. On the other hand, there is the question about whether the accords came only as a result of political interest. We want to work with all the partners in the future so that there is a religious depth and a political vision to this process, which both have been lacking.

Rabbi Melchior and his colleagues are continually working behind the scenes to help make these agreements have real impact on the lives of Jews and Muslims in the region, including in Palestine and Israel. In so doing, they have helped save many lives and have prevented many crises from erupting beyond control.

Conclusion

Rabbi Melchior has been a consistent and committed religious Jewish peace-builder in Israel, and the world, for decades. He has developed sustained relationships with Palestinian religious leaders within Israel and the region for a long time. In addition, he has been a major international pursuer of peace, at international meetings all over the world, some of which he played a major role in organizing. In particular, he was not only one of the leading planners of the historic Alexandria Declaration of January 2002-in the midst of the Second Intifada-with other key partners in the region, but since then, during the past 20 years, but he has successfully implemented the principles of this famous statement in many programs and projects, especially vis a vis the Religious Peace Initiative, which he has pursued with great wisdom and persistence, with important colleagues in Israel, Palestine and internationally. He continues to be a dedicated interreligious peace activist, teacher, preacher, mentor and leader, without ever abandoning the search for peace, despite all the obstacles and challenges. With deep religious faith, commitment and optimism, he promotes peaceful relations among Jews, Muslims and Christians, with courage and conviction, often below the radar, saving lives and keeping hope alive for all of God's children in the region.

Professor Galia Golan: Scholar, Feminist and Peace Activist

Photo by Doron Gild

Professor Galia Golan has been one of the leading peace activists and a professor of peace and conflict studies, as well as Soviet Studies, since her *aliyah* (immigration) to Israel in 1966. She is a world-renowned author and lecturer about Eastern Europe and the Soviet Union, as well as a researcher, lecturer and author of important books on the peace process between Israelis and Palestinians.

After retiring from the Hebrew University of Jerusalem in 2000, she joined the newly formed Department of Government at Reichmann University (previously called the Inter Disciplinary College) in Herzliya, north of Tel Aviv, where she pioneered the establishment of a master's degree program in Conflict Resolution. She continues to teach a research seminar there on the Israeli-Palestinian Conflict.

In recent years, as the political peace process has become frozen, she has been devoting more of her time to peacebuilding activities, especially via a relatively new NGO, known as Combatants for Peace, a Palestinian-Israeli non-profit organization which promotes peace and reconciliation through dialogue and non-violent education, demonstrations and advocacy. Through her intense involvement with Combatants for Peace, Golan has once again discovered the power of dialogue and cooperation with Palestinians in renewed and hopeful ways.

Parallel to her prolific academic career, Golan has always been involved in peacebuilding activities. One of the founders of one of the most important civil society organizations in Israel known as Peace Now, she was involved with this leading peace group in Israel for 30 years in a variety of capacities, from leadership to fundraising. As part of her work with Peace Now she was involved in organizing many of the most significant peace demonstrations in Israel at critical times in the history of the country.

Furthermore, she was also a longtime activist in the left-wing *Meretz* political party, and even contemplated a run for a seat in Israel's *Knesset* (Parliament) at one time, but she decided against it, realizing that she could play a more significant role in the peace movement in extra-parliamentary organizations. She has also been a feminist pioneer in Israel, serving as a founder and Deputy Chairperson of the Israel Women's Network and later as a leader of the organization known as *Bat Shalom*, a women's Israeli-Palestinian peace group. She also created the first Center for Women's Studies in Israel at the Hebrew University of Jerusalem in 1991, another project which combined her academic pursuits with her feminist activism.

Golan has written a beautiful, comprehensive and fascinating autobiography about her long and important career, called *Galia Golan: An Academic Pioneer on the Soviet Union, Peace and Conflict Studies, and a Peace and Feminist Activist*. Even though it has the longest title of a book I have ever read, it accurately sums up her career! In this chapter, I will draw from her autobiography to highlight some of the main milestones of her life.

Early years and education

Born in Cincinnati, Ohio, and raised in Miami Beach, Florida (where I also grew up), Golan also lived in New York City, where she completed her last two years of high school. Following this, she studied at the relatively new Jewish-sponsored university known as Brandeis University in the Boston area in the late 1950s. There she studied with some of the leading social and political thinkers of that era, who had a profound influence on her (as they did on me, when I studied there in the mid-to-late 1960s.) In her autobiography, she describes her seminal years at Brandeis:

> Studying at Brandeis during the last years of the 1950s was an experience and a privilege that cannot be overestimated. I was a philosophy student of phenomenologist Aron Gurvitch, but I also had the privilege to study with (and later become a protegee) of Herbert Marcuse...with all the soul-searching and intellectual turmoil of Brandeis in the late 1950s, it was the most rewarding and impactful period imaginable; it has remained with me and formed me for the rest of my life.

Having studied at Brandeis only a few years later, I fully understand what Golan experienced, since I was privileged to have a similar experience. It was a place of great intellectual ferment, with profound professors and superb students.

During her junior year of college, Golan went to study in Geneva, where she studied psychology and philosophy. During that year, she took a trip to Poland and Czechoslovakia, which was an eye-opener for her, since it was the first time that she had been to a country ruled by a dictator. This sparked an interest for her in Eastern European countries, which was later to become the focus of her academic career. In fact, she was to write her doctoral dissertation on Czechoslovakia.

After finishing college, Golan spent the summer in the Soviet Union as an exchange student with an American group. Following this experience, she received a fellowship to study in Paris for two years, where she learned

French and Polish. While she was there, she reconnected with Professor Marcuse who introduced her to some of the leading Marxist thinkers and activists of the period. Since her mother was living in Europe at the time, this afforded her opportunities to travel to Eastern Europe from time to time, which gave her more opportunities to get to know that part of the world better.

After two years in Paris, Golan went back to the USA, where she worked as an intelligence officer for the CIA for four years in Washington DC, analyzing new developments in Eastern Europe. This was a formative experience in developing her professional interest in the Soviet Union. While she was in the American capital, she participated in many of the activities of the civil rights movement, including protests and marches, especially the historic march with Dr. Martin Luther King in 1963.

Immigrating to Israel

In 1965, Golan came to Israel for a brief summer vacation during which she decided to immigrate to Israel. At that time, Israel was a relatively new, small, socialist country. As a secular Jew, she felt a great sense of history in Israel, and her Jewish identity was connected to a sense of Jewish peoplehood, which she had picked up while living in Europe. After her *aliyah* in 1966, she studied for her doctorate at the Hebrew University of Jerusalem, and went on to become one of the leading professors at that university in Soviet and Eastern European Studies for many years.

In her second year of living in Israel, Golan lived through the Six Day War of June 1967. This was to be a major moment in her life, both in her connection with the young state of Israel as well as in forming her political awareness and activism. She remembers this period well:

> The period of waiting, and the war itself, in many ways sealed my feeling of connection with the country, although it did little to inform me beyond the highly emotional euphoria of the unexpected, three-front dazzling victory. Upon my return to Jerusalem a few weeks after the war, I joined friends in quickly touring the West Bank in the belief that Israel would soon be returning the newly-won territories for peace. That was the impression that the government gave, and that was the general belief at that time; now the Arabs would agree to peace in exchange for return of their territories. My mistake in believing this then was not a misunderstanding of the Arabs. Rather, it was a serous misunderstanding of

the government of Israel. But that became clear to me many years later.

It was not long after the victory of the Six Day War that Israel established its first Jewish settlement in the West Bank, in the city of Hebron, in the spring of 1968. One of Golan's first political acts was to sign a petition against this. This was to be the beginning of a long trajectory of peace activism.

The Beginnings of Peace Activism

As her peace activism developed over the years, Golan began to meet Palestinians. As a result of hearing their narratives, she came to realize the importance of the *Nakba* to them, although by her own admission it took her a long time to do so. Following the Six Day War of 1967, much of her peace work with the Labor party and then Peace Now and other groups in the late 1960s and 1970s was focused on giving back land for peace. For a long time, she and other peace activists were totally focused on 1967 and did not relate much to the experiences of 1948. Later on, in the 1980s, when she began to meet with Palestinians at conferences abroad, this began to change. At one conference, this changed in a fundamental way, as she related in this significant encounter:

> In the 1980s I was at a Track II conference in America. At that time, I was friendly with Professor Rasheed Khalidi, a Palestinian academic who was at the University of Chicago (and later taught at Columbia University). We were good friends because he taught a course on the super-powers and the Middle East and I had lectured in his course. I recall that whenever we met with Palestinians, whether in Peace Now or other groups, the Palestinians always started with '48. I remember often saying 'Why? We can't change the past, why start with '48?' At this conference in the 80s at lunch, when this happened again, I asked Rasheed about this and he answered, 'We start with '48 because this is our legitimacy.' That was a turning point for me, in terms of understanding the other side.

Like many other Jewish peacebuilders in Israel, coming to grips with what happened to the Palestinians in 1948, has been a long and gradual process. At first, there was much denial.

At the same time, Golan remembered that she felt that the 1948 war was a justifiable war since Israel was attacked by the surrounding Arab states and had to fight back to survive. She admitted realizing only much later in life the tremendous costs of the war to the Palestinian side.

> I came to Israel as a young naïve person in 1966. I had experienced anti-Semitism in America and I had lived in France and in Switzerland. I really believed–and I still believe–that we need our own place. I support the creation of the State of Israel. I guess I am a Zionist. But I didn't know the cost to others of our establishing this state.

After signing the petition against the settlement in Hebron in 1968, Golan became convinced that the settlements in the occupied territories were going to be an obstacle to peace. This motivated her to take a courageous step at that time by attending her first meeting of a peace group in Jerusalem.

> I began to be active for peace already when the government began building settlements in the spring of 1968. I thought that if we were going to give the territories back for peace, then we shouldn't be building there. This was the beginning of my disillusionment. At that time, I went to a meeting of a peace group at the Hebrew University since I had friends in the group, where the presenters made a convincing argument which said 'what have we got to lose'–let's give back the territories in exchange for peace–and I found that argument compelling.

Following this, in the 1970s, Golan became involved with the dovish wing of the Labor party which was led by Shimon Peres (later to become President of Israel) at the time. The doves in the Labor party–which included Shimon Peres, Yossi Beilin, Liova Eliav and others–tried for many years to catalyze the Labor Party to actually make good on its commitment to trade land for peace, to no avail. Golan was a central participant in these efforts but eventually she realized that the Labor Party was not serious enough about peace. Later on, from the 1970s onwards, together with other courageous people who helped establish the Israeli peace movement known as Peace Now, she continued to oppose settlement building and expansion, since they believed that this was counterproductive to the peace process.

Over the years, Peace Now would grow into Israel's largest peace organization. In the early 1980s, the activists in the organization led the struggle against the government's push to build settlements in the occupied territories. They organized major demonstrations in Israel's largest cities—Tel Aviv, Jerusalem and Haifa—to try to stop the escalation that would increase animosity between Israeli Jews and Palestinian Arabs in the West Bank and Gaza.

The Peace Process with Egypt and the Beginning of Peace Now

The visit of President Sadat to Jerusalem in 1977 was a game-changer for peace activists in Israel at the time. Golan remembered her excitement and enthusiasm for this visit when it occurred. Later, she lobbied for the peace with Egypt—especially when it seemed that the government of Israel was wavering about actually making the deal—along with friends and colleagues in Peace Now. In her autobiography, she describes the beginnings of her peace activism:

> My peace activism had begun in earnest with the creation of Peace Now in 1978. In March 1978, in the middle of the difficult Israeli-Egyptian peace talks, an open letter of 148 reserve officers and soldiers appeared in the press, urging the government to take a more flexible position and not let the opportunity for peace to be missed... Since they added an address for expressions of support, my husband–who was a reserve combat medical officer–sent in his name. Shortly thereafter, the movement contacted me to give a speech at a small demonstration, and so both of us joined the group building Peace Now into Israel's first and only mass peace movement.

Indeed, as one of the founders of Peace Now, she was gratified that her efforts for peace appeared to be fruitful.

> I was delighted by Sadat's visit, delighted by the Camp David agreements and the peace with Egypt. I remember celebrating with some friends who came over to our apartment with a bottle of champagne. I had been very much opposed to the people who opposed the peace process with Egypt. Peace Now was very involved with lobbying for the peace agreement with Egypt. At one of our first demonstrations, we said that Egypt was holding its hand out for peace and we, Israel, ought to accept this. There was an opportunity here for peace and we didn't want Israel to miss it.

Peace Now, which was successful in encouraging much of the Israeli public to support the peace process with Egypt, was to become the focus of Golan's peace activism for many years, as we shall see in the pages ahead.

The War in Lebanon and the Growth of Peace Now

As Peace Now grew and developed in the late 1970s and early 1980s, one of the main challenges that it faced was how to respond to the war in Lebanon that began in June 1982. After the terrible massacres of innocent Palestinians outside Beirut in the refugee camps of Sabra and Shatilla in September of 1982-which were committed by Lebanese Christians, with the apparent approval of the Israeli army-a major opportunity presented itself. Peace Now took upon itself to organize a huge demonstration in Tel Aviv, which drew more than 400,000 Israeli citizens to protest the war, and especially these massacres, and to demand the investigation of the role played by Defense Minister Ariel Sharon in this terrible incident. It was the largest peace demonstration in Israeli history, which was a watershed moment in Israeli civil society at the time and it revealed the profound interest in peace among large sectors of Israeli society.

My wife Amy and I-and many other people we knew-were part of this outpouring of protest against the policies of the Israeli government at the time. We were exercising our civic responsibility by participating in the largest anti-war demonstration in Israeli history. It reminded me of some of the major anti-Vietnam war protests that I had participated in when I was a student in the USA in the late 1960s. I was proud that I was there with hundreds of thousands of other Israeli citizens who cared about our country. However, this massive demonstration, organized by Peace Now, unfortunately did not end the war in Lebanon very quickly. In fact, it did not prevent the war from continuing for a very long time, for 18 years! Moreover, although it led to an investigation of the role of Ariel Sharon, it did not stop him from becoming prime minister in later years.

Despite the ongoing war in Lebanon throughout the 1980s, the PLO was emerging as a major player in the region, even though it was now operating in Tunis, rather than Beirut. Towards the end of the decade, it surprised Israeli leaders-and world leaders-by recognizing the State of Israel in 1988, via speeches by PLO Chairman Yasser Arafat. These announcements were not taken seriously by Israeli leaders at the time, but they were recognized as important by Golan and her colleagues in Peace Now. Since she had already been engaged in dialogue with Palestinians for several years-from the late 1970s and throughout the 1980s-she acknowledged the recognition of Israel by the PLO as an important positive development towards peace, both for her personally and for the organization with which she was deeply involved, Peace Now.

When the PLO recognized Israel in 1988, it was not a surprise for me. I had read many of the speeches of leaders of the PLO in the documents section of the *Journal of Palestine Studies*. In 1988, Peace Now held a big demonstration urging Israel to acknowledge that the PLO had recognized it. Historically, this was the turning point, and I always refer to this.

Yet, this major event–which was one of the most important demonstrations that Peace Now ever held and which was critical for those in the peace camp in Israel who were arguing that it was time to recognize and deal with the PLO–was hardly recognized by the Israeli leadership or the Israeli people. They refused to believe it or accept it, as Golan recalls well:

> This didn't go down well in Israel. People in Israel didn't look at it, didn't recognize it, didn't accept it, and they still don't. People here didn't see it for what it was. To this day, people ignore what happened in 1988. I was aware of it because I had been following developments within the PLO in my academic research. When I wrote my book on the Soviet Union and the PLO, I sat in the Truman Institute for Peace of the Hebrew University in Jerusalem and I read many years of the newspaper *Free Palestine*, which was published by Saif Hamami in London. I had also been reading the *Journal of Palestine Studies* and I knew about the debate within the PLO about whether or not to recognize the state of Israel... Israelis at the time just didn't believe it. The prime minister at the time, Yitzhak Shamir simply said 'It's not true.' And there was a terrorist attack at the time, which proved to the Israeli government that the PLO did not mean what it said.

The recognition of Israel by the PLO, and their declaration of their intent to enter into a diplomatic process to negotiate for peace, was the precursor of the Oslo Accords, which were to take place a few years later. These accords were to change the situation in Israel and Palestine greatly, although they were not as successful in the long term as they were in the short term.

The Decade of the 1990s–The Oslo Accords and the Growth of Peace Now

Peace Now was a major force for peace activism in the 1970s and into the 1980s. Throughout this period, and into the 1990s, Golan continued and greatly increased her activities for peace via Peace Now and other organizations.

Golan also had been active in developing relationships with key Palestinians, mostly through her work in Peace Now. She had been active in this significant NGO which continually advocated for peace from the beginning. In addition to writing materials in English, she helped organize large demonstrations at which she often spoke. In addition, she lectured to groups from abroad as well as to foreign journalists in Israel. Because of her persuasive personality, she also reached out to well-known people in Israel, including Knesset members, to convince them to sign petitions that Peace Now developed. At one point, when Peace Now was nominated for a Nobel Peace Prize, she asked Abba Eban, who was one of Israel's leading diplomats during Labor party administrations for many years, to sign the recommendation letter, and he agreed to do so.

After the signing of the Oslo agreements in the early 1990s, she and her partners in Peace Now were elated to see real progress towards peace for the first time. She recalls the special moment that she experienced with the announcement of the first Oslo Accord, known as the Declaration of Principles, signed at the White House on September 13, 1993. She celebrated the moment with her fellow peace activists in Peace Now.

> We [Peace Now activists] arranged to view the White House signing by video, at the American Colony Hotel in East Jerusalem, together with Palestinians. I guess we were about 75-80 people altogether, watching on a large screen. When Rabin and Arafat shook hands a great, spontaneous cheer went up – from all of us. Peace Now's Yuli Tamir popped a bottle of champagne and we all celebrated together. My feeling was that this was all unbelievable.

During the period of the Oslo Accords (1993-95), Golan was active as a peacebuilder, both via Peace Now and via a women's Palestinian-Israeli group of activists. Along with her peace activism, she was becoming an important feminist leader, both via her role in Women's Studies at the Hebrew University and via her involvement with the development of the Israel Women's Network (along with Professor Alice Shalvi). After the Oslo peace accords, she was able to combine her feminism and her peace activism.

> During the Oslo period, I was one of the founders of *Bat Shalom*, as part of the Jerusalem Link – an Israeli and Palestinian women's peace group. I was involved in a number of joint events with Palestinian women, including Hanan Ashrawi, Zehira Kemal and other leaders of Palestinian women's groups. We held parlor meetings in Israel and brought women to meet Palestinians in the West

Bank, cooperating mainly with Fatah and the DFLP. The Oslo period was a very heady time, exhilarating, although we constantly heard from the Palestinians about the new check points set up and other problems.

Peace Now was one of the major supporters of the Declaration of Principles and all the Oslo Accords that followed. At the same time, Golan and her colleagues in Peace Now realized that there were many problems with these accords. For her, a critical flaw was the absence of monitoring and the absence of an end game. Nevertheless, Peace Now continued to publicly support these peace agreements and to make the best of them, despite the many obstacles and challenges.

The Assassination of Rabin, the Continuation of the Peace Process, and the Camp David Summit in Summer 2000

Prime Minister Yitzhak Rabin, the courageous leader who promoted and signed the Oslo Accords, on behalf of the state of Israel during 1992-1995 (in cooperation with PLO Chairman Yasser Arafat), was assassinated on November 4, 1995, by a Jewish extremist, who opposed these agreements. This event shook Israel, Palestine, and the Middle East in fundamental ways, and it severely impaired the peace process from moving forward, although it did limp forward for the next several years (until September 2000).

On the night of the assassination, Prime Minister Rabin was speaking at a huge demonstration in Tel Aviv, organized by Peace Now. Golan remembers the impact of the assassination of Rabin on the prospects for peace:

> The slogan of the November 4th demonstration was 'No to Violence, Yes to Peace.' We [leaders of Peace Now] basically organized the demonstration, sponsored by Tel Aviv Mayor Shlomo Lahat, but Rabin did not want his policies identified with the left, so our role was not acknowledged and Lahat would not let us have a speaker. I asked Yossi Sarid, who was one of the speakers, to mention Peace Now, which he did. I left the area only after the demonstration, but I did not hear the shots when Amir shot Rabin. Actually, I learned of that only in the car, on the radio, leaving Tel Aviv. The Oslo 'high' ended with the assassination of Rabin.

During the remaining years of the 1990s, there were still attempts to negotiate peace with the Palestinians. One such attempt was the negotiations towards the signing of the Wye River Memorandum in 1998, which was actually the last peace agreement signed between Israel and the Palestinians. Another one was the effort by President Clinton, in his last year in power, to bring the sides together in July 2000, to reach a comprehensive peace agreement. With the announcement of this summit, there was great excitement in Israel. The summit became known as Camp David II (the first one was the one with Begin, Sadat, and Carter, in 1978, which led to the peace agreement between Israel and Egypt the following year). Many people, including myself, still believed that peace between Israel and the Palestinians was possible at that time.

As a persistent peace activist, Golan remembers the dramatic possibilities of peace that seemed achievable when the Camp David II summit was convened:

> I remember being very optimistic. I had flown back from a sabbatical in California in order to vote and then came home in the summer. Ehud Barak had been elected with a good majority and he promised peace with the Palestinians within a year. I believed him and it looked like it was going to happen at Camp David. Almost no news came out during the negotiations, except that Jerusalem was also on the table. That sounded promising.

Camp David II, which held out so much promise for peace, did not succeed. After two full weeks together, both sides capitulated, went home, and blamed each other for the failure of the negotiations. Golan remembers well the impact of the failure of the two sides to reach an agreement at this summit as well as the activities of peacebuilders within Peace Now at the time. Although she was terribly disappointed, she claims that optimism prevailed. In fact, her optimism shined briefly once again when in fact the talks were renewed in January 2001 in the Egyptian Sinai town of Taba, just beyond the southern border city of Eilat. The Taba Summit between Israel and the Palestinian Authority, which took place January 21-27, 2001, still under the auspices of President Clinton, whose "Clinton Parameters" were presented there, was actually the last gasp of the political peace process. During these talks, members of Peace Now hired a boat and sailed near Taba with pro-peace signs. This was a clever and creative peace demonstration, which was part of Peace Now's aggressive activism at the time. It garnered some publicity but unfortunately did not convince the negotiators to move forward to resolve the conflict, which ironically seemed almost within our grasp at that time.

After that, Golan's faith in the political peace process waned. However, even though political despair set in, she and other peace activists became more and more active in peacebuilding organizations. They saw that the politicians were not serious about peace. They were bogged down in narrow political concerns. In contrast, the peacebuilders or peace activists felt that developing good relations between Palestinian Arabs and Israeli Jews—and creating effective programs and projects that could advance mutual understanding and cooperation—was the imperative of the moment and of the years ahead.

The outbreak of the Second *Intifada* and its impact on peacebuilding

Following the failure of the Camp David II summit–and after the provocative walk on the Temple Mount by Ariel Sharon (who was a member of the Knesset for the Likud party at the time)–the Palestinians began a major uprising which was to be known as the Second *Intifada* (shaking off of the occupation), which would last for five long years. When it began, Prime Minister Ehud Barak placed all the blame for the outbreak of the *intifada* on Arafat and the Palestinians. He insisted that Arafat had planned it all along, irrespective of Sharon's belligerent walk on the Temple Mount. He repeated incessantly that "we don't have a partner for peace," which became the mantra for many Israeli governments that followed.

Not everyone, however, believed or accepted this mantra. For example, Golan was wary and critical of this excuse.

> This business of the 'no partner' is awful. It really got me angry. Barak knew that he had a partner. They [representatives of Israel and Palestine] kept talking throughout the month of September 2000. It was infuriating. Evidence indicates that this was a deliberate deception on the part of Barak.

In a comprehensive essay entitled *Deception and Israeli Peacemaking since 1967*, Golan went into great detail about this particular communications strategy of Barak, as well as of five additional cases in the history of Israel's mostly failed attempts at peacemaking during the past 50 years or more. By studying archival material and intelligence reports, she came to the conclusion that Barak and his media advisors did not present an accurate picture of what happened at the Camp David II summit.

> By refraining from stating what really happened at Camp David and claiming that Israel had presented a 'generous offer' that was

met with total intransigence, the Barak government appears to have sought purposely to deceive the Israeli public. In fact, the 'no partner' comment was prepared before the conference in case of failure... More to the point, negotiations actually continued immediately after Camp David and throughout the month of September [and later at Taba, Egypt, in January 2021]. The 'no partner' claim was politically expedient. Clinton himself explained that it was needed to bolster Barak's political position, since he had gone to Camp David as the head of a minority government and would soon face new elections. But the 'no partner' claim became a powerful act of deception, as it was frequently repeated, and it became ingrained in the political discourse and public opinion. It set in motion the shift to the right in Israeli society, justifying a hardening of Israeli positions under subsequent governments. The 'no partner' claim was fortified and supposedly proven true by the outbreak of the Second *Intifada* in September 2000. And so, to maintain the original deception, a second deception was introduced: Israel accused Arafat of planning the violent Second *Intifada* when, in fact, he had sought to prevent its outbreak.

In her essay, Golan clearly demonstrated her deep knowledge of the peace process as an academic, not just as a peace activist. In fact, she was to write some very important books about the peace processes late in her academic career which examined deeply the successes, failures and near breakthroughs for peace.

Through her research, Golan went on to prove this claim of the second deception by referring to Israeli intelligence sources—including senior sources in the Israeli Security Agency (Shin Bet) and the Israeli Police—most of whom said that the *Intifada* was a spontaneous outburst on the part of the Palestinian population and that it had not been planned in advance. A documentary film entitled *A Million Bullets in October* (directed by Moish Goldberg, 2007,) revealed that from the end of Camp David in the summer of 2000, until and including the Taba talks in January of 2001, Barak actually believed that Arafat was interested in reaching a peace agreement, although he publicly adhered to the 'no partner' line.

Golan was very active in Peace Now during this time. After the failure of the Camp David II talks in summer 2000, she and other leaders of Peace Now met with Palestinian leaders to ascertain why, in their view, the talks had failed. At these meetings, she heard much criticism by the Palestinians of Barak's behavior at the Camp David talks. While both sides claimed that the leadership of the other side was more intransigent, leading to the breakdown in these talks, Golan had learned from discussions with Palestinians that they viewed Barak as the major obstacle in achieving progress at Camp David. Golan and others in the Peace Now camp tended to agree with this. In her autobiography, Golan recalled how the leaders of Peace Now urged him to pursue peace, even at the last minute, at the Taba talks.

> The last generally unnoticed Peace Now action in support of negotiations in this period came with the Taba meeting in January 2001. The meeting itself was a last-ditch effort by Barak to reach an agreement that might get him re-elected in the upcoming election. We organized a boat full of people carrying signs of support from the sea just off the coast of the Taba meeting.

This boat protest by Peace Now gained a lot of media attention, but unfortunately did not persuade the politicians and diplomats to seal the deal for peace. The meeting at Taba was the last serious effort at reaching a comprehensive peace agreement in the history of the Palestinian-Israeli conflict. But the search for peace by peacebuilders would continue.

The Disengagement from Gaza and the Takeover by Hamas

After the end of the Second *Intifada* (2000-2005,) the leaders of the State of Israel, led by Prime Minister Ariel Sharon, came up with an idea which was intended to help the cause of peace. In the summer of 2005, they decided to unilaterally disengage from the Gaza strip. This involved removing all Israeli settlers, settlements and soldiers and turning over the territory to the Palestinians in Gaza. This also took place in four settlements in the Northern West Bank. The official statements of the government at that time announced that if this went well, Israel would continue to withdraw settlers and soldiers from the West Bank–but this did not happen, and it is not clear that this was ever really the intention of the government.

Golan was one of the founding members of the left-wing political party known as *Meretz*, with which she was active for a long time. She was invited to run for a Knesset seat with *Meretz* but she declined to do so. She preferred to be part of the political party but not to be a politician. *Meretz* was always advocating for peace with the Palestinians. Golan's husband David, whom she met and married in Israel in 1972, was one of the founders of this party too, when it was called *Ratz* (the Movement for Civil Rights, founded by

Shulamit Aloni.) This party always had a strong human rights and civil rights agenda.

When the disengagement from Gaza took place, *Meretz* was critical of the policy because of its unilateral nature. The *Meretz* leaders thought that it should have been a negotiated settlement. However, Golan broke with her party on this and she was supportive of unilateral disengagement for practical reasons.

> I was active in *Meretz* at the time. *Meretz,* which represented the left wing in Israel, said that what was wrong with the disengagement was that the Israelis did not negotiate with the Palestinians. But my view was different. I felt at the time that if Israel had tried to negotiate with the Palestinians, it would not have worked! They wouldn't have gotten anywhere. [Prime Minister Ariel] Sharon was absolutely right. Just get out of there! They could never had reached an agreement with Abu Mazen on the evacuation there.

Moreover, in her research on peacemaking since 1967, Golan studied the motives of Sharon and Olmert (and others) with regard to the disengagement from Gaza. She spoke with several people from within Sharon's inner circle who knew what was happening. In addition, she read the book by Dov Weissglass, one of Sharon's closest advisors, entitled *Ariel Sharon, Prime Minister, a Personal Examination.*

> In this book, Dov Weissglass tells the real story, which was that Sharon asked for estimates or evaluations from the National Security Council, as to what would happen if Israel were to evacuate four settlements, 15-19 settlements or all the settlements. I believe that Sharon was looking into evacuating all the settlements—or almost all of them—because he was concerned over the demographic issue and the possibility of a bi-national state. These were the same reasons used by other Israeli hardline politicians such as Yitzhak Rabin, Tzipi Livni and Ehud Olmert. They wanted to get out of the territories. They thought that the occupation was bad for us and that it was leading to a bi-national state.

The disengagement from Gaza did not, however, produce the hoped-for result of peace between Israel and the Palestinians in the Gaza strip. Instead, Islamic radicals took over the area after a quick civil war between *Hamas* and *Fatah.* The leaders of *Hamas* were total rejectionists who did not believe in or support the Oslo Accords.

The take-over of the Gaza Strip by *Hamas* proved to be a real obstacle to peace. Moreover, the fact that the Palestinian people were deeply divided between *Hamas*-ruled Gaza and the *Fatah*-led West Bank, was a source of great consternation for peacebuilders like Golan.

> The *Hamas* takeover after the Palestinian elections and the joint government–which nobody would talk to since *Hamas* was a part of it–and the violent overthrow by *Hamas* which included throwing *Fatah* people out of the windows!–all of this made for the final separation [between *Fatah* and *Hamas*]. This was ironic because the negotiations were never about Gaza. It was always understood that the Palestinians would get the Gaza Strip! The negotiations were always over the West Bank. The division between the Palestinians played into Israel's hands. Israel wanted to divide the Palestinians. The essential problem was that once *Hamas* took over and we had the violence of the rockets from Gaza, this was a perfect excuse for the right-wing in Israel to say 'you see what happens when you evacuate!' That became a mantra–like the 'no partner' mantra–wherever you pull out, you are going to get rockets! This did not help with Israeli public opinion!

Once *Hamas* was ruling Gaza, this made the peace process very complicated. In Ramallah, the President of the Palestinian Authority, Abu Mazen, was promoting non-violence and was trying to negotiate with Israel, whereas in Gaza the *Hamas* used violence or, as they called it, *armed resistance*. Also, the split among the Palestinians created a severe problem for the Palestinians themselves. *Fatah* and *Hamas* were in a situation of enmity; in fact, they were bitter opponents! *Hamas* is a religious (fundamentalist) movement, an off-shoot of the Muslim Brotherhood, and *Fatah* is a nationalist one. Golan described their relationship succinctly:

> They were always at loggerheads. The secular *Fatah* people never liked the Muslim Brotherhood. The lack of reconciliation between these two camps is bad for the Palestinians. And Israel used this to avoid peace and say that we can't speak to them because they speak in two voices.

Yet, despite the failure of the disengagement to lead to any semblance of peace, the political peace process limped on. After Ariel Sharon suffered a severe stoke and was no longer able to function on the political stage, Ehud Olmert of the new *Kadima* party became prime minister and made a surprisingly strong effort to negotiate for peace with the Palestinians.

The Annapolis International Peace Conference and Talks between Prime Minister Olmert and President Abbas

In November 2007, President George Bush of the United States convened another peace summit in Annapolis, Maryland, not far from Washington DC. The conference did not achieve much but it did lead to more direct negotiations between the sides. Back home in Israel and Palestine, Prime Minister Ehud Olmert and President Mahmoud Abbas (Abu Mazen) met many times over several months for intensive negotiations.

By many accounts, both sides were very close to reaching an agreement, but due to several factors–including and especially the corruption trial of Ehud Olmert, which led him to resign–such an agreement never took place. Yet, it was the closest both sides have ever come to reaching a comprehensive Israeli-Palestinian peace agreement, which is why Golan, in her book *Israeli Peacemaking Since 1967*, called it a *near break-through:*

> Olmert's efforts produced only a near breakthrough due to some, if not all, of the negative factors at play. The critical factor would appear to have been the corruption charges and the resignation of Olmert, which prevented any continuation which might have produced a breakthrough. But contributing to this were the political weakness of Olmert, the spoilers who corroded his political base and decimated his coalition, to a large degree due to ideological objections, alongside Abu Mazen's own weakness due to the split among the Palestinians and the spreading strength of *Hamas*, both leading to a cautious approach by Abu Mazen.

Olmert's approach worked well with Abbas (Abu Mazen). The impression was that the Olmert-Abu Mazen talks were serious and that Olmert really saw Abu Mazen as a partner for peace–he tried to change the paradigm of 'we don't have a partner for peace.' Golan remembers this well:

> I have talked with Olmert a few times about this. To his credit, he tried to tackle this from the psychological angle. He welcomed him to his official residence with the Palestinian flag raised; he tried very much to treat him as an equal. Olmert gave a talk at a conference we did on the issue of trust-building at Tel Aviv University. He talked about how he felt that it was very important to create trust between them, which was very smart and good. Abu Mazen sang the right music whenever he met with Olmert. He did it very much on purpose—he was totally conscious of what he was doing.

Abu Mazen talked about this in his autobiography (which has been published in Hebrew).

In the end, however, despite all the good intentions and intensive talks, it was another peacemaking failure, which did not lead to a resolution of this seemingly intractable conflict. It seemed that the politicians and diplomats were incapable of reaching an agreement that would have been for the mutual benefit of their peoples, and would have prevented futile wars between Israel and the Palestinians. Instead, Israel was to fight four wars with the *Hamas*-led Palestinians in Gaza between 2008 and 2021.

The Impact of the Gaza Wars: Moving from Peace Now to Combatants for Peace

Golan felt that all of these wars in Gaza were leading Israel away from the peace process with the Palestinians. In addition, they caused dissension within the peace camp in Israel:

> In all of the Gaza wars, the leaderships of Peace Now and *Meretz* was divided as to whether to oppose these wars or not. For example, during the 2008 war, when I was abroad then for something else to do with peace, we had a phone call among six people in the leadership of Peace Now. Three of us said that we must come out against this war and three others said that we should not do so because we would lose our public, which was in favor of the war. Later, I noticed that the three people who were against the war were all from *Meretz* and the three who were for the war were from Labor.

In 2014, as a result of the third Gaza War, Golan left Peace Now–which had, in her view moved towards the center–and joined Combatants for Peace, a joint Israeli-Palestinian organization which was more to the left than Peace Now. She described this move poignantly in her autobiography:

> The final straw was the 2014 war against Gaza. A friend from *Meretz* called me to a meeting of a small group that wanted to organize a demonstration against the war. At that meeting, we were three or four from *Meretz*, some from *Hadash* [a joint Jewish-Arab left-wing political party] and one or two from Combatants for Peace. I volunteered to raise money for the demonstration, along with Mossi Raz, a former Director of Peace Now. Since we were fairly well-known abroad from our activities in Peace Now, the person who organized the fund-raising for Combatants for Peace set

up an internet campaign using our pictures and statements, and we successfully solicited contributions. Combatants for Peace organized the demonstration under its slogan *There is Another Way.* After that, I officially left Peace Now and joined Combatants for Peace.

In recent years, Golan has become very active in Combatants for Peace. This relatively new organization appeals to her since it was a very active, grassroots movement, entirely joint Israeli and Palestinian, composed of former fighters from each side. Moreover, Combatants for Peace advocates non-violent opposition to the occupation of Palestinian areas by the Israeli military. Golan became a member of the steering committee and a member of their Tel Aviv-Nablus group, and she helped to create an organization to help with fundraising and publicity in the USA–American Friends of Combatants for Peace. In her work with this joint Israeli-Palestinian organization, Golan has developed great respect for her Palestinian counterparts and for the communications strategy of the organization:

> I am in awe of the Palestinians in CFP. They are mainly *Fatah* people. They are under lots of pressure from their community because of the anti-normalization attitudes of the people. I have tremendous respect for these people since they are taking chances and they will come out and work with us.

> Remember—the Palestinians were all in jail in Israel. They came to the conclusion, for one reason or another, that violence was not helping them. So, they have chosen the path of non-violence. The organization believes in communication, and I think that it is important to show Palestinians that there is a partner on the Israeli side and to show Israelis that there is a partner on the Palestinian side. I have never been one of these people who says 'let's make the occupation better, let's take blankets and food and God-knows-what,' but that is a lot of what Combatants does. Their positions are good. We do the annual joint memorial ceremony. And now we also do an annual memorial for the *nakbah*. This is very important. This is important for Palestinians to see, even though they know that we don't represent a large proportion of the Israeli public.

With her extensive feminist background, it is not surprising the Golan got involved in organizing and participating in a new women's group within Combatants for Peace.

We had a women's group and I have met Palestinian women there who had never met an Israeli citizen who wasn't a soldier! They have horrible memories from childhood of Israeli soldiers coming in to their homes in the middle of the night. This is real. For them to meet Israelis who know this and who listen is very important and meaningful. I think it makes a difference and it is important. We have to know what is important to them and they have to know what is important to us.

Golan remains a peace activist with Combatants for Peace, which has become her most important outlet for peacebuilding work in recent years. The mission statement of this organization, from the Combatants for Peace website, speaks directly to her at this point in her life.

This egalitarian, bi-national, grassroots organization was founded on the belief that the cycle of violence can only be broken when Israelis and Palestinians join forces. Committed to joint nonviolence since its foundation, CFP works to both transform and resolve the conflict by ending the Israeli occupation and all forms of violence between the two sides and building a peaceful future for both peoples.

This is an important organization which I too have come to know in recent years. I have attended their joint memorial commemoration three times and found that the way they memorialized the dead on both sides of the conflict and looked toward a peaceful future was extraordinarily meaningful. In addition, I have met and interviewed one of the Palestinian founders of this organization, Sulaiman Khatib, who shared his forward-looking approach with me:

I am optimistic. The dream is to live in dignity and freedom for everybody from the river to the sea, whatever the solution is. My experience has taught me: We can't just sit and wait for an agreement. We have to be involved in the here and now. What keeps me moving? The people I meet every day.

I also read a beautiful memoir about Khatib, written by a young American Jewish peace activist, Penina Eilberg-Schwartz entitled *In This Place Together: A Palestinian's Journey to Collective Liberation*, which explains in a beautiful way not only the motivations of one Palestinian peacebuilder to found Combatants for Peace but also much of the background for the establishment of a new nonviolent movement for peace. In addition, this book talks a great deal about "third alternative thinking"–learning and telling both the Israeli and Palestinian narratives of the history and of the current state of the Israeli-Palestinian conflict and then integrating them into one collective narrative–which is in fact one of the main themes of the book, if not its central message. In Khatib's note at the beginning of the book, he reinforces this message:

> By telling my story, I want to humanize the headlines as much as possible. To show the complexity and the beauty and the ugliness and the pain and the hope to share what I went through, what our communities–both Palestinian and Jewish–continue to go through. I hope to use my little bit of knowledge to give a different look, from different sides... To hold multiple narratives is not easy. It is not easy to carry contradictions in your soul. It's much easier to see one side of the story, to blame the other, to live in victim-hood, to feel that all the world is against you, that everyone wants to kill you. But this is not reality. The history of Palestine and Israel has been told in many ways, and if we want a better future, we must gather the pieces and form them into a new shared story.

Golan has joined with Khatib and other Palestinian and Israeli peace activists to struggle for peace in this new way. Over the course of her career, she made a transformation from activism for peace in the mainstream Labor party and then the left-wing *Meretz* party, and in her civil society involvement through Peace Now and then to Combatants for Peace. In her autobiography she wrote:

> There is a saying (belief?) that generally one is radical as a young person and with maturity becomes conservative. It has definitely been the other way round for me, at least since immigrating to Israel.

Golan has clearly found her peacebuilding home within Combatants for Peace.

Conclusion

Professor Galia Golan is without a doubt one of the most persistent Israeli Jewish peacebuilders, as well as a scholar, teacher and writer about the Israeli-Palestinian peace process over many decades. She has been involved in advocating for peace since she came to Israel in the late 1960s via some of the most important political parties and non-governmental organizations in Israeli society. She does not rest and is continually coming up with new ideas and new ways to implement them, particularly through Combatants for Peace. In addition. Golan is a prolific writer and critic of the mistakes made in the peace process over the decades. She has written some very profound and perceptive books and articles on this topic which are eye-openers for anyone who reads them. Moreover, she has written a wonderful autobiography, which summarizes her professional and activist career. Golan is a peacebuilder with a vision and a program of action. She has always merged her scholarly side and her activist side in her professional and personal life in her own unique way.

Hadassah Froman: Sharing the Land in Peace

Photo by Amy Kronish

Hadassah Froman is an Orthodox Jewish religious woman, teacher of Judaism, healer, a pioneer in Jewish-Muslim Dialogue, and a pursuer of peaceful coexistence with her Palestinian Arab neighbors. Froman lives in the settlement of *Tekoa* in the West Bank, just south of Jerusalem in *Gush Etzion*, the Etzion Bloc. In addition to her peace work in her local area, she often participates in public programs for peace in Jerusalem and elsewhere. In recent years, she has also specialized in teaching about the *Zohar* (one of the most important texts of Jewish mysticism of the medieval period) and she teaches poetry to young people in schools and in the Israeli army.

Froman is the widow of the late Rabbi Menachem Froman, who was famous throughout Israel and Palestine (as well as internationally) for his unusual groundbreaking work in reaching out to radical Palestinian Muslims in serious attempts at peacebuilding, dialogue and reconciliation. Rabbi Froman was an iconoclastic religious Zionist settler who believed deeply in peace and in developing good relations with his Palestinian neighbors. He built strong and sustained relationships with Muslim religious leaders in the West Bank as well as with the leaders of the *Hamas* movement in the Gaza Strip. He knew them well and developed a deeply religious as well as national dialogue with them, gaining their admiration and trust. Because he had these special connections, he was able to help people like Rabbi Melchior (one of the peacebuilders featured in this book) in approaching Muslim religious leaders to be part of bold initiatives for peace. He also developed very positive relationships with Muslim religious leaders who were part of the Palestinian Authority in Ramallah, and he even gained access to President Yasser Arafat, with whom he and his wife met several times.

As we shall learn from her directly, Hadassah Froman often joined her husband, Rabbi Menachem, in forging meaningful relationships with Palestinian religious and national leaders for over 30 years until his death in 2013. Since then, she has been carrying on his legacy through her commitment to peacebuilding through dialogue and teaching, especially with a relatively new organization in her area known as *Roots/Shorashim/Judor* (the name of the organization is in English, Hebrew and Arabic). She and her colleagues in this new NGO believe that the land of Israel/Palestine can be shared by members of the two peoples, neither of whom is going anywhere. Since 2014, they have been developing good relations between Palestinian Arabs and Israeli Jews, especially with young people, at their center, called *Mercaz Karama*, the Dignity Center, near a major intersection in the Etzion Bloc. In addition to their peacebuilding work, Froman and her colleagues are involved with a creative and ambitious Israeli-Palestinian political peace-making movement, called A *Land for All—Two States, one Homeland* which is gaining some traction in Israel, Palestine and abroad. They have developed a thoughtful and comprehensive vision and statement of principles, whereby both peoples can share the land, while creating two states at the same time. We will learn more about this movement from Froman and others in this chapter.

Early Life and Family

Froman was born in 1950 and raised on an Orthodox religious kibbutz, Kibbutz Lavi, in the Lower Galilee in a fervently Zionist family, for whom the state of Israel was of central importance. The founding of the state in 1948 was a seminal religious and national event for her and her family. According to Froman:

> The establishment of the state of Israel was not just a political act; it was also the fulfilment of Divine Providence. It was a miracle. It was part of the religious-historical process of *geulah* [redemption] of the people and the land of Israel. At the same time, my father, who died five years ago at the age of 94, imparted the idea to me that we had to learn to live with the Arabs, to solve the conflict with them.

Kibbutz Lavi, which was founded in 1949 by young people from the religious Zionist youth movement known as *B'nei Akiva*, is known to this day for some of the moderate ideas of its rabbinic leadership. Her father was one of the pioneers on this kibbutz. She recalls nostalgically her father's commitments to Judaism and Zionism as well as to learning to live with the local Arabs, which included relating to what happened to them in the 1948 war.

> I came from a family of *Hapoel Hamizrachi*, the movement for Religious Zionism. My father was a religious Zionist Jew. He was also a classical left-winger at the same time that he was very Zionist. He was also a super intellectual person. He dreamed all his life of settling and working the land of Israel, which is what he did. Until the age of 94, he woke up every morning to work in the fields of the land of Israel, at Kibbutz Lavi, a religious kibbutz in the lower Galilee, where I grew up. He worked in the orchards of the kibbutz. Also, until his very last day, he prayed every day. His dream was to die in his orchard. In addition, as a serious intellectual

person, he was always learning about the world and studying *Torah*. At the same time that he was very Zionist, he was also very leftist—he combined the two together very well! He believed that the Jewish citizens of state of Israel needed to learn to live with the Arabs in our midst and that the state needed to recognize and even express forgiveness for the wrongs done to the Palestinian Arabs during the *Nakbah* [the Arabic term for 'the great catastrophe,' i.e., the loss of the 1948 war and the ensuing loss of lands and creation of a large number of refugees].

Froman's reminiscences about her father's religious Zionism, combined with Labor Zionism, and mixed with left-wing ideas about cooperating and learning to live with the local Palestinian Arab population, reflect a mixture of views which existed and thrived together in the early decades of the new state of Israel. Yet, they were somewhat unique when integrated within one person. Unfortunately, his outlook was the exception not the rule. Most Jews in Israel in its first decade were not sensitive to the needs of the Arabs within their midst. It was as if they were invisible. Similarly, Palestinian nationalism was virtually unknown within Israeli society between 1948 and 1967. It was denied and subdued, not just by the Jews in Israel but also by the Arabs, who were referred to as *Israeli Arabs*, thus negating their Palestinian identity. It wasn't until Benny Morris and other "new historians" who wrote more accurate histories of what happened, based on their extensive study of archival materials, that Jews in Israel and abroad began to learn the more complicated and difficult history of the founding of Israel.

In contrast to her father, Froman's mother was less political. She generally kept her right-wing views to herself. However, she was very attached to nature, agriculture and the land of Israel, but she did not love the collectivism of kibbutz life. Her mother's attachment to the land of Israel definitely rubbed off on her daughter since she decided later in life to be one of the pioneers in the settlement of the land of Israel in the West Bank after the 1967 war.

After graduating high school, Froman served in the Israel Defense Forces, following which she studied briefly at the Hebrew University in Jerusalem and then at a religious college for girls in Jerusalem where she learned Jewish texts and pedagogy. During her studies, she married Menachem, and after living briefly in Jerusalem, they were among the first settlers in Kibbutz Migdal Oz, in *Gush Etzion* (the Etzion Bloc) in the West Bank, south of Bethlehem, where she served as a kindergarten teacher. Three years later, she and her husband moved to Tekoa, to join the original nucleus of Russian Jews who had settled there after 1967. She has lived in Tekoa ever since.

Following the Six Day War of June 1967

The victory of Israel over the Arab states in the June war of 1967 opened up new opportunities for religious Jews who felt a strong connection to the land of Israel. A new messianic movement arose called *Gush Emunim* (Bloc of the Faithful), the movement to settle all of the land of Israel. Its members began to settle in the occupied territories. Hadassah Froman and her husband Rabbi Menachem Froman were among this group—they regarded themselves as "pioneers."

However, in contrast to most of the other Jewish settlers in the new territories captured by Israel, Hadassah and her husband believed in sharing the land with the Palestinians who lived there! They respected their human rights, their dignity and their right to their own historical-religious narrative. Over time they developed a unique religious-humanist philosophy, which Froman carries on today, along with other colleagues, since her husband's death in March 2013.

> My choices later in life were much more complex. On the one hand, we–Menachem and I–decided to be pioneers in the settlement movement in Judea and Samaria with *Gush Emunim*; on the other hand, we expressed a great deal of objections and sensitivity to overzealous nationalism, and to harming the human rights of Palestinians. Gradually, we came to recognize the right of Palestinians to national rights. Menachem was a leader in this. This was a complex ideology of this and that, i.e., living in the settlements in Judea and Samaria [the terms that Jewish settlers use for the occupied West Bank] and at the same time recognizing that there was a Palestinian national movement with its own legitimate national aspirations. Menachem had grown up in the Labor movement, and he saw the settlement enterprise as a continuation of their pioneering in the land of Israel from the beginning of the Zionist movement.

Froman's ideology is a hybrid of seemingly contradictory ideas. On the one hand, she believes that Jews have the right to settle in all parts of the land of Israel. On the other hand, following the teachings of her husband, she also believes that the Palestinians have a right to be there too, and she supports human rights for them, as well as for Jews:

> I believe in respect for every Palestinian as a human being, and for his property. This has always been very basic for us. For Menachem, this extended to respect for the Palestinians' national aspirations. He also was looking for ways to live together—Israeli Jews and Palestinian Arabs—with their two world views and national identities. I have always been, and I still am, his student. I became a follower of his philosophy of Jewish humanism. For Menachem, this was religious humanism. He felt that both Jews and Muslims were connected to this land in very deep religious and national ways. Accordingly, Menachem's religious philosophy was different than the usual Zionist ideologies which were more concerned about how to rule over another people.

Froman has clearly inherited her husband's philosophy and practice of religious humanism and very much made it her own. In fact, she has become one of the leading proponents of this ideology, not only in the West Bank, but throughout Israel.

Froman and her family of ten children settled in the village of Tekoa, where she lives until today, along with many of her children and grandchildren. During all the years that she has lived there, she and her husband have been committed to developing positive relationships with the local Palestinians. Yet, as we shall see, when the Oslo Accords came about in the early 1990s, their peace activism was to increase and become more important to them, even though they did not support all the details of these peace agreements.

The Impact of the Oslo Peace Agreements in the early 1990s

The Oslo Peace Accords of the early 1990s were a watershed moment for the advancement of the possibility of peace between Israelis and Palestinians in the region. Some people hailed them; other rejected them completely. In between, people like Hadassah Froman were ambivalent about them. In fact, she had rather mixed feelings about them:

> On the one hand, I remember that it was a very emotional time because we felt that this was a real step towards peace. On the other hand, there was also a feeling that this was a missed opportunity, that this peace was one of separation, and trading territories for peace, rather than recognizing the very strong connection that we as Jews have to the land of Israel. We felt that somehow the peace should have recognized this, but it did not. We felt that this *shalom* [peace] was not *shalem* [harmonious], i.e.,

163

that this peace was not a full one, and that therefore there was not
a great likelihood that it will actually come to fruition.

Despite these ambivalent feelings, Froman recalls that this was a time for
the development of some new concepts for peace, as well as for cultivating
more significant and sustained relationships with Palestinians, especially religious Muslim Palestinians.

On the one hand, during the period of the Oslo Accords [1993-
95], there was a push for more dialogue and encounters with
Palestinians. On the other hand, these accords motivated my husband, Menachem, to come up with a suggestion for peace that was
more nuanced. He wrote about this in many articles which were
printed in the press in Israel. His suggestions for peace included
his religious vision for peace, which was missing in the Oslo
Accords. He thought that the Oslo Accords were just political and
were lacking the religious dimension. He was involved with Rabbi
Melchior [another peacebuilder portrayed in this book] in discussions at that time about a concept of a *religious peace*. Menachem
established lots of good relationships with religious leaders from
Hamas and with religious leaders from all over the world, as well
as with Palestinian religious leaders in Palestinian society in Israel
and with the Palestinian Authority which was being developed at
that time. He also had a good working relationship with Shimon
Peres [one of the architects of the Oslo Accords] during that period, a relationship that strengthened and developed over time.

Froman and her husband Menachem were unusual proponents of peace,
especially within the settler community in the West Bank and Gaza. They
continually developed creative and innovative ideas for living peacefully
with Palestinians. They saw both the value and the limitations of peace accords, along with all their complications and challenges. The complexities
would only increase in the next decade, as political attempts to reach a comprehensive peace agreement between Israel and the Palestinians were
unsuccessful.

After the Failure of the Camp David II Accords in Summer 2000

In the summer of the year 2000, the last attempt to reach a comprehensive
peace arrangement between the Palestinians and the Israelis failed after two
weeks of intensive negotiations at the Presidential retreat known as Camp
David in the hills of Maryland. The Israeli team, led by Prime Minister

Ehud Barak (who had been elected in a landslide victory in 1999), and the Palestinian delegation led by Chairman Yasser Arafat, could not find the right formula to allow them both to sign a peace accord, under the aegis of President Bill Clinton of the USA. On the one hand, this was a great disappointment to most people who were seeking peace. On the other hand, it opened up some new opportunities.

In a very unique way, Froman recalled the failure of the Camp David II talks. She felt that it gave more impulse to seeking new ways to make peace, based much more on religious ideas, not just secular ones.

> I remember that Prime Minister Ehud Barak took the negotiations as far as they could go. And when they failed, the idea that only his way – the way of a political agreement — was proved to not be enough to bring peace. In fact, we thought that it was impossible. This strengthened our idea that a religious peace was necessary, not just a political, secular one. We believed that in order to reach a religious peace, one has to go about it in a different way. Since the religious foundations for peace are part of the root of the problem, we felt that the religious dimensions of peace must be included in the talks between Jews and Palestinians, and not left out as a separate matter. For example, we need to discuss the issue of our religious approaches to the Temple Mount, and not simply leave them out of the talks. I learned through my talks with Palestinians that most Jews in the world do not understand the sensitivity of the Palestinian Muslims' attachments to the Temple Mount, *Harem El Sharif*. My husband developed a thesis which demonstrated that the Temple Mount was at the heart of the conflict, and he developed a model for how to deal with this.

During this period, Froman was engaging in more and more dialogical discussions with Palestinians in her area, which greatly enriched her understanding of their religious and national narrative. Over time, she would deepen and increase her talks with Palestinians, which would not only expand her own religious Jewish identity to include the other, but enable her to become a persistent pursuer of peace. This would continue to occur even during momentous developments in the war and peace processes, including the disengagement from Gaza and the wars between Israel and the Palestinians in Gaza, about which Froman had very mixed feelings.

Responding to the Disengagement from Gaza in 2005

One of the boldest moves for peace in the history of the conflict was the unilateral disengagement from Gaza by Israel, which took place in the summer of 2005. It was a very controversial decision in Israeli society, one fraught with both hopes and dangers. In the end, it would turn out to be a huge failure as far as peace was concerned. On the contrary, it would lead to several wars between Gaza, which was controlled by *Hamas*, and the state of Israel.

Hadassah Froman, and her husband Rabbi Menachem Froman, were among those who opposed the disengagement by the government of Israel from the Gaza Strip. They had developed relationships with many Palestinians inside Gaza. In particular, they were distressed by the way that the disengagement was accomplished.

> My husband Menachem was connected to people in Gaza. He and I would go there periodically. He had a very special relationship with the head of the Palestinian police of the Palestinian Authority, Nasser Yousef, who was a *Sufi*. Menachem was a Jewish *Sufi*, since he studied Jewish Mysticism and Hasidism. We would go in and out of Gaza. I accompanied him sometimes, but more often he went without me, since I was home with the children. Menachem had very good relationships with members of the leadership in Gaza, and with religious leaders there before the disengagement.
>
> Concerning the disengagement: Menachem told Nasser Yousef, before it actually happened, that if there would be a unilateral disengagement by Israel from Gaza, that this would turn Gaza into a center of terror. He also wrote articles about this in the media and was interviewed by the media about his views on this. He felt that this was the wrong way to go about this. In his discussions with Nasser Yousef, the Palestinian leader told him that there was an ancient synagogue in Gaza that could be preserved and that a Jewish neighborhood could be built in the center of Gaza and all of Gaza would be changed! This could have changed the whole story of Gaza to something different, according to Nasser Yousef. Also, with regard to the whole idea of disengagement, Menachem and I thought it should be done via negotiations, which could have left Jewish communities in Gaza under Palestinian control. This was before *Hamas* took over in Gaza.

Rabbi Froman also met with Prime Minister Ariel Sharon and spoke to him at length. Sharon let him speak, listened to him, but at the end dismissed him. This was a serious attempt of a religious peacebuilder to influence the political process. Unfortunately, it did not work. Rabbi Froman and Hadassah Froman–along with most of the settler community–were deeply disappointed by Prime Minister Sharon's decision to pull Jewish settlers out of Gaza, and they were especially upset with the forceful way he did it, in typical Sharon "bulldozer style." According to Hadassah Froman, the process was much too violent and counterproductive.

> The disengagement was implemented with violence by the Israeli military against settlers–they removed all the settlements with force–and therefore we opposed the way that the disengagement was implemented. We believed that the separation of the two sides would lead to violence, and this is what actually happened. Menachem and I were very opposed and disappointed by the whole way that the disengagement was done, and with the results of it in Gaza. Running away from Gaza only served to strengthen the violent elements within Gaza. The sense was that the violence on the part of Palestinians won them a victory–they forced the Israelis to run away!

Froman and her husband also believed that dialogue would have been better than a forceful pull-out.

> Menachem and I believed that you needed to enter into dialogue with the root of the problem. In the Palestinian community, the religious matters are the root—they are at the center of their identity! It is impossible to resolve the conflict without this 'root work,'like 'root canal' in dentistry.

The Fromans believed that if religious Jews could talk to religious Muslims reaching agreement was possible. Indeed, they thought that interreligious Jewish-Muslim dialogue could lead to sustainable accords:

> Menachem did not think that they [the *Hamas* leaders] were *tzadikim* [righteous people] but without them, nothing real would be resolved. He would go to meet with the *Hamas* religious leaders often. At other times, he talked with the *Hamas* leaders about a *hudna* [a long-term truce]. Imagine where we would be today if we had implemented a *hudna* with *Hamas*. I don't know if it would

167

have succeeded, but perhaps we would be in a totally different place.

Froman accompanied her husband on many of his visits to Gaza and in his work for peace and reconciliation with her whole heart and soul, for many years.

> In retrospect, I am sorry that I did not do more with him. I was home raising ten children. But I did accompany him on much of his work for peace. (But he did not take me to meet religious leaders of *Hamas* because they were not open to meeting with women.)

Froman was a committed partner in peacebuilding with her husband for many years. Despite all the ups and downs of the peace process, they continued their peacebuilding work together, until he died in March 2013. More than 4000 people from all walks of life, including many Palestinians, attended his funeral in Tekoa in the West Bank. After his passing, Hadassah continued her peace work on her own, in partnership with Israeli Jews and Palestinian Arabs in her region, the Gush Etzion Block, south of Jerusalem.

Increasing Local Peacebuilding

One of the last major attempts at bringing Palestinians and Israelis together to negotiate for peace was the effort by Secretary of State John Kerry, over nine months, during 2013-2014. A great deal of time, money and resources were invested in this process, but it failed. The leaders on both sides remained very stubborn and would not commit to genuine negotiations that could have brought a peace accord.

Despite this setback in the political peace process, people on the ground were continuing to engage in people-to-people dialogue and education. Hadassah Froman was one of these people. She and some Palestinian friends decided to re-commit to peacebuilding among Palestinians and Jews in their area.

> After Menachem died, some Palestinians came and said to me: 'he was a teacher for you and for us, let's do something together that he dreamed about.' It was an initiative on the part of these Palestinians. They felt a deep moral religious imperative to do something in memory of Menachem. They came from the nearby village, *Bet Umar*. This family at one point had members who were very active in the *intifada* who were arrested and sat in Israeli jails for a long time. While they were there, they had time to read and

to think, and they begin to read philosophy and especially Ghandi on non-violence, and they began thinking about non-violent ways to resolve the Israeli-Palestinian conflict. And then, their eldest son was killed by an IDF soldier for no good reason, in an unacceptable way.

These Palestinians adopted a philosophy of non-violence. They wanted to use this to help steer the Palestinian people in a new way. Naturally this appealed to Hadassah Froman and other Jews in her area who reacted positively to this initiative of some Palestinians whom they regarded as very brave.

> We felt that the fact that they wanted to do it here, with us the settlers, was a very meaningful, courageous step. These Palestinians have a plot of land near the main intersection in *Gush Etzion*, which they have dedicated for our joint work together. The idea was to create a *mirkam enoshi*, [a human tapestry], a special place for coexistence, a place for gathering and meeting and encountering one another. I was one of the people who helped establish this very special place—an Israeli-Palestinian piece of land—and to this day it is alive and functioning! We call this peacebuilding organization *Roots/Shorashim/Judor*. Things are happening there all the time.

According to Rabbi Hanan Schlesinger, one of the main movers in the *Roots/Judor/Shorashim* organization, Hadassah Froman has been very instrumental in making this happen. She was there at the founding of the organization in January 2014, and she has remained a consistent presence and force in the movement. The center that they have established, which is called *Mercaz Karama*, the Dignity Center, is at a main junction in the *Gush Etzion* area, south of Bethlehem, close to where many violent incidents have occurred over the years. According to Rabbi Schlesinger:

> This is the only place in the West Bank where Palestinian Arabs and Israeli Jews can sit together in dignity. Palestinians cannot enter my town freely in the West Bank and Jews don't enter Palestinian villages, both due to fear. The new center is like a mental health clinic. More and more Palestinians and Israeli Jewish are coming there to encounter the other out of the realization that we are sick, that we have been suffering from fear and trauma for a long time.

169

There were a few years when Froman was involved with an Israeli-Palestinian women's group. In addition, there have been Israeli and Palestinian youth groups that were very active. According to Schlesinger, these *dignity centers* are growing and developing in the West Bank, with new ones being established in the Jordan Valley and in the northern West Bank, known by some Jews as the biblical *Samaria*.

This peacebuilding work has become the focus of Froman and her Jewish and Palestinian partners in recent years. The work includes both dialogical encounters as well as opportunities for serious learning about each other's religion.

> We have invested a lot of personnel and money to continue to make this happen. And we have two groups of interreligious encounters—one for adults and one for youth—we learn about Islam and Judaism together. Some of the Palestinian Muslim teachers are *Sufis*—they are open to learning about Jewish Mysticism, since they know about Muslim mysticism. Rabbi Yaacov Nagen, from Otniel, is very involved in this with us.

Why has Froman become so invested in this local peacebuilding work, in her area of the West Bank? At a certain point she asked herself this question:

> In the context of all the big political things going on, and growing hatred in the area, and feelings of destruction, and politicians who don't do what they should be doing, and the army with all of its problems, including causing many unnecessary issues in the area, I asked myself: 'what can I do in this complicated situation? What can a small group of Palestinians and Israelis do together?' My answer has been to help to create this small oasis of peaceful coexistence.

> This small place which we have set up receives thousands of people from around the world and from Israel all the time, including students from pre-army academic courses, schools, universities, who come there to learn about what we are doing. We have created a place where we can put the issues on the table in a comprehensive manner-settlers and Palestinians-and we discuss them in depth. We are showing people that there is another way to live here, that there is no choice but to continue to develop more and more methods and skills for coexistence here. And we need to focus on

justice and equality and life that is good for both peoples living on this land. We don't need more wars and more separation. On the contrary, we can live together on this land. Rather than separate from each other, we need to connect with each other.

In addition, Froman feels that this project–even though it is small in size–has a message for the world.

My husband Menachem did things on a grand scale, with the international media, and he knew people from all over the world. He went very far. I am a smaller person and I am doing smaller work. But I feel that the work that I am doing here over many years is reaching many circles of influence. We are working with many influential people who have the will and the ability to affect change in many educational and social settings. We are doing this even though there are many forces of violence and opposition to what we are doing. I can't say for sure that I and my colleagues will win the day. Nevertheless, I am committed to this way that I have developed together with local Palestinians in the area where I live. I believe that a little bit of light can defeat a lot of darkness!

In addition to her involvement with this organization, Froman is also involved with two other like-minded organizations or movements, which are conducting dialogues and promoting cooperation between Jews and settlers in the West Bank: *Siah Shalom* (Talking Peace) and *Eretz L'kulam* (A Land for All). Both groups believe, as she does, that somehow the land can be shared by all who live on it, and that creative political solutions can be developed to meet the needs of both peoples to live in Peace.

Talking Peace was created by Dr, Alik Isaacs, a scholar of Jewish and western religious thought, along with Professor Avinoam Rosenak and Sharon Leshem Zinger. In a recent article in the Israeli newspaper Haaretz entitled *Can God Solve the Israeli-Palestinian Conflict*, Dr Isaacs was quoted as saying: "If we don't manage to listen to and engage with constituencies that have opposed the peace proposals in the past, it's not possible to achieve peace in the future." Talking Peace facilitates workshops with both religious and secular Israeli Jews and Palestinian Arabs, from the West Bank and within Israel, including those who have deeply opposed the peace efforts in the past on both sides. Like Froman's efforts, this is a non-political organization which is focused on listening deeply and creating new opportunities for communication and cooperation. During the last 10 years, the staff of Talking Peace has worked with Israeli and Palestinian community leaders, rabbis, diplomats, women leaders and more, and they have trained nearly 100 facilitators to conduct meaningful dialogical encounters that have long-lasting impact.

Similarly, A Land for All, is trying to bridge deep gaps between Palestinians and Jewish Israelis who live in the West Bank. However, this movement has more of a political vision. They believe in the creation of two states in one open land for both Palestinians and Israelis in some sort of confederation. They have developed a detailed vision and plan for how this can come about and in recent years, this movement is gaining some traction in Israel and abroad. While many observers think that their ideas are naïve and impossible to achieve, they nevertheless are offering a clear and detailed vision which includes a statement of principles and detailed ideas of how this could be implemented over time.

Froman also partners with Rabbi Tamar Elad-Applebaum (who is featured in the chapter in this book on Envisioning the Future) in public programs for peace and coexistence in Jerusalem. For Froman and her partners this peace work is a matter of religious faith. Together with religious Muslims, Christians and Jews, she fervently believes that Israeli Jews and Palestinian Arabs can somehow learn to live together in this piece of land.

> It is definitely based in faith. Based on our religious beliefs in our common humanity, we are engaged in our work on a daily basis, every day, slowly and steadily. This is a matter of belief and practicing what you believe! I believe that we are observing the mitzvot [commandments] between human beings and God and between us and our fellow human beings at the same time.

Without a doubt, it is her deep religious Jewish faith which keeps her going. However, her unique understanding and interpretation of Judaism is different than many (perhaps most) other Jews who live in the West Bank since it catalyzes her to be involved in ongoing efforts for coexistence and reconciliation with her Muslim and Christian neighbors.

Conclusion

Hadassah Froman is a very special modern Orthodox Jewish woman peace-builder in Israel. She has developed her theology and her practice—along with her husband Rabbi Menachem Froman, until his passing in 2013—in serious, substantive, and sustained ways over many decades. In recent years, together with Jewish and Palestinian colleagues and partners in her area—the Gush Etzion bloc, south of Bethlehem—she has participated actively in a groundbreaking new peace organization called Roots/Shorashim/Judor to maintain and support peaceful coexistence in the region. She is committed to this work with all of her heart and soul, since it derives from her profound religious belief system, which is central to her life. In addition, Froman partners with many other peacebuilders throughout Israel in promoting her ideas about the importance of learning to live in harmony with the local Palestinian Arabs and the possibilities of living in peaceful coexistence with Palestinians in general. Moreover, as an Orthodox Jewish feminist, she has been particularly instrumental in bringing Jewish and Palestinian women together to learn about each other's religions and cultures, as a form of bridge-building towards mutual acceptance and understanding. Also, she has spoken to many groups from all over Israel, as well as from abroad who visit her in her region, about the importance of developing good relations with Palestinians from her unique religious point of view. In so doing, Froman has been a model and a source of inspiration to people throughout Israel and Palestine, as well as internationally. People have come to know her as a deeply religious Jewish woman who promotes peaceful living with love and devotion out of a deep sense of commitment and commandment.

Part Three

Reflecting on the Past and Looking Towards the Future

Profiles in Peace

Envisioning a Better Future

I have always believed that it is important to envision a better future, rather than always being mired in the despair of the past and obsessed with the obstacles found in the present moment. One of my professors at the Harvard Graduate School of Education, Professor Rabbi Israel Scheffler, called this *Blue Skies Thinking*. If one has a vision of what one would like to see for oneself and one's people, this guides one's work in the real world. All good organizations–as well as countries and communities–have some kind of vision, which is often found in a mission statement or a Declaration of Independence or some other foundational document.

All of the peacebuilders who are the heroes and heroines of this book have a vision of a better future, for their people, and for both peoples–the Palestinian people and the Jewish people–who have been engaged in this seemingly intractable conflict for more than 100 years. They are all people of courage and commitment, since their peace work over many decades has usually challenged the conventional wisdom of the time. What makes them remarkable is that they have persisted in their work for peace, and continue to do so, despite the huge obstacles in their way. They have been able to see beyond the daily political problems and personalities because they have values and beliefs that are central to their thinking and to the professional and personal lives that they live.

Envisioning a better future is essential for peace activists since they need to have a good sense of where they want to get to and what they want to achieve, both of which will guide their theory (or theology) as well as their practice.

Many years ago, I attended workshops in Jerusalem with regard to conflict resolution and the Israeli-Palestinian conflict with Professor Jay Rothman, who used to teach at Antioch College and later at Bar Ilan University in Israel, and now is a consultant in this field. At these workshops, I realized that while learning about the history of the conflict is important (which is why the first chapter of this book is about history and context), it is not the whole story. All too often groups that engage in discussing the conflict begin with history and never move forward since they can't agree on the historiography (the interpretation of history) and only learn that they have very divergent narratives. Instead of focusing only on history, Professor Rothman urged us peacebuilders who were working on the grassroots level to develop a vision for the future. What would we like to see for our people?

For both peoples? What processes–political, psychological, religious, spiritual and educational—can help us bring the real closer to the ideal in our societies? And what is our role in defining progress and designing projects that can help us achieve our goals of peaceful coexistence over time?

Accordingly, I asked each of our peacebuilders these questions:

What is your vision for the future? What would you like to see happen? How do you see the roles of diplomatic peacemaking as well as civil society peacebuilding? How are they interrelated?

In addition, I have asked four young peacebuilders, who have participated in peacebuilding programs as participants and organizers for many years, to share their dreams and hopes for a better future. Their reflections will appear at the end of this chapter.

Palestinian Peacebuilders

Professor Mohammed Dajani has been one of Palestine's most persistent peacebuilders over time. In particular, since he founded his organization known as *Wasatia* ("Moderation" or "the Middle Way") in 2007, he has spoken out for the values and ideas that he deeply believes. Through publications, articles, interviews, books–and through social media–he has articulated his views continually and consistently, despite threats to his life and despite the fact that his ideas are often not accepted by the Palestinian establishment in the West Bank.

In many of his writings, he has discussed the vision of *Wasatia* and how it relates to the future of Palestine.

> The doctrine of *Wasatia*, or 'centrism' lays out a middle ground between secularism and fundamentalism in the Islamic world. Generally speaking, it represents the mainstream of the Muslim masses. *Wasatia* in Palestine supports the peaceful democratic aspirations of Palestinians. *Wasatia*, an Islamic movement guided by the Quran and Prophetic traditions, should avoid being too radical, too political, or too rejecting of the peace process. It should practice diplomacy, creativity and brilliance in dealing with the international community.

Dajani has promoted both a moderate vision and practice of Islam, as a professor, publicist and activist, who has developed a comprehensive secular-cultural philosophy of Islam. Not only has he studied the Koran carefully, but he has put the ethical principles of peace and reconciliation

178

into practice. Moreover, he has served as a guide for other Muslims–perhaps the large Muslim middle ground in Palestine and elsewhere–who are looking for a way in the world other than that of extremist fundamentalist Islam, which is portrayed in the media too often as if it is the real Islam. Indeed, Dajani has spent much of his time and energy combating Islamic extremism and offering a reasonable alternative. For example, he has said clearly:

> Rather than remaining bystanders, moderate Muslims need to join forces in recognition that their religion and its central texts have been hijacked by a small group of minorities for political ends. Furthermore, moderation would erode the occupation's raison d'être by helping Palestinians and Israelis see their overlapping goals. A good starting point would be mutual recognition.

In his vision for the future, Dajani hopes that the Occupation by Israel of Palestinians in the West Bank would end and then Israeli Jews and Palestinian Arabs would be able to get on with their lives. He believes that his path of moderate peacebuilding will eventually catalyze change in the hearts and minds of both peoples. In his many lectures and writings, Dajani has explained how moderation will help end the occupation:

> It will help Israelis and Palestinians realize the overlap in their desires. Israelis, who are concerned with personal and national security, will see the neighboring Palestinian community as a moderate culture seeking a better life for their families. Similarly, Palestinians will see the Israelis as seeking peace and security in order to secure a prosperous future for their society. As such, the raison d'être for the occupation fades away.

In addition, Dajani has been a major promoter of the concept of reconciliation between Israeli Jews and Palestinian Arabs. Not only has he said repeatedly that this idea is rooted in both Judaism and Islam, but he believes that it is necessary for Palestinians and Israelis in order to create a better future for both peoples.

> Both the Islamic and Jewish traditions fully support the concept of reconciliation. There is justification for the peace process in the texts of both faiths. Thus, we need to work with, not against each other. We must perceive the other not as an enemy in conflict, but a partner in peace.

Dajani's concept of reconciliation–which he believes is the key to a more healthy and productive future for both Palestinians and Israelis–is clearly

179

not just a theoretical one. If more people would adopt it, it could lead to much pragmatic progress for peace. In fact, other Palestinian peacebuilders have adopted similar visions for the years ahead.

Another such Palestinian peacebuilder, who is one of the heroes of this book, **Bishop Munib Younan**, approaches the future from his unique Palestinian Christian perspective. He has been a religious leader in Palestine and the world for a long time. He served as the Bishop of the Lutheran Church in Jerusalem for 20 years, and he was the president of the World Lutheran Federation for seven years, the first Palestinian Christian to hold this position. His efforts for peace in Israel, Palestine and internationally earned him the Niwano Peace Prize from the prestigious Niwano Foundation in Japan. Locally, he remains involved in interreligious peace work through the Council of Religious Institutions of the Holy Land, of which he was a founder and has been a core member for a long time. As such, he has come to believe that religious leaders with whom he has worked in partnership for a long time, have a very important role to play in helping to resolve the Israeli-Palestinian conflict in a just and fair way, now and in the future.

> We have the role as religious leaders, even those of us in the older generation, to educate our young people about the possibilities of peace. This can be done in synagogues, in mosques, and in churches. In addition, we religious leaders must always present a vision for justice and not allow the politicians to lead us. We must lead them. We work for the collective good and for the values of peace and justice and reconciliation, and the value of dignity which God gave to every human being. This is the reason we have to lead them and challenge them, even if they don't like it.

Like most (but not all) of the other peacebuilders in this book, Bishop Younan still believes that the best political solution to the Israeli-Palestinian conflict is a two-state solution. But he sees beyond the political framework to a better system of human relations that must be developed in the years ahead which will be based on the development of mutual trust and respect for the human dignity of the people on both sides of the conflict.

> As far as the bigger picture goes, I would like to see a two-state solution, based on the '67 borders. But I don't want to see a Palestinian soldier standing opposite an Israeli soldier. I don't want to see any soldiers; rather, I would like to see a demilitarized situation, where we can really trust each other, work with each

other, and have economic growth for both sides. In addition, there is a lot we can learn from the Israeli economy. Israelis are good in medicine, agriculture, and hi-tech. They have established themselves in the years since 1948. Palestinians are innovative, creative and open to learning, and open to living with the other. Some people depict us as terrorists. We are not terrorists. We want to live our lives with dignity.

A two-state solution which is only a political framework is clearly insufficient. Two states that would continue to engage in violence and wars would be counter-productive. Therefore, any political/diplomatic agreement that will be reached by the peacekeepers in the future will be insufficient if it does not lead to the end of the conflict. Bishop Younan has stressed this in his speeches and writings over many years.

I would like see the end of the conflict, with no more wars and no more violence. We can all benefit from economic growth. Today is different than 70 years ago. Today, Palestinians are aware that justice depends on Israel's security. This is a symbiotic relationship. As a religious leader, I feel that one of our functions is to continue to encourage this two-state vision as the best solution for both peoples.

The fact that Bishop Younan has emphasized throughout his career that *both sides* in the conflict will benefit from peace has been one of his outstanding contributions. I vividly remember that he presented these balanced ideas in a magnificent sermon that he gave at his installation as Bishop of the Lutheran Church in Israel, Palestine and Jordan, in the beautiful Church of the Redeemer in the Christian quarter of the Old City of Jerusalem in 1998, (a position that he held for 20 years, until 2018). Since that time, he has genuinely understood that peace, security and justice are all necessary for both Israeli Jews and Palestinian Arabs.

As a visionary, Bishop Younan sees beyond the narrow political framework of two states and imagines a useful confederation in the region.

In the future, after the two-state solution begins to take form, we can think of ideas like a confederation. Or we could adapt the European model of a European Union for the Middle East, in which we would include Israel, Palestine, Jordan, Iraq, Lebanon and Syria. Every country would have its own political independence, but there will be interdependence with various policies that affect everybody. This is very important. And I believe it is possible–if there is a will, there is a way!

As a prominent Christian religious leader in Jerusalem, thinking about Jerusalem has always been close to Bishop Younan's heart. As a peace activist, he has always struggled for peaceful and just solutions to the question of how Jerusalem can somehow be shared among Jews, Christians and Muslims, and he has developed both theoretical and practical solutions for this.

> The issue of Jerusalem has to be carefully considered. I have been active in the Council of Religious institutions of the Holy Land where we have consulted experts, politicians and diplomats about Jerusalem. When we speak of Jerusalem, we are speaking specifically about *the Holy Basin*, which is the most complicated area of the city since the holy places for the three religions are there. We can find a solution for that, with the idea that the three religions will have a say, to protect the Holy Places.

In addition to practical ideas, Bishop Younan believes that Jerusalem has a special mission in the world. In both the present and the future, Jerusalem should be a unique city due to its holiness and spiritual history.

> As a religious leader, I feel that Jerusalem must be a city of peace, coexistence and tolerance, where the three faiths share in this city. I would like to see that the holy places are places of worship and prayer, not centers of conflict. Jewish, Christian, and Muslim places should be fully respected. That is a key for peace. Once you respect the other's holy place, there will be less conflict between the people of the different religions and nationalities in Jerusalem. I think that this idea is not messianic, but actually possible.

Bishop Younan is both a messianist and a pragmatist at the same time. This is what has made him such an important peacebuilder in Israel and Palestine for so long, and why his legacy is important for future generations.

Another Palestinian peacebuilder, **Huda Abuarquob**, who lives in the West Bank in the village of Dura, near Hebron, has her own views of a possible future. Like Bishop Younan, she envisions a future which would be mutually beneficial to Palestinians and Israelis alike.

> In my vision for the future, I would like to see Palestinians and Israelis enjoy freedom, justice and equality. In addition, I would

like to see walls of separation come down, and in their place, I would hope that opportunities can be developed for a dignified partnership that will lead to prosperity and security **for** all people in the region. Moreover, it will be important that there be an acknowledgement that both peoples belong to this land.

Abuarquob actively endeavors to bring this vision to realization through her work with the Alliance for Middle East Peace (ALLMEP) since 2014, for which she serves as regional director. In this role, she helps to raise the capacity of many of the 150 member organizations so that they can bring about the changes that they all seek. She does this by creating opportunities of engagement with each other—Palestinian Arabs and Israeli Jews—which are based on equality, justice and freedom for all. This is a strategy which she plans to continue in the years ahead.

I plan to continue to support the work of the member organizations of ALLMEP–all of whom are engaged in peacebuilding programs one way or another in the region–by doing advocacy work internationally to bring about much needed attention to the work of peacebuilders in the context of the Israeli-Palestinian conflict. I will continue to convene more key diverse people in the region to support this vision. In so doing, I will continue to strive to change the status quo, and to work for a just solution of the conflict for both peoples. In addition, I see my peacebuilding work as essential for maintaining hope and as a key element of resilience and steadfastness (the Arabic word for this is *summud*).

Maintaining hope–in the light of so much despair, destruction and depression–is one of the major goals of all peacebuilders. For some, like Bishop Younan, it is a religious obligation, emerging from his deeply rooted Christian theology.

Jewish Peacebuilders

Bishop Younan is not the only one with messianic hopes for the future. Rabbi **Michael Melchior**–who has been the leading Jewish Israeli religious peacebuilder for decades–is also very much a messianist, but from a Jewish perspective:

We Jews believe in the Messianic hope. I am one of those who came here to Israel because I believe in the vision of what this country can be, a kind of light for the whole world. I don't think

that we can have a secure future existence if we don't have peace.
I believe that peace is the essence of existence.

Unlike many other religious and political leaders in Israel, who have become pessimistic and think that peace is only a dream but has become
impossible due to the shift to the political right in Israeli and Palestinian
societies, Rabbi Melchior still feels that peace is possible. He has not given
up, and will probably never give up.

> I fervently believe–and I say this after a very long journey with the
> other side and also with our side–that peace is within reach. Also,
> I believe that when we see hands stretched out towards us, we have
> to accept those hands, and we have to create that kind of future.
> It's possible to go down a slippery slope to hell, it's easy. But it's
> also possible to use this momentum which has been created in re-
> cent years in the world and in our part of the world to create a
> better world, a world of peace.

Rabbi Melchior has often stated that from his Jewish religious perspective
it is possible now, and in the years ahead, for the followers of Judaism to
live together with the followers of Christianity and Islam. Moreover, he has
demonstrated this over and over again in his work with Christians and
Muslims through the Alexandria Process and via the work of the Religious
Peace Initiative, which he has been leading with courage and continued
commitment for many years. In so doing, he has argued forcefully for a long
time that we need both a political peace and a religious peace. In addition,
he and his colleagues in the Religious Peace Initiative see their role as
mediators between conflicting sides in the conflict and he can say with confidence that his mediation work has saved many lives.

> I believe that it is not only essential to *tzur me'rah* [desist from evil]
> –as we have done in our efforts in recent years to save lives–we
> have saved thousands of lives in recent years via our mediation
> work – but we also have to do *aseh tov* [to do good deeds]. We need
> to show people that the followers of Islam and Judaism and
> Christianity all can really live in peace together. I believe that this
> is possible. When we do this and when people will realize that
> peace is possible, then that will be paving the path towards this
> goal. We can help change the minds of the vast majority of
> Palestinians and Israelis who just want to end the conflict and get
> on with their lives, but they don't believe that it is possible yet.
> This will pave the path also then for the politicians to do what they

have to do because eventually it has to be also a political peace, not just a religious peace. We need to remove the obstacles–the psychological, practical and political obstacles–to peace. This is our role, now and in the years to follow.

Rabbi Melchior brings examples from other places in the world where reconciliation between enemies was considered to be impossible but happened because of courageous and determined leaders. This gives him hope that change can occur also in the Palestinian-Israeli conflict. It does not have to go on forever. Like other conflicts that have been resolved, this one can be concluded too.

> I have seen changes in other parts of the world, such as the relationship between the Catholic church and the Jewish people, which throughout the ages was much worse than the relationship between Islam and Judaism. Like relationships between countries, like Germany and France, or like many other countries which have lived in centuries of bloody wars. At a certain stage you reach a conclusion that there is another way. We don't need major catastrophes to occur in order to get to that conclusion. We've had enough bloodshed.

Similar to Bishop Younan, Rabbi Melchior is not just a messianist–he is also a pragmatist. Not only is he a rabbi, but he has operated in political circles and knows them well since he was a Member of Knesset (Israel's parliament) for several years and he served as a minister in the government and as a political peace negotiator. He has argued for a long time that the two-state solution is the best way to resolve the Israeli-Palestinian Conflict and that it is still possible. Even though it is complicated, it can be developed with the help of political leadership as well as with people in civil society– including and especially religious leaders and followers–at the grassroots levels. He says this for both practical and religious reasons, which is his way of promoting a vision of peaceful coexistence which insists on keeping hope alive.

> I sincerely believe that we can have a two-state solution. In the beginning, we will need all the security measures and all the guarantees, but eventually we can have open borders and different kinds of relationships of trust with each other. But it will take time to overcome a lot of the animosity that has developed. The process will be both bottom-up and top-down. We will need to work on both levels. In my speeches to young people around the world, I

try to keep hope for peace alive. I share this messianic hope with people in the Muslim and Christian faiths. We have to create a world to which the Messiah would like to come!

Not all peacebuilders are as optimistic as Rabbi Melchior. In stark contrast, **Professor Galia Golan** has become very pessimistic about the possibilities of a peace agreement being achieved between Palestinians and Israelis. Perhaps this is because she has studied the conflict so intensively and has written books and articles on the subject. Or maybe her pessimism is due to the fact that she has seen how badly political leadership has deteriorated on both the Israeli and Palestinian sides of the conflict. In any event, Golan does not see an end in sight via the political/diplomatic peace process.

It is very difficult to be optimistic these days, given the way the Israeli public has voted in the recent four elections. The center right and even far right-wing parties far outnumber the votes to the left or even left-center. It would be foolhardy to expect the election of an Israeli leader in the near future who might enter genuine negotiations with the Palestinians for peace. If Netanyahu would not agree to the necessary compromises, one can hardly expect right-wing Naftali Bennet to be forthcoming. Also, Yair Lapid, his new partner in the leadership of the recently formed 'unity' government, launched his political party in 2012 in the settlement of Ariel in the West Bank.

Golan's familiarity with Israeli politics has led her to a very sober assessment of the political scene in Israel. Indeed, leading Israeli politicians have not spoken up for peace–or entered into negotiations for peace with the Palestinians in a long time. The Netanyahu era – which lasted for 15 years– was one in which peace with the Palestinians was not pursued. He was finally outsmarted by a new government coalition of right, center and left political parties in May of 2021, but it does not look like any of his successors will be any better on the peace front, even if they may turn out to be less autocratic and not corrupt.

On the Palestinian side, President Abbas, who was only elected for four or five years, has ruled for 14 years as a mini-dictator. Accordingly, the political situation is not much better in Palestine, which also continues to face divided rule, with Fatah and the PLO ruling in the West Bank and Hamas reigning in Gaza and pursuing continual wars and violence with Israel.

What then could change? Golan believes that the only possibility for a political peace would arise if outside pressure from the leadership of the United States or the European Union forced a peace agreement on Israel and Palestine, but she is not optimistic about this either. In her view, this is very unlikely.

Golan is also disturbed by growing tensions between Palestinian Arabs of Israeli citizenship and Israeli Jews within Israel's borders. Another byproduct of the Netanyahu years was constant incitement of Jews against Arabs, which led to much violence in 2021 in mixed cities in Israel. She believes that this civil strife has become so severe that it could tear Israeli society apart, leading to very dire consequences. In addition, creeping annexation and ongoing oppression and humiliation of Palestinians in the West Bank and East Jerusalem will more than likely lead to more violence in the Occupied Territories. It is significant to note that settler Jews call the West Bank or Occupied Territories by the biblical names of Judea and Samaria, and have no intention of ever trading these areas for peace. All of this has created a negative atmosphere for possible political peace, which has influenced Golan's thinking about the prospects of a return to a real political peace process. She states her views about all of this seriously and succinctly:

> The outburst of Jewish and Arab fighting within Israel during the recent conflict [the mini-war between Israel and Hamas in May 2021] hardly bodes well for the future. Civil strife may one day lead to the end of Israel, regardless of the Occupation, but, at the least, a third *intifada* [violent uprising by Palestinians in the West Bank] seems likely in the not-too-distant future, if outside actors do not take a more direct and energetic role.

Despite her well-grounded political pessimism, Golan is still active as a peacebuilder, mostly through her work in Combatants for Peace, an Israeli-Palestinian NGO, which she believes is doing important work. She believes in the vision of this organization, which states:

> In keeping with our values, we work towards a two-state solution in the 1967 borders or any other mutually agreed upon solution that will allow both Israelis and Palestinians to live in freedom, security, democracy and dignity in their homeland. For over a decade, we have embodied and served as a model for our humanistic values. We envision Combatants for Peace as a strong, significant and influential bi-national community–a community that

exemplifies viable cooperation, co-resistance to the Occupation and to violence, which forms the basis for future coexistence. Through joint nonviolence in the present, we lay the foundations for a non-violent future.

Golan still has dreams of a better future.

As for my dreams: I would like to see an end to the Occupation, along the lines of the Olmert-Abbas proposals, based on two independent states bound by cooperation agreements in various fields. I would also like to see an end to the Israeli-Arab conflict as per the Arab Peace Initiative. Within Israel I would like to see *Meretz* converted to a fully joint Jewish and Arab party with two (one Arab, one Jew) in every party position, every committee, and in the Knesset list.

Representing another Jewish viewpoint altogether, another Jewish peacebuilder, **Hadassah Froman**–one of our heroines in this book due to her commitment to reconciliation, mutual understanding and sharing the land of Israel–is less interested in the big political picture and more interested in local peace work in her region in the West Bank, known as *Gush Etzion*. The Etzion Bloc is located just south of Jerusalem, where Froman and her family have lived since 1970 and where she feels that it is somehow possible for Palestinian Arabs and Israeli Jews to live together now and in the future.

In the context of all the big political things going on, and growing hatred in the area, and feelings of destruction, and politicians who don't do what they should be doing, and the army, with all of its problems, including causing many unnecessary issues in the area, I asked myself: 'what can I do in this complicated situation? What can a small group of Palestinians and Israelis do together?' This small place, the Center for Dignity, which we have set up in the Gush Etzion block, receives thousands of people from around the world and from Israel all the time, including students from pre-army academic courses, schools, universities, who come to learn about what we are doing. We have created a place where we can put the issues on the table in a comprehensive manner, settlers and Palestinians, and we discuss them in depth. We are showing people that there is another way to live here, that there is no choice but to continue to develop more and more methods and skills for coexistence here. And we need to focus on justice and equality and life that is good for both peoples living on this land. We don't need more wars and more separation. On the contrary, we can live together on this land. Rather than separate from each other, we need to connect with each other.

For Froman, this is not just an abstract philosophy or ideology. Instead, it is a matter of theology and practice for her. She is a believer and a practitioner. As such she believes that the land which the Jews call Israel-and which the Palestinians call Palestine-can be shared. Moreover, she doesn't just talk about her dreams. She works to bring the real closer to the ideal every day, in her own way.

> This is a matter of religious faith. I believe that Israeli Jews and Palestinian Arabs can somehow learn to live together in this piece of land. It is an issue of belief and of daily work, every day, slow and steady. This is a not just a matter of belief but also of practicing what you believe!

All six of these peacebuilders-whom we have followed and listened to carefully throughout this book-envision a better future for Jewish Israelis and Palestinian Arabs in the land which they share. They do not all agree on political solutions. But they all have dreams of a better life for all of God's children in this land, whether it is called Israel or Palestine or perhaps some combined new name in the future. Moreover, they have all put their principles into practice. They have been building peaceful relations between peoples and people on the ground for decades and they continue to do so, each in his or her own way and they don't plan to give up. Instead, they persist for peace since they have a vision of how this will benefit their people as well as the people on "the other side." This characteristic is their greatness and their legacy for future generations.

Young Jewish Israeli and Palestinian Arab Peacebuilders

Rabbi Tamar Elad-Applebaum
Photo courtesy of Rabbi Tamar Elad-Applebaum

Rabbi Elhanan Miller
Photo by Naomi Zeidman

Hoda Barakat
Photo courtesy of Hoda Barakat

Tareq Saman
Photo by Stephanny Paola Vicuna

In addition to the peacebuilders profiled in this book, there is fortunately a new generation of peacebuilders arising in Israel and Palestine. There are many people and organizations active for peace in the region. The Alliance for Middle East Peace (ALLMEP), an umbrella organization with which I was affiliated as a founding member when I was the director of the Interreligious Coordinating Council in Israel (ICCI), lists over 150 peace-building organizations on their website, which are active in a wide variety of peacebuilding programs and projects in Israel and Palestine.

I have chosen to bring the voices of four young peacebuilders, with whom I have worked in recent years. I could have brought many more. These four people–two young men and two young women, two Jews and two Palestinians–represent some of the hopes and dreams that our six peace-builders have expressed. In important ways, they are the continuation of the philosophies and activism of these leaders, each in their own way.

Rabbi Elhanan Miller is a recently ordained modern orthodox rabbi in Israel. Previous to this, he was a journalist covering Arab and Palestinian affairs for the *Times of Israel* and other media outlets. He learned to speak Arabic from a young age and served as a translator in the army. In his years as a student, he began to get involved in dialogue programs between Jews and Arabs in Jerusalem, first under the auspices of the Jerusalem Inter-national YMCA and then with the Interreligious Coordinating Council in Israel (which I directed for 23 years, from 1991-2014). After participating in one of our dialogue programs for young adults, he served as a translator for these groups, and he often joined other young adults with me to meet and speak to groups that visited Israel which took an interest in our inter-religious peacebuilding work. Since then, he has set up his own non-profit organization called *People of the Book* whose goal is "to introductive basic concepts in Jewish faith to Muslim audiences and vice versa." Through in-novative videos and creative interfaith conversations, this project fosters mutual understanding between Jews and Muslims and contributes to grass-roots peacebuilding.

Miller's participation in peacebuilding programs as a student had a major impact on his life.

> They were crucial for my worldview. On a personal note, they were the first opportunity I had to use the Arabic I had learned in the army. I started learning Arabic in 7th grade out of curiosity and love for languages and for Arabic specifically. I was trained in col-loquial Arabic and spoke Arabic through the army. I worked for

over three years in the army as a translator but I never interacted with Arabs. They were passive actors that I would translate for intelligence. It wasn't a human interaction in any way.

When I started the first dialogue group at the Jerusalem International YMCA–the program was called MVP–Moderate Voices for Peace–and it was directed by Amy Kronish–that was an extremely formative experience for me. It took place over a full year. It was extremely well-organized and well-facilitated. The facilitators were fantastic. That was the first opportunity for me to really engage in meaningful conversations with Palestinians. It was such a positive experience and so interesting, that I decided to join the ICCI group of Jewish Israeli and Palestinian Arab young adults the following year. I had this appetite to continue.

Later on, as a translator, Miller helped us at ICCI to develop a method which we found was very helpful in creating a good atmosphere for dialogue. He and others served as neutral translators from Arabic to Hebrew and vice versa. This allowed two facilitators–one Palestinian Arab and one Jewish Israeli–to facilitate the dialogue. Miller felt that this was very beneficial.

I think it's important to have two facilitators for the simple fact that it gives the participants the feeling of representation and balance. I think it's also very important for there to be translation, because it allows people to speak in their own language. It does make the process more cumbersome and a little bit more boring and drawn out, and everyone has to say less, because everything gets translated. But I think, especially if you have people whose English isn't so proficient, which is often the case, then you need a translator. I found that the model of two facilitators and a neutral translator to be a very useful one.

Since Miller has become deeply involved in peacebuilding work through dialogue and more recently through religious and interreligious activism, he has become somewhat of an optimist although he remains aware of the obstacles and challenges facing those who are trying to bring peace to the region.

I am an optimist and believe that peace is possible. Our agreements with Egypt and Jordan are proof of that, though they may be [examples of] cold peace. My vision is a two-state solution: a nation state for the Jewish majority with full civil rights for the 20% Palestinian minority living within it, and a nation state for Palestinians which Jews will hopefully be able to continue living in as residents, but will likely choose not to realistically. I think governmental peacemaking is only possible when there's a strong grassroots movement pushing in the same direction.

Yet, Miller is also realistic. He does not think normalization will happen in the foreseeable future, certainly not before a comprehensive peace agreement is signed with the Palestinians. Widespread normalization is predicated on the sanction from Arab governments, and this is very difficult in the Middle East. He also feels that religious leaders have a limited role in Israel and Palestine since only a few religious leaders will go against the grain of their societies. Nevertheless, Miller remains an optimist, insisting that solutions can be found to all outstanding issues.

Another serious young Jewish peacebuilder, **Rabbi Tamar Elad-Applebaum**, also has an optimistic vision for the future. This is based on her many years of involvement in peacebuilding programs and projects, including some that she has designed and implemented with partners in Jerusalem and beyond. For Elad-Applebaum, it all began with the death of her brother more than 20 years ago, when he was serving in the Israel Defense Forces in the West Bank.

> This all began when my brother, Nadav, was killed. July 5, 2001. He was a paratrooper. He was in the army then in the Hebron area. He had been studying at a yeshivah, where he was known as a good-hearted person who liked to volunteer for things. His death was a life-changer for me We were very close, even though there was a difference of seven years. The fact that my brother fell as a soldier in the line of duty, as part of the Israeli-Palestinian conflict, was undoubtedly a formative experience in my life. During the year after he died, I began to get involved with many peacebuilding activities. I felt at the time that this was my responsibility. I discovered a whole group of people who had similar experiences of loss, broken-heartedness and pain, which catalyzed them to become involved in peace work.

During that period, many other people whom Elad-Applebaum knew well, died as a result of the conflict: Arik Frankental, the commander of Nadav's unit, and a cousin of her husband, was killed in a terrorist attack; a graduate of her youth movement, known as in *Bnei Akiva*, and a friend of hers from school all died. To her sorrow, she knew too many people who were killed during this period. This was a very difficult time for her, since it was during her student years when she was in her early twenties and was studying to become a rabbi.

> This was a very troubling time, when we suddenly learned about the meaning of the conflict, not through words or ideas, but through people who were killed. My feeling was that my brother died not because of war but because of the conflict. It was crucial for me to understand this deeply. We have a serious conflict here. I still remember the eulogy given by Aviv Kochavi [now commander-in chief of the Israel Defense Forces] at Nadav's funeral. It was at that time that I realized the great responsibility that those soldiers who were killed had on their shoulders.

Since the early 1990s and the Oslo Accords, Elad-Applebaum developed a deep sense of personal responsibility for trying to do her part to deal with the conflict. Her brother's stories about his personal encounters with Palestinians while he was a soldier influenced her greatly, catalyzing her to seek out Palestinians whom she could encounter and with whom she could cooperate.

> I realized that I had a responsibility to those who had died due to the conflict. Nadav told me about conversations that he had with Palestinians in the villages near Hebron, and about questions that he had. This has stayed with me ever since then. These experiences are what set me on my path as someone who was interested in encountering Palestinians as human beings, and as someone who thought that this conflict needed to be brought to an end.

It was during that time that Elad-Applebaum began to get involved in peace-oriented activities. For example, she joined the circle of Arabs and Jews who had lost a loved one to the conflict, which was organized then by Yitzhak Frankental. This organization later became the Parents Circle-Bereaved Families Forum, one of the leading peacebuilding organizations in Israel and Palestine. This spoke to her very personally. She was also a member of the religious peace movement known as *Oz V'shalom* (as was Rabbi Melchior when he was young). Among other things, they organized a meeting in Gaza. There were also programs for young adults and students. She attended many of these programs and discovered how important it was for her to meet and hear what Palestinians were thinking and feeling. Because of her involvement with this religiously-based peace movement, the idea that religion should be a force for peace became important to her. Also, during that time, she participated in a group for siblings who had lost a loved one due to the conflict.

> Through discussions in this group, it became important to me that this constant bereavement must end and that I need to take some responsibility in my personal and professional life, as a rabbi-to-be, to do what I could to help end the conflict.

Indeed, this is what Elad-Applebaum has done in her professional life, especially as the founder and spiritual leader of a very special Jewish religious community in Jerusalem know as *Kehillat Zion* (the Community of Zion). Since 2013, when the community was founded, she has provided her members with a multitude of opportunities to encounter Palestinians both on an interreligious basis as well as a national basis and to cooperate with them on joint projects towards a shared society. She did this even though that she knew that members of *Kehillat Zion* would be left-wing, right-wing and in the middle.

> I felt that it was my responsibility to give the community exposure to the 'other.' I felt that this could happen in several ways. The first way was to go to meet people from other religions and other nationalities. The second way was via cooperative projects, such as our *Beit Midrash Bein-dati* [Interreligious Study Group], as well as *Hesed* [charity]projects, like *the Blue Door*, which collects used items for poor Jews and poor Palestinians in Jerusalem. A third thing that we did was to begin to learn Arabic. We provided subsidies to members of the community to learn Arabic.

In addition, Elad-Applebaum has been instrumental in bringing many people from the outside to the community. She brought religious groups of Christians and Muslims to the synagogue to meet her congregants and to allow them to experience their spiritual form of Jewish worship, as well as to study together and to talk with the congregants about their situation. Together with her lay leadership, she has created an open community that welcomes guests from other religions and nationalities from the outside on a regular basis.

But she and her leadership in her community did not stop there. They also have been engaged in many activities that helped develop political consciousness among their members. They went to *Sheikh Jarrah* (the Palestinian neighborhood in East Jerusalem where many Palestinians have been facing evictions from their homes) to learn about what was happening there. They also went to other places in East Jerusalem to see and learn about other problems facing the Palestinian community. For example, they took people to East Jerusalem on a study tour organized by *Ir Ammim* (a non-profit organization which promotes coexistence for Palestinians and Israeli Jews in Jerusalem) to learn about the issues which Palestinians face in that part of Jerusalem on a daily basis.

In addition, she attended a very special four-day program in the West Bank (sponsored by a Jewish Israeli organization known as *Encounter*) to speak to Palestinians and learn about their situation. Not only did she attend the Encounter seminar in the West Bank but she arranged for members of her community to join so that they could attend this as a group project. They spent four days in Bethlehem and in Hebron.

Moreover, whenever she organized joint public prayer occasions–as with her *Ma'aminim* (Believers) program which takes place in a central location in Jerusalem before an audience of hundreds of people on evenings in May or June–she and her colleagues bring voices of Palestinians from East Jerusalem to Jewish audiences. Also, she does this public program and other programs in two languages–Hebrew and Arabic–as a symbolic and practical way of showing respect to both Israeli Jews and Palestinian Arabs in Jerusalem.

Furthermore, she and other members of her community have been involved with the *Tag Meir Forum* (a pluralistic Jewish umbrella organization, which combats hate crimes and racist vandalism and murders all over Israel and especially in the West Bank). This is a very important peacebuilding organization in Israel, which I helped to found several years ago. Elad-Applebaum and members of her community have become central partners in this coalition and they attend, organize and speak at many of the activities and programs, including solidarity visits to families who have been injured by hate crimes. Elad-Applebaum feels that her activism in her religious community is unique to her synagogue and to her personally as the rabbi of this innovative and inspiring institution (full disclosure: I am a member of her synagogue).

> We are one of the very few religious communities in Israel–with people from the right and the left both politically and religiously–which place these activities in the center of our mission as a community. All of these programs are central to my rabbinate, to who I am as a rabbi as a leader of a community. All of these

197

programs are intrinsic to my religious faith as a Jew. I believe as a
religious Jewish person that peace and reconciliation–and our ability to live here together and to recognize our mutual suffering–are
very important to our mission as a Jewish people which has returned to live in its land.

All of this activism and engagement are based on Elad-Applebaum's vision
for a better future for both Palestinian Arabs and Israeli Jews both in national terms and with regard to Jerusalem as a special place of possible
peaceful coexistence.

My thoughts about the future have changed over the years. I have
listened to my Palestinian partners a lot. What I would like to see
are two states for two peoples. I would also like to see Jerusalem
become a holy city, in which there will be a shared life for all citizens. There should be a way for people to express their national
feelings of belonging as well as their religious faiths. I would like
to see a set of relationships in Jerusalem where everyone respects
the other in a good and positive way. I would like to see Jerusalem
as a 'place of prayer for all peoples' [Isaiah 56:7]. I would really
love to see Jerusalem as a city which provides the opportunity for
all human beings to dream about their lives. Our lives should be
filled with holiness and human dignity. There should be a place
for everyone. It should be a city of *hesed,* where lovingkindness and
justice are found among all the people, as our classical biblical
prophets described it. I feel certain that this is possible.

For Elad-Applebaum, her dream for the future is also a distinct possibility.
She believes that it can actually happen! A two-state solution can be arranged, and an agreement can be reached to end the conflict.

I would like to see normalized relations and the absence of wars!
This will be the end of the conflict! In my imagination, Jerusalem
would be a place where the richness of diversity would be a central
part of our lives, and we would see it as a gift from God. It would
be a place where Jews would understand Arabic and Palestinians
would understand Hebrew, where respect for everyone's human
rights would be a major value. This may sound utopian, but this is
what I would like to see. I see myself as one who is part of the camp
in Israel in which can be found believers in a better future for everyone here, people who share a prophetic utopian vision for
Jerusalem and for Israel. I believe that religions have a major

responsibility here—they have a joint responsibility to repair and heal this world, to make it a better place.

Jerusalem is a city which must be shared by Jewish Israelis and Palestinian Arabs, as we will see when we hear from young Palestinian peacebuilders (below).

Young Palestinian Peacebuilders

Tareq Saman grew up in the eastern part of Jerusalem, in a neighborhood known as Shuafat, where part of the neighborhood is a former refugee camp, comprised of Palestinians who fled Israel in the 1948 and 1967 wars. After completing high school, he attended the Hebrew University of Jerusalem, where he studied Hebrew language and education. As a fluent Hebrew speaker, he spent many years teaching Hebrew to Palestinians in Jerusalem, who require this skill in order to find gainful employment.

During his student years at the Hebrew University, Saman decided to join his first dialogue group with Israeli Jews. In 2008, he joined the Israeli-Palestinian Young Adult dialogue group of the Interreligious Coordinating Council in Israel (ICCI), the organization which I founded and directed for 24 years. This was during the first war between Hamas and Israel, which was a very difficult time for dialogue. Previous to this, he had participated in a formal course for dialogue during his last year of studies at the Hebrew University. Saman remembers well the impact that this dialogue experience had on him.

> Until then, I had not really had a chance to have serious discussions with Jewish people. In that class, we had a lot of good conversations. The course that I took at the Hebrew University on dialogue was good preparation for me for this next step. I was interested in having more conversations with Jews. Until that time, as a Palestinian, the only Jews I met were soldiers at checkpoints or clerks in the offices of the National Insurance or the Ministry of Interior. When I heard about the dialogue group for students and young adults which was offered by ICCI during the 2008 academic year, I was interested in it.

Saman actually left the ICCI dialogue group during the middle of the year due to issues involved with the war between Israel and Hamas that year. It was difficult for him to be in a group when some of the Jewish Israelis in the group were also soldiers in the Israel Defense Forces at the time. But after the war was over, in a remarkable act of reconciliation, he returned to

199

the group. He adapted to the atmosphere of dialogue and found that this group experience was a good place for him to engage in serious conversation with Jews his age. One of the things that Saman liked to do in this group— as well as with groups from abroad with whom he met, as a representative of ICCI—was to have Jews hear his views on the Israeli-Palestinian conflict, and particularly what it was like to grow up in Jewish-controlled Jerusalem.

> I liked to share with Jewish students my feelings about my identity and what it is like to be a Palestinian in Jerusalem. This was very important for me, especially before we had social media, like we do now. The other side saw Palestinians only as 'terrorists.' I wanted to give them the real story. We are normal people, just like the Jewish students are normal, and we each have our distinctive ideas and identities. Yet, we need to know more about each other. Through the dialogue, I learned how the other person saw the situation from their side, and they learned how I saw it from my side. Also, I found more people from the 'other side' who shared my beliefs and my approach. I am still in touch with some of the Jewish people from this dialogue group. Over the years, I have seen some of these people and kept up the conversation.

Based on his positive experience in dialogue with the young adult group of ICCI, Saman went on to be a counsellor for three summers at a unique summer camp in upstate New York entitled Face-to-Face/Faith-to-Faith. This program was a very special interfaith youth program which brought together teenagers from South Africa (Blacks and Whites), Northern Ireland (Protestants and Catholics), cities in the USA, and Israel/Palestine. My organization, the Interreligious Coordinating Council in Israel (ICCI) was the Israeli partner in this program, which was originally co-sponsored by Seeking Common Ground and the Auburn Seminary (Presbyterian) in NYC (later the program was run only by Auburn Seminary). This year-round program included local dialogue groups in each country and an intensive two-week summer experience in a Presbyterian camp in upstate New York (which was made kosher and vegetarian, so that all the students and staff could eat together). Following the camp experience, the young people returned to their countries to continue the dialogue and to prepare and implement action projects.

For Saman, his experience as a counsellor in the Face-to-Face program added new experiences and insights to his expanding identity.

My experience with Face-to-Face in the USA was totally different than my dialogues in Israel. This was the first time that I met people from other conflicts in the world. There are many other conflicts in the world other than the Palestinian-Israeli Conflict. I learned that some of the conflicts are similar to ours and others are very different. Also, it was good to meet people who supported my work in dialogue in Israel and Palestine. I met people from South Africa, Northern Ireland and from the USA and I learned from them how they dealt with their conflicts, and in the cases of South Africa and Northern Ireland, I learned how they emerged from their conflicts and entered a 'post-conflict' situation.

In addition, Saman had a chance to meet American Jews.

Since then, one of my best friends is an American rabbi named Reuven. We are in touch all the time. When he came to Israel, he stayed in my home. When I visited him in the USA, I stayed in his home. Even though he is right-wing politically, we are able to listen to each other, to discuss issues as friends. Even though he is pro-Israel, I feel that he has come to understand my Palestinian narrative of the conflict and this is important to me. Also, since we are both educators, we both care about the next generation. We want the next generation to learn about the humanity of the other, and to hear each other's narrative.

When Saman met people from South Africa and Northern Ireland at the Face-to-Face/Faith-to-Faith camp in upstate New York, he discovered that he was often jealous of them because they lived in countries where their conflict had been resolved and they lived in a post-conflict situation, in which there is no more ongoing violence between the two sides. In contrast, in Israel/Palestine, the situation was surprisingly different.

Here, we don't even have the same name for the country: the Jews call it Israel, and we, the Palestinians, call it Palestine. And it is the same land! Our conflict is very different. For example, Palestinians continue to live under occupation, whereas teenagers from Northern Ireland thought that that the world 'occupation' meant only 'job.' They were not familiar with this term which we use every day.

Later on, Saman studied at Brandeis University, in a special Master's program called *Coexistence and Conflict Resolution*. During his two years there, he learned about many conflicts in the world, including some that he had never heard about before. During his studies, he discovered that in other conflicts in the world, many more people have been killed than in the Israeli-Palestinian Conflict. On the one hand, this opened his horizons to understand more about conflict but on the other hand, it made him more pessimistic about the possibility of seeing a resolution to the Israeli-Palestinian Conflict.

> One of the things that I learned about other conflicts is that they do come to an end. There are solutions. In contrast, it seems to me that there is no solution to the Israeli-Palestinian Conflict. There appears to be no end in sight. It is very hard to find a win-win solution here. It looks like that one party will win and one will lose.

After Saman came back from getting his MA at Brandeis University, he worked as co-director of Kids4Peace in Jerusalem for a while. Following this, he became the director of the Department for Arab students at the Bible Lands Museum in Jerusalem. In both jobs, he continued to use the knowledge and experience that he had gained from participating in peace-building dialogue groups, as well as the knowledge garnered by studying at one of the best universities in the USA. In his work at the Bible Lands Museum, among other responsibilities, he oversees a dialogue program with Palestinian and Israeli students who are 4th graders–from a Jewish Israeli school in *Beit Hakerem* and a Palestinian Arab school in *Beit Hanina*. They used art from the museum, they have tours in the museum, and they learn about the history of this land, which belongs to three religions, Judaism, Christianity and Islam.

> This is an Abrahamic area—Israeli Jews and Palestinian Arabs are all attached to this land. This program is very experiential. The students also learn about how this idea could be relevant for the present situation and for the future. This is a program that has been running for 25 years. It began in 1995, after the Oslo agreements in the early 1990s and continued through and after the Second Intifada in the early 2000s, during hard times. It was stopped for one year during the corona pandemic but it will start again. This program is one way that I continue my peacebuilding activities from past years.

With all this practical and professional experience, Saman has been able to develop his own vision of the future, especially with regard to the city of

Jerusalem, where he grew up and lives to this day with his wife and son. Moreover, his dreams for a better future for Jerusalem and the region are influenced not only by his strong Palestinian identity but also by his personal religious experience as an observant Muslim.

> I believe that this land should be a place where Jews, Christians and Muslims can practice their religion. They all should be able to live here, to be connected to this land. The religious identities here are very central. For example, Jerusalem, *Al Quds*, is a holy place for the three religions and should be open to all three. As I look toward the future, and think about how we can all live together, I don't have much faith in the politicians.

Saman apparently would love to see a situation where the nationalisms– both Palestinian nationalism and Jewish-Israeli nationalism (especially the most extreme expressions of both)–are less important than they have been in recent decades. Rather, what is more important to him is that Jews, Christians and Muslims can live side by side in this land, especially in Jerusalem. Jerusalem–*Al Quds*–should not only be a city of coexistence for the people who live there, but it should also be open for everyone around the world to come to visit. With these views, Saman's Muslim religious world view is actually very similar to those of young Jewish religious peace-builders such as Rabbi Elhanan Miller and Rabbi Tamar Elad-Applebaum.

Hoda Barakat was born in the USA and grew up in the USA, the Kingdom of Saudi Arabia, Jordan and Palestine. In Palestine, she went to high school in the West Bank city of Nablus, one of the major Palestinian cities in the northern West Bank and an area of much conflict between local Palestinians and Israeli settlers and soldiers in the area. After this she attended Al Najah National University in Nablus where she earned a BA in Civil Engineering (2007) and later received a MA in Management (2018).

Barakat worked as the Palestinian facilitator for ICCI alumni programs for youth and young adults for one year (2012-2013). Together with a Jewish Israeli facilitator, she recruited young adults who were graduates of ICCI's dialogue programs to join the new alumni network and they facilitated dialogue sessions as well as organized conferences. During that year, she also worked for another peacebuilding organization, based in the USA, known as Hands of Peace. She went on to work for Hands of Peace for 14 years, first as regional coordinator (2007-2013) and then as Regional Manager (2013-2021) and eventually left the organization after she got married in 2020.

Hands of Peace is an American-based peacebuilding organization that has been bringing Israeli Jewish and Palestinian Arab youth (ages 15-18) to the USA for intensive three-week dialogue and action programs during the summer months since 2003. The "Hands," as the youth in this peacebuilding organization are known, participate for four years, and some are even involved for as much as seven years, gaining extensive experience in dialogue and activism. Originally based in Chicago it also brings youth to San Diego. In addition to these programs, it has developed leadership programs for youth as well as action-oriented opportunities for alumni.

Barakat became involved with peacebuilding programs after her sister attended Hands of Peace as a teenager, where she had a very good experience. The following year, she was asked to be a chaperone on the program, and then she joined the staff. At first, she was asked to help with recruitment for the program, but then she joined and stayed with it for many years.

While working with Hands of Peace, one of the longest lasting peacebuilding programs for Israeli and Palestinian youth, she and her team sponsored regional programs in Palestine and Israel. They planned and implemented three or four overnight seminars each year. This was in addition to the summer experience in the USA, which was designed for first year participants. In the second year, a small group of them would travel to the USA as leaders. In subsequent years, she was constantly in touch with the participants of these programs, and in recent years, the organization has added programs for alumni.

Over the years, Barakat saw that this program had significant impact on the Palestinian and Israeli young people who were fortunate to participate in it. Despite the complexity of the process, she witnessed significant personal growth and deeper understanding of the conflict among many of the young people.

> The situation is very complex, and as we saw from the [ongoing] violence, it is sometimes even desperate. Yet, one of the things that I learned from my work with Hands of Peace and other dialogue groups is that it is a very personal process. I saw many remarkable shifts in the thinking and the lives of the teenagers who came into the program. Some of the changes were unbelievable. Young Jews and Arabs demonstrated a great ability to change and to develop themselves. Many of them discovered their own stereotypes and even their own racist thoughts that they hadn't realized before. Many of them also developed awareness of how privileged they

were and how they did not do much to try to solve the conflict. Others realized that they understood themselves too much as victims of the conflict. It was moving and powerful to see how much some of these young people changed and developed their awareness of the other. During the 14 years that I worked there I saw great changes in many individuals.

Not only did many young people undergo profound personal transformations through this program concerning how they saw the other, but Barakat also went through her own process of personal and professional growth and development.

I went through a similar process. I was forced to see the other. Many of my own prejudices and stereotypes changed and developed over time. I was constantly faced with the questions of what is justice and what is fair. Ten years ago, I thought that the solution to the conflict only had to be fair and just for my people. Now I can't say that any more. I realize that it must be just and fair for both peoples. Now I see the other and I realize that the solution to the conflict has to be fair for them too. I cannot ignore the other anymore. I am now cognizant of the fact that in order for us to have a sustainable peace I need a solution which is also good for the nearly seven million [Jewish] people who live in Israel. This was definitely not on my radar when I began working in this peace-building program. Previous to this, I just thought about myself and my situation, without reference to the other side. Now I realize that in order for peace to work, I have to figure out a way to live with the other side. I don't have to love the solution, and I may not get everything that I wanted to get, or what I feel entitled to get, but I need to be realistic about what can be done and what can't be done.

As far as her dreams for the future, Barkat appears to prefer a one-state solution although she does not say so explicitly. In her hopes and dreams for the future, she has a vision for full equality for Palestinian Arabs and Israeli Jews. This is her main concern.

I really don't care who rules me and who holds the majority. I just care that we have one country where everyone gets the same rights. I don't care what you call it. I don't care which religion is the dominant one. I just want to live in a place where I feel that I am worthy and equal to everyone around me. If a kid in Gaza has the same

rights as a kid in Tel Aviv, you can call it 'Israel' and I don't care.
As long as everyone is equal!

Barakat shares a dream that many Palestinians have. She wants to see an end to the Occupation-the discrimination, oppression, and humiliation of the Palestinians in the West Bank. Instead of the status quo, she envisions a future in which Palestinians would be fully equal with Israelis. She is less concerned about the political framework-one state or two states or whatever creative negotiators may come up with in the future. Her vision is simple and straightforward. She wants dignity and human rights for all. She would like to see equal treatment under the law, equal services, and fair treatment for all people in the region.

In addition to the six outstanding veteran peacebuilders profiled in this book, these young Israeli Jewish and Palestinian Arab peacebuilders—and many more like them who are active in the field—give us hope for the future. They and their colleagues have the potential to prepare their societies for ways to emerge from the Israeli-Palestinian conflict and live without constant war and violence. With increased financial and popular support over the years, the goal is that they will influence the politicians and diplomats to change direction, to negotiate for peace, and build the infrastructure for peaceful living for all citizens of Israel and Palestine in the years and decades ahead.

Afterward: Is Peace Possible?

Researching and writing about the lives of the six peacebuilders featured in this book has been a labor of love for the past few years. Through this process, I have gotten to know them better and have come to appreciate their contributions to peaceful coexistence between Palestinian Arabs and Israeli Jews over many decades, despite all the obstacles and challenges which they faced and continue to face. In so doing, I have learned a great deal about the qualities needed to be a peacebuilder in the ongoing conflict that we live with in our region, the Israeli-Palestinian conflict. These qualities include courage, commitment, persistence, resilience, and hope—characteristics which are shared by all the peacebuilders in this book, and many more who are active in civil society in Israel and in Palestine.

Writing the book has also sharpened my own thinking about the intertwined fields of peacemaking and peacebuilding, as well as helped me to clarify some of my own ideas about the role of peacebuilders now and for the future. In this brief afterward, I will share some of these thoughts.

Peacemaking and Peacebuilding

I have argued in this book that peacebuilding is currently the only game in town at the moment, since the "peacemakers" (the politicians, diplomats, international relations experts) on both the Palestinian and the Israeli sides of the conflict have unfortunately abandoned the search for a political solution. At this juncture, I would like to state clearly that ultimately we will need both peacemaking (politics and diplomacy) and peacebuilding (the work of people and groups in civil society via NGO's) to resolve and transform our conflict in this region. In other words, we will need a political/diplomatic solution to the conflict, to be negotiated by the leaders of both sides to the conflict, undoubtedly with the help of mediators from the international community, such as the president of the United States and his advisors. I understand that this kind of solution, or even the beginning of such a process, does not seem imminent but we need to keep in mind that it is essential for the common future of both Palestinians and Israelis. Without it, we will face ongoing conflict, more violence and wars, which are counter-productive to a better future for all concerned. A comprehensive political solution to the conflict here is in the interests of both peoples—the Jewish-Israeli people and Palestinian people. The status quo is not good for either side in the long run.

In this book, I have chosen to focus on peacebuilding, rather than on peace-making (except for the introductory chapter on history and context.) The reason for this decision is that that most of the writing about efforts to achieve peace in Israel and Palestine has focused on the political-diplomatic aspects of what is known as "the Peace Process." I have felt for a long time that much of what is written about this in newspapers, articles and books, is about the failures of this process, as well as all the multiple obstacles to achieving success. The multitude of reasons why the peace process has not succeeded are well-known by now, including intransigent leadership, rejectionist extremist groups which incite to hatred and lead to repeated wars, growing fear and frustration in both Palestinian and Israeli societies about the possibilities of peace, and religious extremism which has combined with ultra-nationalist fanaticism. It is noteworthy that these phenomena which have not allowed the peace process to move forward for the last two decades can be found on both sides of the conflict, not just on one side (there is a tendency in many quarters for people to only blame one side for the continuation of the conflict).

I have focused in this book on the work of six outstanding peacebuilders (and I could have included many more, about whom I have written in my blog posts for the *Huffington Post* and *the Times of Israel* during the last 10-15 years.) Why? Because their stories are not well known in the world, and I want more people to know about their amazing work. Because in the absence of any progress in the political peace process, it is essential not to give up, and to pursue peaceful relations between Israelis Jews and Palestinian Arabs in whatever ways are possible. And because the more that peacebuilding efforts increase and multiply, the more likely it will be that they can influence the political decision-makers to renew their efforts for political peace agreements via negotiations between representatives of the two governments. We need support for peace from the grassroots, from the ground up, as well as from the political echelons, from the top down.

At the end of the day, I believe that both peacemaking and peacebuilding will be necessary for us to achieve peace in our region. In the long run, they complement one another, influence one another and are essential components for developing sustainable peace between Israel and the Palestinians.

Is Peace Possible?

During my career of over 30 years in the field of interreligious dialogue and peacebuilding–which has included my lecturing at universities, synagogues, mosques, churches, community centers as well as speaking at international conferences and seminars and briefing groups that came to visit in Israel and Palestine-I was often asked: is peace possible between Israelis and Palestinians?

My answer was always yes, although it became more difficult to say this over time.

During the hopeful decade of the 1990s-which was characterized by peace agreements between Israel and the Palestinians, as well as historic peace agreements between Israel and the Vatican and Israel and Jordan-it was much easier to say with confidence that peace was possible. After all, the Oslo Accords of the early 1990s had broken the ice and proved that reaching a peace agreement with the Palestinians was in fact possible. All of the peacebuilders featured in this book remember the Oslo Peace Agreements fondly, even if some of them were disappointed by some aspects of these accords.

But after the Second *Intifada* (uprising) between 2000-2005, mutual trust between Palestinian leaders and Israeli leaders was deeply damaged, and even though there were some efforts to bring the two sides to the negotiating table during the presidency of Barak Obama, they did not succeed. In fact, the last diplomatic agreement between Israel and the Palestinians was made in 1998 (24 years ago!) at the Wye River Plantation outside of Washington DC under the tutelage of President Bill Clinton, with Bibi Netanyahu and Yasser Arafat signing the document for each side.

Nowadays, it is much harder to say that peace is possible, but I still think that it is correct. Why?

First, we have learned from contemporary history that some seemingly intractable conflicts have actually come to an end. Who would have imagined back in 1977 that President Anwar Sadat of Egypt would come to speak in Israel's parliament, the *Knesset*, and announce his willingness to make peace with Israel? Egypt had been Israel's arch enemy since its establishment in 1948 and had fought several major wars with the young Jewish state! Who would have believed that Yasser Arafat, the head of the Palestine Liberation Organization-which had committed countless terrorist attacks against Israel for decades-would change course and announce his commitment to enter into negotiations with Israel in 1988, and then to actually do so in 1992 and 1993 with the historic Oslo back-channel negotiations and then the Oslo Accords?

Similarly, who could have thought that peace between Protestants and Catholics in Northern Ireland was possible in 1998 after decades of horrifying terror and counter-terror called "the Troubles?" And yet, in April 1998, a surprising peace agreement was reached between the conflicting sides, with American intervention, that has lasted to this day. Similarly, it was inconceivable that the oppression of the black population in South Africa which went on for decades would ever end. But Nelson Mandella rose to the occasion, as did Fredrik de Klerk, who was the leader of white-ruled South Africa, and they made an historic agreement which ended the apartheid regime in that country, despite all the despair and lack of hope that was the conventional wisdom there for a very long time.

As a result, I do not accept the political determinism of many pundits in our region (and outside of it) who say that peace between the Palestinians and Israelis is impossible and that it will never happen. I do not accept this. On the contrary, I believe that it can and must happen, for the mutual welfare of both peoples. And I believe that all of the peacebuilders portrayed in this book–and many others–share this deep belief despite all the challenges and obstacles they face continually.

Let me illustrate this idea with a story from my own experience as one who directed a peacebuilding organization for nearly 25 years.

During my career as the founder and director of the Interreligious Coordinating Council in Israel (ICCI), I oversaw many programs that were devoted to dialogue and peace. Among the most important and effective programs that I was involved with for 11 years was a program called *Face to Face/Faith to Faith*. This international program, which was founded by a Jewish woman from Denver, Colorado, and a Christian woman minister from New York (originally from Louisville, Kentucky), brought together diverse teenagers (black and white, Jewish, Christian and Muslim, Palestinian Arabs and Israeli Jews) from four regions of the world (Israel/Palestine, South Africa, Northern Ireland and the USA) for a year-long program, which included an intensive two-week summer camp experience at a facility run by the Presbyterian Church of the USA in upstate New York. The full year program also included dialogue sessions in each home country as well as projects to be implemented by the end of the year by the youth in their home settings. After its initial years, the program was administered by Auburn Seminary in New York City under the leadership of Rev. Katharine Henderson, who became a trusted colleague and a good friend.

Each year, there was a fundraising event in New York City to raise money for the next year of the program. One year I attended one of these events, which took place in a beautiful venue in Manhattan and was attended by hundreds of people. As part of the program, a moderator interviewed six young graduates of the program who were on a large stage under a huge banner that read "Peace is Possible." It was an impressive and inspiring evening, which I have never forgotten. Ater the program, when I asked some of the young people what they thought of the banner, they told me that they agreed with its message. They said that they had just lived for two full weeks over the summer with their former enemies and they discovered that peaceful living was indeed possible with them, through dialogue and sincere attempts at mutual understanding and cooperation.

I understood what these young people were telling me. They had experienced peaceful coexistence and they knew that it could work. In my work with hundreds of youth and young adults over many years, I repeatedly saw that their positive dialogue experiences with "the other," their perceived "enemy," had made them optimistic about the possibilities of peace. This led me to appreciate the positive power of dialogue, which is all too often undervalued and considered less important than political negotiations. In addition, I learned from them, as well as many others in the field, that dialogue is not enough.

Dialogue and Action

Many years ago, one of my Israeli Arab Muslim colleagues told me that, in his view, dialogue that does not lead to action is insufficient. Over time, I came to agree with him, and I endeavored to include an action component in all of the encounter programs that I supervised, directly or indirectly. I too became critical of dialogue programs that were only "feel good" experiences, which permitted liberal Jews to feel satisfied that they had done something to bring about the end of the conflict, but in actuality, they had not taken the brave step of moving out of their comfort zones in order to make serious change.

It is no accident that all of the peacebuilders in this book have been involved in action programs for many years, and are still involved in many ways, some of which are very public and others which are behind-the-scenes efforts at bridge-building and mediation. Action is implemented in many forms, from storytelling, to educational programs, to solidarity visits to advocacy projects, which urge the politicians to end the Occupation and the terror (otherwise known as "armed resistance") and renew negotiations for peace.

By now, most peacebuilders have internalized the idea that if they want to have a serious and systematic impact on their communities, they need to focus on action programs, not just on talking.

All of the peacebuilders featured in this book are heavily involved in action programs in many ways through a wide variety of organizations: Huda Abuarquob via the Alliance for Middle East Peace, Professor Mohammed Dajani through *Wasatia* (the Middle Way), Bishop Younan through the Council of Religious Institutions of the Holy Land, Rabbi Melchior through the Religious Peace Initiative of *Mosaica*, Professor Galia Golan through Combatants for Peace, and Hadassah Froman via Roots/ Shorashim/Judor in the West Bank. As we have seen, they are deeply committed to their work in these peacebuilding organizations (and others) which not only provide them with some hope in the present and for the future, but provide the rest of us with inspiration and ideas for what is possible and what we can do to improve the situation.

The Influence of Interaction with the Outside World

Most of these peacebuilders spent a significant amount of time outside of Israel and Palestine, a fact which clearly broadened their perspectives about peaceful coexistence in many ways. Rabbi Melchior grew up in Norway, and was active in interreligious dialogue there before he came to live in Israel. His experiences in developing Jewish-Muslim coalitions were formative ones, which influenced his ability to do similar things in Israel and the region, and his meetings with Palestinians and Jewish peace activists began while he was still in Norway. Professor Golan grew up in the USA, was educated at Brandeis University, spent time in Europe before coming to live in Israel, and attended many international conferences and seminars which affected her deeply, especially when she began meeting Palestinians at these events in the 1980s. Hadassah Froman's husband, Rabbi Menachem Froman, attended many international events, where he met like-minded pursuers of peace, who had a great impact on his development as a religious person of peace, as well as deeply influencing his wife. Professor Dajani spent ten years in the USA, where he earned two doctorates in political science, and has attended countless seminars and conferences abroad. Similarly, Bishop Younan studied theology for several years in Finland, and during his presidency of the World Lutheran Federation for seven years— and as a leader in the international interreligious movement for peace known as Religions for Peace—he has interacted with peacebuilders all over the world, which has greatly enriched his knowledge and experience. Also,

Huda Abuarquob, who studied and worked for several years in the USA, and has attending seminars and workshops in many places in the world on peace and reconciliation, has become one of the most serious and strategic peace activists in Palestine.

I too have greatly benefited by my many international encounters with people of peace in many seminars, workshops and conferences during my 30 years in the field of interreligious dialogue and peacebuilding. I have met people of peace in many places of former conflict-such as Northern Ireland, Bosnia-Herzogovenia, Spain, Japan, Germany, England and more-who have inspired me and catalyzed me to action over many years. I have been active in the Alliance for Middle East Peace, from its inception in 2004, and I was deeply involved in programs and projects with Religions for Peace since my organization in Israel-the Interreligious Coordinating Council in Israel-was the Israeli chapter of Religions for Peace for many years. In addition, I attended conferences on peace sponsored by the Vatican at Assisi as well as participating in an important seminar on Religions and Peace at the Vatican in 2002. I have met people from more difficult and complicated conflicts who managed somehow to help to resolve their conflict, so I know that the seemingly impossible obstacles to peace can be overcome with the right leadership and the will of the people. These fascinating and inspiring encounters have not only strengthened my knowledge about peace work around the world but they have also bolstered my resolve to continue to write about those who pursue peace persistently in many places (especially in Israel and Palestine), to be an activist for peace and reconciliation, and to believe that it is possible to achieve peace, even in my region, where the conflict seems to be so intractable.

Loving Peace and Pursuing Peace

In my tradition, the Jewish Tradition, there is a famous saying from a tractate of the *Mishnah* (a foundational Jewish text from the rabbinic period, approximately 2nd century CE) known as *Pirkei Avot*, the Ethics of the Fathers, which has guided me in my life and in my professional work in interreligious dialogue for peace for a long time. This text reads:

> Hillel taught: be a disciple of Aaron: Loving peace and pursuing peace. Loving our fellow human beings and attracting them to the study of Torah.

I have always found it fascinating that this important rabbinic sage chose the biblical Aaron as a model Jewish leader because he loved peace and pursued it.

In an excellent comprehensive article in the journal *Conservative Judaism* (in 2000), Rabbi Reuven Hammer, the former Professor of Rabbinic Literature at the Schechter Institute in Jerusalem, explained why and how the rabbis elevated Aaron to the model Jewish leader, how Hillel painted such a glowing and warm portrait of Aaron when the *Torah* text is so critical of him and his actions. Despite the ambivalence of the *Torah* toward Aaron, especially after his role in the incident of the Golden Calf, Aaron becomes the high priest and therefore the leader of the priestly group. Rabbi Hammer wrote:

> Hillel has given us a two-part description of the basic qualities of Aaron, which he calls upon his students to emulate. These basic qualities are (1) love of peace (*shalom*) and (2) the love of all human beings. Each of these 'loves' has an operative definition, a way of translating the emotion of love into action. The love of peace is demonstrated by the pursuit of peace. The love of human beings is shown by bringing them closer to *Torah*, the teaching of God. It is important to note that Hillel speaks of the love of human beings and does not confine himself to the love of Jews.

Hillel made Aaron the archetype not only of the ideal Jew but the ideal Jewish leader, one who leads through love rather than fear, with persuasion rather than force.

In another work, *Third Party Peacemakers in Judaism*, which focuses on Aaron as a peacebuilder, Rabbi Daniel Roth, Director of the Religious Peace Initiative of *Mosaica* in Israel (who works with Rabbi Michael Melchior, one of the heroes of this book), teaches us about the importance of the archetype of Aaron in Jewish Tradition. In so doing, he brings to bear the earliest rabbinic commentary on this *Mishnah* about being the disciples of Aaron in the post-*Talmudic* tractate *Avot d'Rabbi Natan*, which states:

> A *lover of peace and a pursuer of peace:* Even if you run after it from city to city, from district to district, from country to country, do not desist from making peace. For it is equal in weight to all the other *mitzvot* (commandments) in the *Torah*... and Scripture says, 'Depart from evil and do good; seek peace and pursue it.' (Psalm 34:15) Rabbi Yosei says: If a person sits in his house and does not go out to the marketplace, how will he make peace between

people? Rather, by going to the marketplace, he sees people fighting and enters between them and effects a compromise between them.

Rabbi Roth emphasizes that this commentary stresses that to be a "pursuer of peace" one must proactively go out to make peace wherever there is conflict. It is not enough to passively be a "lover of peace." One must take the initiative, not simply wait for conflicts to come to you to be resolved, but rather one must participate in action programs, either individually or as a group.

All of the peacebuilders in this book—and many more that I know in the field—are not just "lovers of peace." They are active pursuers of this ideal, through their persistent involvement in peace work over many decades, through their many important initiatives which have brought thousands of people closer together, and through their visions for a better future, which continue to inspire us every day. In so doing, they bring us closer to the values which we hold dear–the love and dignity of every human being and the priority for *shalom, salaam,* peace to bring social, religious and political harmony to this world.

Profiles in Peace

Selected Bibliography

Abuarquob, Huda. "Feminism in Israel. Feminist, Peacebuilder; An Interview with Huda Abu Arquob." *Fathom*, February 2018.

https://fathomjournal.org/women-and-feminism-in-israel-palestinian-feminist-peacebuilder-an-interview-with-huda-abu-arqoub/

—. "Promoting Implementation of Resolution 1325 in Palestine." *Palestine-Israel Journal*, Jerusalem, vol. 25, nos. 3 and 4, 2020.

Barakat, Zeina M. From Heart of Stone to Heart of Flesh: Evolutionary Journey from Extremism to Moderation. Munich. Herbert Utz Verlag, 2017.

—. *Al-Wasatia: Moderation in Times of Extremism,* Moderation and Reconciliation Studies Center, Ramallah, Palestine, Wasatia Publishing, 2018.

Barakat, Zeina M. with Mohammed S. Dajani Daoudi, Munther S. Daoudi, and others, editors, *Teaching Empathy and Reconciliation in midst of Conflict,* Jerusalem and Jena, Germany, Wasatia Publishing. 2016.

Baumbart-Ochse, Mohammed Dajani Daoudi, Svenja Gerthess, and Rabbi Ron Kronish, *"The Practice and Promise of Inter-Faith Dialogue and Peacebuilding in the Israeli-Palestinian Conflict"* for the Academic Peace Orchestra Middle East of the Peace Research Institute Frankfurt. August 2014. Policy Brief No. 35. Frankfurt, Germany.

Braunold,and Abuarquob. "A Bigger Threat than BDS: Anti-normalization." *HaAretz*. July 2, 2015.
https://www.haaretz.com/jewish/.premium-worse-than-bds-anti-normalization-1.5374940

Covey, Stephen. "The Third Alternative in the World." *The Third Alternative*, by Stephen R. Covey, NY, Free Press, pp. 375-415. 2011.

Corrymeela Community, Interreligious Coordinating Council in Israel, St. Ethelburga's Centre for Peace and Reconciliation. *Principles of Group Facilitation: An Exploration of Good Practice*. London. St. Ethelburga's Centre for Peace and Reconciliation, 2010. (This document can be found on the website of www.ronkronish.com.)

Dajani, Mohammed. *Wasatia: The Spirit of Islam*. Jerusalem: Wasatia Publishing, 2009.

—. *The Future of Jerusalem*. Jerusalem: Wasatia Publishing, 2012.

—. Exploring American Studies: A Success Story. Jerusalem: Al-Quds University, 2013.

—. Big Dream/Small Hope: Peace and Reconciliation Vision. Jerusalem: Wasatia Publishing, 2014.

—. Wasatia: The Road to Reconciliation. Jerusalem, Wasatia Publishing, 2014.

—. The Holy Books as Guiding Lights. Jerusalem, Wasatia Publishing, 2015.

—. Wasatia: The Straight Path from Denormalization to Reconciliation. Jerusalem: Wasatia Academic Institute, 2018.

—. "Hamas and Palestinian Religious Moderation." *Palestine-Israel Journal of Politics, Economics, and Culture*. Vol. 13, No. 3, 2006, pp. 10-15.

—. "Big Dream/Small Hope: A Peace Vision." *Crosscurrents*, Summer 2008: 191-219.

—. "The Arab Peace Initiative: Lost in the Translation." *Crosscurrents*, December 2009: pp. 532-539.

Dajani, Mohammed, ed. *Jerusalem From the Lens of Wasatia*. Jerusalem: Wasatia Publishing, 2010.

Dajani, Mohammed and Zeina Barakat. "Israelis and Palestinians: Contested Narratives." *Israel Studies*. vol. 18, no. 2, Summer 2013, pp. 53-69.

Dajani, Mohammed and Gershon Baskin. "Israeli-Palestinian Joint activities: Problematic Endeavor, but Necessary Challenge." *Bridging the Divide: Peacebuilding in the Israeli-Palestinian Conflict*, edited by Edy Kaufman, Walid Salem, and Juliette Verhoeven, Boulder, Colorado: Lynne Rienner Publishers, 2006, pp. 87-110.

Dajani, Mohammed and Munther Dajani, *Dajani Glossary of Islamic Terms*. Jerusalem, Wasatia Publishing, 2015.

Dajani, Mohammed, editor with others, *Teaching Empathy and Reconciliation in Midst of Conflict*. Jerusalem: Wasatia Publishing, 2016.

Eilberg-Schwartz, Penina, with Sulaiman Khatib. *In this place together; a Palestinian's journey to collective liberation*. Boston, MA, Beacon Press, 2021.

Epstein, Nadine. "Mohammed Dajani Daoudi: Evolution of a Moderate." *MOMENT magazine*, July/August 2014.

Golan, Galia. *Galia Golan: An Academic Pioneer on the Soviet Union, Peace and Conflict Studies and a Peace and Feminist Activist*. Springer Nature, Switzerland and Jerusalem. Springer Publishing and the Hebrew University, 2019.

—. Israeli Peacemaking Since 1967: Factors Behind the Breakthroughs and Failures. London, Routledge, 2015.

—. "Deception in Israeli Peacemaking since 1967." *Israel Studies Review*, vol. 34, issue 1, Spring 2019, pp 1-26.

—. *Israel and Palestine: Peace Plans and Proposals, From Oslo to Disengagement*, second revised edition, Markus Wiener Publishers, Princeton, NJ, 2007, p. 237.

—. "Building Peace from Below: The Israeli Peace Camp." *The Journal of South Asia and Middle East Studies*, 2020.

Hammer, Reuven. "The Apotheosis of Aaron." *Conservative Judaism*, vol. 53, no. 1, Fall 2000, NY, pp 20-33.

Horovitz, David. "When an Ex-Fatah Palestinian Neighbor Took up a Zionist Author's Challenge." *The Times of Israel*, June 12, 2019. https://www.timesofisrael.com/when-an-ex-fatah-palestinian-neighbor-took-up-a-zionist-authorros-challenge/

Kronish, Ronald. *The Other Peace Process: Interreligious Dialogue, A View from Jerusalem*. Lanham, MD, Hamilton Books, 2017.

—. "The New Peace Atmosphere in Israel." *Dade Jewish Journal*, September 16-22, 1993.

—. "The Other Peace Process." *The Jerusalem Post*, February 2, 1997.

Kronish, Ronald. ed. Coexistence and Reconciliation in Israel: Voices for Interreligious Dialogue. Mahwah, NJ. Paulist Press, 2015.

Landau, Yehezkel. email letter to Ron Kronish, January 5, 2022.

John Paul Lederach. *Building Peace: Sustainable Reconciliation in Divided Societies*. Washington DC, US Institute for Peace, 1997.

Melchior, Rabbi Michael. "Establishing a Religious Peace." *Coexistence and Reconciliation in Israel: Voices for Interreligious Dialogue*. ed. by Ronald Kronish, Mahwah, NJ. Paulist Press, 2015.

Mitchell, George J. *Making Peace: The Inside Story of the Making of the Good Friday Agreement*. NY. Alfred A. Knopf, 1999.

Mitchell, George J. *The Negotiator, a Memoir. Reflections on an American Life*. NY, Simon and Schuster, 2015.

Morris, Benny. *1948: A History of the First Arab-Israeli War*, New Haven, CN. Yale University Press, 2009.

Rabin, Yitzhak. Speech on the Occasion of the Signing of the Declaration of Principles in Washington DC, September 13,1993. https://www.mfa.gov.il/mfa/foreignpolicy/peace/mfadocuments/pages/remarks%20by%20pm%20yitzhak%20rabin%20at%20signing%20of%20dop%20-%2013.aspx

Roth, Daniel. *Third-Party Peacemakers in Judaism: Text, Theory and Practice*. NY. Oxford University Press, 2021.

Savir, Uri. *The Process:1,000 Days That Changed the Middle East*. NY. Random House, 1998

White, Canon Andrew. *My Journey So Far*. Oxford, England, Lion Boks, an imprint of Lion Hudson plc, 2015.

Wright, Lawrence. *Thirteen Days in September: The Dramatic Story of the Struggle for Peace*. NY, Vintage Books, a division of Penguin Random House, 2014.

Younan, Munib. *Witnessing for Peace. In Jerusalem and the World*, Minneapolis, Fortress Press, 2003.

—. *Our Shared Witness. A Voice for Justice and Reconciliation*, Minneapolis, Lutheran University Press, 2012.

About the author

Rabbi Dr. Ron Kronish served as the Founder and Director of the Interreligious Coordinating Council in Israel (ICCI), Israel's premier interreligious organization from 1991 to 2014. A graduate of Brandeis University, with a BA in psychology, he is an ordained Reform rabbi and holds a doctorate in education from the Harvard Graduate School of Education.

Rabbi Kronish lectures and teaches in Israel and North America. In recent years, he has taught as an Adjunct Professor at Drew University's Center for Religion, Culture and Conflict in the Drew Theological School; at Brandeis University's master's program in Conflict Resolution and Coexistence in the Heller School for Social Policy and Management; and at the Schechter Institutes for Jewish Studies in Jerusalem.

Rabbi Kronish blogs for *The Times of Israel* https://blogs.timesofisrael.com/author/ron-kronish/and is a contributor to The Jerusalem Report.

For more information, see his blog: https://www.ronkronish.com/

He lives in Jerusalem with his wife Amy since 1979.

Books

The Other Peace Process: Interreligious Dialogue, A View from Jerusalem, (Hamilton Books, an imprint of Roman and Littlefield, 2017)

Coexistence and Reconciliation in Israel: Voices for Interreligious Dialogue, (editor) (Paulist Press, 2015)